# For Enquiring Minds

# For Enquiring Minds

## A Cultural Study
## of Supermarket Tabloids

*S. Elizabeth Bird*

The University of Tennessee Press
Knoxville

Chapter 6 is a revision of the author's "Media and Folklore
as Intertextual Communication Processes," which appeared in
*Communication Yearbook* 10 (1987): 758–72, © Sage Publications.
Reprinted by permission of Sage Publications, Inc.

The paper in this book meets the minimum requirements
of the American National Standard for Permanence
of Paper for Printed Library Materials.

The binding materials have been chosen
for strength and durability.

Library of Congress Cataloging in Publication Data

Bird, S. Elizabeth.
    For enquiring minds : a cultural study of
supermarket tabloids / S. Elizabeth Bird. 1st ed.
        p.        cm.
    Includes bibliographical references and index.
    ISBN 0-87049-728-6 (cloth : alk. paper)
    ISBN 0-87049-729-4 (pbk. : alk. paper)
    1. Tabloid newspapers—United States.
    2. Journalism—Social aspects—United States.
    3. United States—Popular culture.
I. Title.
PN4888.T3B5        1992
302.23'22'0973—dc20                91-13989        CIP

*In memory of my mother,*
*Eileen Elizabeth Bird*

# Contents

# Illustrations

# Acknowledgments

Many people gave their time and shared their thoughts with me to produce the raw material for this book. Globe Communications provided invaluable assistance at various points during my research; staff members answered all requests for information courteously and helpfully. In particular, I thank the 1986 editorial staff of the *National Examiner*, who allowed me to visit and interview them, and who also permitted me to place an announcement in the paper requesting readers' letters. Special thanks to former Editor William Burt, former Associate Editor Cliff Linedecker, former Photo Editor Ken Matthews, and current staff members Sheila O'Donovan and Anthony Leggett. I am deeply grateful to the readers of the *National Examiner* who took the trouble to write to me, especially those who also agreed to be interviewed. They remain anonymous in the text, but their contribution was immeasurable.

Working with tabloids has its own special problems. "Trash" is supremely ephemeral, and old issues are almost impossible to obtain. I am, therefore, especially grateful to Mrs. Mary Ferrell of Dallas, Texas, whose personal library of John F. Kennedy memorabilia includes some rare tabloids of the 1960s and 1970s. She allowed me to visit her home to study her "scandal sheets"; I appreciated her hospitality very much.

Thanks are also due to Jay Mechling and two anonymous readers who reviewed the manuscript for publication. Their comments were thoughtful and constructive; some of their suggestions have helped make this a better book than it might otherwise have been. As always, the flaws that remain are mine. I would like to thank James W.

For Enquiring Minds

Carey. He has not yet read the entire manuscript, but his words of encouragement over the last few years have meant more to me than he probably knows.

I owe an immense debt of gratitude to Carol Orr, the director of the University of Tennessee Press. She saw the seed for a book in a conference paper, and she nurtured that seed for five years. Without her initial suggestion and continued support, this book would not have been written.

I thank my husband, Graham Tobin. His comments on the manuscript were invaluable—but above all, I thank him for his love, support, and belief in the book, even when I had my doubts.

# For Enquiring Minds

# Introduction

The young woman was talking about her favorite tabloid hero, actor Sylvester Stallone. "He's gorgeous! And my boyfriend almost, almost looks like him, almost—he's got like maybe five months to lift weights to look like him." As I thought about her comment, I started to wonder. Here is a woman in her twenties, raising three children alone, and working two jobs to support them. Her real world of work and social relationships is also filled with the images of the lives of many others—celebrities, "ordinary people" doing extraordinary things. Which is more "real," the persona of Stallone, or that of her boyfriend? When she is with her boyfriend, does she see him, or does she see Stallone? How is her relationship with Stallone incorporated into her relationship with this actual man who is attempting to remake himself? While I cannot really answer these questions, this personal debate brought home to me the need to explain a phenomenon like tabloids not as something unique and neatly self-contained but as untidily situated among numerous other strands of culture.

Culture is about connections—between people, ideas, values. Anthropologists have for years used connective metaphors to define culture, such as networks, structures, or the "web of significance" (Geertz 1973). I call this book a cultural study, and in it I try to enter into the web and follow some of the strands of significance. My aim is not simply to write about supermarket tabloids as if these were something one can detach from the web and hold up for examination. For the Stallone fan, tabloids are one facet of life among many. Tabloids, like any kind of cultural phenomenon, exist alongside and because of other cultural phenomena. They complement the star sys-

-1-

tem, the other popular media, the class system, and the gender system. They exist because of television, newspapers, movies, and a vast range of folk narratives and values.

In studying any medium and its users, it is almost overwhelmingly tempting to see it as somehow separated from culture. I find myself talking about "my tabloid readers" as if the fact that certain people had contributed to my study gave them some special identity that was defined by one small activity in their lives. Yet tabloids, like television, movies, newspapers, and oral tradition, reflect and feed into each other and may only really be understood in relation to each other. For while culture may be conceptualized as a web, the metaphor is not quite enough. The connections between components of a culture are not actually neutral, as a web might suggest. Rather, some components act on others, changing them. Victor Turner, talking about culture today, suggests a rather more precise metaphor—a "hall of mirrors" (1985, 245). The suggestion here is that cultural phenomena are indeed interconnected but that each does not exist in some objective space. Rather, everything reflects off everything else in ever-repeating images. One component is not only linked to everything else but also affected and changed by it (I do not say distorted, because that implies the existence of something undistorted). The shape of the image depends on where one is situated, and it is impossible to see the whole from the outside.

If, perhaps, we return to the tabloid-reading Stallone fan, we see her reading of stories about her idol situated somewhere in this hall of mirrors. The tabloid stories bounce off and add to the established "image" of Stallone derived from previous reading and viewing, that image reflecting his movie roles. Her image of masculinity, derived from a myriad other oral and media sources, in turn bounces back onto her boyfriend, whose persona reflects a not-quite-complete image of Stallone. From my position along another trail of connections, I then reflect upon her.

The "hall of mirrors" metaphor is closely related to many arguments about postmodern culture and its intertextuality (Jameson 1984). Indeed, the notion of intertextuality runs through this study as I try to show how an understanding of tabloids is possible only if

# Introduction

we take into account their relationship with other media, and especially with older, oral traditions. Postmodern theorists are very much at home with the idea of culture as a hall of endlessly repeated images. However, while acknowledging the contributions of the postmodernists, I believe the metaphor of the hall of mirrors applies to culture in general, not just to postmodern culture.

For instance, Caughey (1984) argues convincingly that anthropologists have focused exclusively on the "real" social world while neglecting the "imaginary" social world. This world, he asserts, is peopled with figures that have no physical existence. In a simple society, any individual's imaginary social world may include spirits, ancestors, dream figures, or the characters of myth and folklore. We may dismiss these as hallucinations or fiction, but individuals have real social relationships with them that have real effects in their lives. People act on the results of their social interaction with spirits; social relationships between real people are influenced by social relationships between the living and the dead. Even in the simplest culture, an individual is placed in a hall of mirrors that reflects endless images of real and imaginary social worlds.

In contemporary society, the mirrors have proliferated. To the imaginary social worlds of spirits, dreams, and folklore are added the infinite images of of media and their imaginary figures. And, as Caughey points out, many people spend a great deal of time relating to these figures—through fantasy, daydreaming, personal storytelling, interpersonal gossip, and creation of mutual narratives. Relationships with media figures can be time-consuming and even more "real" than many daily interactions in the "real" world. As Caughey mentions, sometimes they can even replace the real world, as they seem to have done for John Hinkley and Mark Chapman. Tabloids are not unique but simply one more supplier of images for the intertextual hall of mirrors.

A central point that emerges from my text is that tabloids, their readers, and to a somewhat lesser extent, their writers, have continued a tradition that, while obviously dependent upon print, is rooted in oral tradition. An important theme of the book is the situating of tabloids in a tradition of oral, folk narrative. Ong (1982) introduces the useful concept of "residual orality" to illuminate the inter-textuality of oral and literate traditions. He points out that, even in a culture that is predominantly literate, many people (perhaps most) retain a grasp of culture that is rooted in orality rather than literacy. Tabloids, as I shall show, bear all the hallmarks of a residually oral tradition, illustrated in their history, content, writing style, and reader response.

In my first chapter, I trace the roots of tabloid journalism, sug-gesting that standard histories of the press do not pay enough atten-tion to the connections of journalism with traditional narrative. The theme of intertextuality, of connectedness, is important here. The his-tory of the press often seems to be one of great press figures making innovations, and a neglect of cultural context. In the nineteenth cen-tury, when the groundwork for today's tabloids was essentially laid, newspapers grew alongside all kinds of street and folk literature. The legacy of that tradition is still flourishing today.

My second chapter examines the content of the tabloids in terms of themes and formulas that recur consistently; chapter 3 looks at how tabloid writers work to produce that predictable content. My fourth and fifth chapters explore tabloids from the readers' point of view, showing how indeed the papers intersect with other aspects of peoples' lives—such as leisure, other media, class, and above all, gender. Once again, connections and the intertextuality of the oral and print traditions are significant.

Chapter 6 brings together the three elements of producer, content, and reader, showing how the three work together to produce the par-ticular cultural phenomenon of the tabloid. Finally, I provide a short conclusion placing my work within the larger discourse of cultural studies and sounding a cautionary note about a trend toward the uncritical celebration of popular culture.

One important issue that has emerged in that discourse on cultural studies has been the question of the stance of the researcher, particu-larly with work than can be described as ethnography of popular cul-ture. I am often asked whether I enjoy tabloids and whether I share the enthusiasm of the readers who talked to me. Many scholars of popular phenomena do indeed seem to choose a topic they have been

# Introduction

drawn to as a fan. In the contemporary spirit of ethnographic self-reflection, I should admit that, while I have developed a strong appreciation of the importance of tabloids in many people's lives, I did not begin my study as a fan, and I do not end it as one. After the initial excitement of reading material considered somehow taboo by virtue of its "trash" status (Brown 1989), I began to find the papers predictable, repetitive, and eventually, depressing.

I think the reasons for that are, at least in part, tied to the issue of orality versus literacy. Critics, inescapably mired in the analytic, literate tradition, detest media like tabloids because they are formulaic, sensational, and altogether too excessive. Tabloid readers, more comfortable in a concrete, residually oral tradition, love them for the very same reasons. It sometimes seems to be assumed that an academic who studies popular culture can study it as a fan, from the inside. There are problems with this, however. Of course academics are unabashed fans of popular culture—of "high" culture, even. But, whether fans or not, if a particular form of culture then becomes an object of their study, I believe they should never assume that their appreciation of it is or can be identical with that of many other enthusiasts.

Academics are more steeped in literacy than almost any other cultural group, and we carry that literacy-based mind-set almost everywhere we go. When we start to analyze a cultural phenomenon, whether tabloids or the *New Yorker*, we think not only about the particular phenomenon in question but about everything we have read about it and other related phenomena. We may be part of it as fans, but we are also apart as inveterate analysts, and we should not forget that. With the increasing self-awareness of ethnographers about their enterprise has come a realization that we can never be ethnographers and "natives" at the same time. Clifford Geertz, for example, has moved from the aim of understanding the "native's point of view" to the less ambitious one of understanding "what it might be like" to belong to a particular culture (1988). My equally modest goal has been to try to explain "what it might be like" to see tabloids as an important part of one's life, and how these papers do indeed fit into the lives of millions.

# 1

# Tabloids
# Past and Present

We intend to interest you mightily. We intend to dramatize and
sensationalize the news and some stories that are not news. . . . If
you read it from first to last and find anything therein that does not interest you, we want you to write and tell us about it.

—Bernarr MacFadden,
introducing the *Daily Graphic*, 1924

The *National Enquirer* has been branded a "disgrace to journalism"
by William F. Buckley (1981, 508), and, along with other weekly
"supermarket" tabloids, characterized as the epitome of "low-taste"
media (McDonald 1984). Patrick Brogan probably speaks for many
"serious" journalists when he crisply dismisses the tabloids: "In
America, all this stuff can be shovelled off into the incinerator without a second thought . . ." (1979, 39). Yet the combined weekly circulation of the six major supermarket tabloids hovers around ten million, with readership estimated at fifty million (Nordheimer 1988);
the *National Enquirer* alone sells well over four million copies a
week. The tabloids clearly offer millions of Americans something
they do not find in other media.

The publications in question are the weekly "supermarket" tabloid papers, a familiar sight in the checkout lanes of supermarkets,
drugstores, and convenience stores. Ownership of the six major tabloids is now divided between MacFadden Holdings Inc., which owns
the *National Enquirer,* the *Weekly World News,* and the *Star,* and

Globe Communications, which publishes the *Globe,* the *Sun,* and the *National Examiner.* In addition, there is *News Extra,* a small, cheaply produced weekly based in Canada, which is not widely available in the United States. The *Enquirer* and *News* have editorial offices in Lantana, Florida, not far from Globe's base in Boca Raton, Florida, while the *Star,* until 1990 part of Rupert Murdoch's holdings, is head-quartered in Tarrytown, New York.

As any checkout-lane browser knows, the tabloids serve up a mixture of celebrity gossip, human-interest features, usually with a "sensational" twist, stories about occult and psychic phenomena, UFOs and so on, and large doses of advice, self-help tips, and medical news. They almost never cover politics, except at the level of the personality story, such as the *Enquirer*'s notorious coverage of Gary Hart's relationship with Donna Rice. Usually working with several weeks of lead time, they have little interest in fast-breaking "hard" news stories.

The 1980s were the decade of the supermarket tabloids, when their characteristic formats developed and circulations peaked. Four tabloids, the *National Enquirer, Star, Globe,* and *National Examiner,* had the greatest circulation growth of all magazines in the United States in 1982, reaching a combined figure of 11.4 million (*BusinessWeek* 1983). But, although tabloids really made their mark on American culture in the 1980s, they were hardly new. Rather they represented the highly successful recipe that blended modern marketing techniques with an editorial mix that had been brewing for generations.

## Early Tabloid Ancestors

Although the term "tabloid" refers only to the half-broadsheet size of the papers, it is now almost invariably used to refer to the "sensational" tabloid—the paper whose stock in trade is the human-interest, graphically told story, heavy on pictures and short, pithy, highly stereotyped prose. The weekly tabloid in its present form is a phe-

# Tabloids Past and Present

nomenon of the 1970s and 1980s, but the current papers are the heirs of a long tradition in journalism, whose roots may be traced back hundreds of years. Journalists today seem to prefer the idea that the tabloids have nothing to do with "real journalism," and indeed they often draw inspiration from sources that daily journalism would find less than credible. Nevertheless, although tabloids and folklore are cousins, journalism is another branch of the family, and the history of tabloids is one strand in the broader history of journalism.

The concept of news itself has been traced back to the very beginning of human society, and no doubt the urge to know what our neighbors are up to is universal (Stephens 1988). For present purposes, however, I will begin the search for tabloid ancestors in the seventeenth century, when we see the direct, printed ancestors of today's tabloids. In Europe and America, broadside ballads and newsbooks flourished, packed with tales of strange and wonderful happenings—murders, natural disasters, unusual births, and omens. The distinction between early newspapers and ballads was hazy at most: "Some of the early forms of popular newspaper were simply single printed sheets; while these gave topical items in prose, the broadside ballads would give news in verse. Need we be too pedantic about the difference between a ballad and a newspaper?" (Shepard 1978, 24). Both covered stories such as this: "The Two Inseperable Brothers, or a true and strange description of a Gentleman (an Italian by birth) about seventeene yeeres of age, who hath an imperfect (yet living) Brother, growing out of his side, having a head, two armes, and one leg, all perfectly to be seen. . . . Admire the Creator in his Creatures" (Rollins 1969, 13). Verse 12 describes the "imperfect" brother:

> It like an infant (with voyce weake)
> Will cry out though it cannot speake.
> as sensible of paine,
> Which yet the other feeleth not,
> But if the one be cold or hot,
> that's common to both twaine.

Other ballads collected by Rollins also tell stories that could grace the cover of any modern tabloid. There is the "Sad accident" of the man who was buried alive for three days in 1661 but survived. A ballad on a great fire of 1662 includes a verse about a woman who was saved because she changed her mind about staying in a certain house—now virtually a journalistic cliché in any disaster coverage. Today's poltergeist appears in the seventeenth century as a phantom drummer who threw children out of bed, and the miracle cure is represented by the crippled "Happy Damsel" who was cured after reading the Bible.

Murders were covered in lurid detail, usually climaxing in the penitent confession and execution of the culprit. Readers' fantasies were catered to in lavish descriptions of events like royal weddings: "News reports on royal pomp and circumstance dwelt on the details because the events depicted were more extravagant and magnificent than anything else in their readers' experience" (Stephens 1988, 103).

Stephens argues that the spread of ballads and newsbooks owed less to favorable social conditions than to developing technology: "The cataclysm that created them was the arrival of the printing press, with its ability to spread accounts of more or less typical outbreaks of murder, lust and sin to an audience whose size was unprecedented but whose appetite for sensation was, more or less, normal" (1988, 117).

Much of the material in these sheets was drawn straight from oral tradition or relied on word-of-mouth reports, often stressing that sources were eyewitnesses or, at the very least, credible—the "insiders" of their day. To satisfy the demand, printers often recycled old tales with new dates and locations; undoubtedly they did much recycling that was less conscious, publishing and republishing the apocryphal tales that later became known as "urban legends" (Brunvand 1981). For instance, Rollins includes "A warning by the example of Mary Dudson," who swallowed a small snake which grew and eventually killed her. Almost three centuries later, the New York *World* reported on a girl who died and was found to be harboring a living viper which she had swallowed as an egg or young one (Nov. 4,

1924, cited in Rollins 1969, 132). Likewise, the New York *Tribune* reported on a London girl who had swallowed an octopus, although the paper failed to trace her (Sept. 28, 1924, cited in Rollins, 132). The tale, after which Schechter (1988) names his book, *The Bosom Serpent*, resurfaces regularly in oral tradition and print; both Schechter and Brunvand (1984) trace it from ancient beginnings to contemporary oral circulation. Modern tabloids are full of the same kind of "dreadful contamination" accounts.

A characteristic of the seventeenth-century news and ballad books was their moralizing tone. Mary Dudson's fate was a warning; through the Italian Siamese twins we can admire God's work. The same tendency is noted by Nord in his examination of the "teleological" roots of American journalism in seventeenth-century Puritan writing: "All occurrences—perhaps especially 'strange and wondrous' ones—were clothed in religious, and therefore public, meaning" (1988, 2).

Puritan writers like Cotton Mather and Samuel Danforth collected accounts of the same kind of momentous events that were covered in ballads and newsbooks. Their methods are virtually identical to those of modern tabloid reporters: "The sources ranged widely, from the classic works of antiquity to the best scientists of the age to folklore to the average person with a story to tell. The role of the writer was not to conduct systematic empirical research, but rather to report the empirical statements of others. Such a methodology was empiricism without science. It was, in a word, journalism" (Nord 1988, 19).

In such works as *An Essay for the Recording of Illustrious Providences*, Mather "assures the reader that this information comes from reliable sources, eyewitnesses wherever possible" (Nord 1988, 21). The purpose of this accumulation of tales was to provide meaning, to demonstrate divine providence. Nord suggests that the moralistic character of seventeenth-century writings disappeared by the eighteenth century, although the early news media continued to cover this "litany of predictable unusual events": "what had been divine providence had become by 1729 simply the news" (1988, 32). However, other research suggests this was not quite the case; Nordin

(1979), for example, found a strong moral and religious component in the colonial press of 1700 through the 1780s. As in the ballads, the dying speech of the convicted murderer was a staple topic, as was the whole range of "predictable unusual" events such as disasters and strange births. Then, as now, the critics railed against the press of the day for its unwholesome interest in things sensational.

## The Penny Press

Although Nordin suggests that "sensationalism in the early Boston press was so pervasive that it exceeded the levels of even the most sensationalized popular newspapers of the nineteenth century" (1979, 302–3), journalism historians tend to attribute the growth of the human-interest and "sensational" style (rather than subject matter) to the 1830s, with the growth of the "penny press." Benjamin H. Day's New York *Sun* and James Gordon Bennett's *Herald* targeted a growing mass of semiliterate urbanites with their human-interest stories (Mott 1963; Emery 1972). Even though some now argue that the importance of the penny press in journalism history has been overrated (Nerone 1987), innovations of this period did change newspapers forever. When Day founded the *Sun* in September 1833, he was aiming at a mass newspaper market for the first time. The *Sun* sold for one cent on the street, compared to the six-cent subscription price that put other newspapers out of the reach of working people. It was also smaller and more portable than other newspapers, foreshadowing the popular appeal of later tabloids. From 1828 to 1840, newspaper circulation grew from 78,000 to 300,000, most if not all attributable to the growth of the penny press (Schudson 1978).

Equally important were the writing style and tone adopted by the *Sun* and other penny papers. While newspapers until then were very much "establishment" media, aligned with business and political interests, the *Sun* "was the first American newspaper written less for merchants and politicians than for the general reader" (Whitby 1982, 24). According to Whitby, "the tone of the *Sun* was based on the language of the common man and reinforced its motto, 'It Shines for

All' with plain talk that was athletically lean and representative of realistic human conditions" (1982, 25). No longer devoting large amounts of space to lists of facts and figures, the paper's aim was to tell a good human-interest story, appealing to readers' feelings as much or more than their intellect: "It is noteworthy that the word 'sensationalism' is virtually absent from the annals of journalism until the advent of these papers" (p. 27).

To tell stories effectively, the *Sun* evolved a simpler, more direct news style, using vivid, active language and colloquialisms, and breaking up stories into more manageable paragraphs (Whitby 1982). It is the writing style rather than the subject matter as such that marks off the penny press from its newspaper predecessors—the colonial press discussed by Nordin indeed covered sensational subject matter, but the style was far from the human-interest narratives of the penny press era, usually lacking the "sensory detail" (Francke 1986) that the penny press pioneered. The short, clear, active style became the model for journalism from then on—tabloid journalism simply developed the style at its most formulaic.

Standard journalism history tends to suggest that this style was something quite new, neglecting to consider the non-newspaper roots of this kind of journalism in the broadside ballads which continued to influence and be influenced by newspapers throughout the nineteenth century. For in the nineteenth century, alongside the penny press and other newspapers, the broadside ballads and chapbooks also took advantage of greater literacy and continued to sell in the hundreds of thousands. They maintained the gruesomely moralistic tone that had characterized the seventeenth- and eighteenth-century versions, with predictable patterns for such events as murders. Typical of the genre is this verse from a ballad on the murder of "Mr May" in 1836:

A frightful sight the body was, when found upon the road—
His head all beat to pieces, and weltering in his blood;
His teeth knocked from their sockets, were strewed all around,
And clots of Mr May's life-blood was trodden in the ground (Collison 1973, 43).

Graphic descriptions of the murder itself were usually followed by accounts of the trial and execution, typically enlivened by the penitent last speech of the convicted murderer (Burt 1958). Nineteenth-century mass-circulation newspapers and ballads were closely entwined in form. Cohen, in her analysis of just one type of story, the "murdered-girl stereotype," suggests that both newspapers and ballads "tell the story from the same moral stance, express the same interpretation of character, and are interested in the same details. . . . The shared pattern consists basically of a plot formula that has an attendant company of other formulae, such as stereotyped scenes, stereotyped actors, and stereotyped phrases" (1973, 4). Thus particular "types" of story were recognized by ballad writers and journalists alike, and the varying details gradually disappear to accommodate the known "story." Journalists, with their ability to construct long accounts very quickly, used the same techniques as ballad writers and oral balladeers before them; the concept of recognizing "the story" still guides journalists today (Bird and Dardenne 1988). But this kind of formulaic narrative construction is clearest in the writing style that became known as "human-interest" and that developed in its most stereotyped form in the mass-circulation newspapers and later tabloids.

In order to provide the rich detail the human-interest story needed, the 1830s penny press began using reporting techniques that later became standard journalistic practice. While previous newspapers had relied mostly on documents such as court records, Bennett added observation and interviewing—the "legwork" we now associate with journalism—as essential reporting tools (Francke 1986). Bennett developed the use of such methods in his extensive 1836 coverage of the notorious Helen Jewett murder case (which also spawned eleven chapbook accounts, including one by the editor of the *Police Gazette* [Schiller 1979]). Bennett's reporters visited the scene of the crime and interviewed other prostitutes at the brothel where Jewett had worked. He then took the opportunity to editorialize on the "guilt of society . . . the atrocity of permitting establishments of such infamy to be erected in every public and fashionable place in our city" (quoted in Schiller 1979, 59). In addition, Bennett used his paper to try to prove that the accused murderer, Richard Robinson, was convicted in a coverup intended to avoid embarrassing influential brothel customers. This kind of crusading, in which the penny papers "spun available facts into a pattern expressive of basic class tensions and antagonisms," (Schiller 1979, 65), was a new development in journalism, one that later tabloids continued.

While Nordin had argued that the moral and religious component had disappeared from crime news by the nineteenth century, that assessment seems premature. Certainly the religious dimension is largely absent, and the parade of unusual events—floods, sea serpents, strange births—is now indeed simply news, still covered enthusiastically but not given any special "meaning." But moral judgments, like those made by Bennett, were not absent, especially in crime news—moralizing continued into the tabloids of the 1980s. Crime news in newspapers and ballads frequently offered a moral point, even if it was not quite as blatant as seventeenth- and eighteenth-century warnings. Papers like the *London Illustrated Police News* and its later American counterpart the *Police Gazette* reveled in the gory details of murders, followed by accounts and engravings of contrite murderers going to their deaths, characterized by a "shamelessly hypocritical style . . . serving up hardcore violence under the pretext of moral improvement" (Schechter 1988, 88).

The penny press did transform newspapers and ultimately removed the market for such media as ballads and chapbooks. Toward the end of the nineteenth century, the search for the ancestors of tabloids focuses squarely on newspapers rather than the other forms of street literature that influenced them. The human-interest story continued to be central in mass-market newspapers throughout the nineteenth century, with observation and interviewing techniques developing more completely. The second half of the nineteenth century saw wide use of the "sensory detail" that such techniques produced, often resulting in stomach-turning descriptions, such as the Cincinnati *Enquirer*'s account of the victim's corpse in the famous Tanyard Murder case of 1874: "The skull had burst like a shell in the fierce furnace heat; and the whole upper portion seemed as though it has been blown out by the steam from the boiling and bubbling brains" (quoted in Francke 1986, 9).

## The 1880s

Although illustrations were used in the newspapers and ballads of the earlier nineteenth century, these publications had to rely largely on their writers' graphic abilities to tell the story. As technology developed, it became possible to use illustrations more liberally, and another foundation stone was laid for the heavily illustrated tabloid. The first illustrated daily newspaper was the *Daily Graphic*, founded in 1872. It featured editorials, personality features, verse, foreign news, and "graphicalities." Murder stories were popular, and these often included composite pictures, similar to the "composographs" that were used by later tabloids (Bent 1927). The *Graphic* achieved a daily circulation of around ten thousand but folded in 1879.

It was not until a little later that conditions were right for the successful precursors of the tabloids. The 1880s were a period of great energy and urban growth, with city life gradually becoming the norm for more and more Americans. The time was right for the development of newspapers as a truly profitable enterprise, as the technology was now available to mass-produce papers more cheaply, including illustrations and advertisements. In addition, waves of immigration and nationwide school attendance had by the late nineteenth century produced even more of the barely literate people who were the intended audience for mass-circulation news.

When Joseph Pulitzer bought the moribund *New York World* in 1883, he began the movement that became known as yellow journalism. He reduced the price of the paper from two cents to a penny and embarked on a crusade against government corruption, white slavery scandals, and other exciting topics. Pulitzer vowed to concentrate on "what is original, distinctive, dramatic, romantic, thrilling, unique, curious, quaint, humorous, odd, apt to be talked about" (Bessie 1938, 44). By 1886, the *World*'s 250,000 daily circulation was the largest ever, and the *Sun* was struggling. Since its inception, the *Sun* had taken a class-conscious populist approach, supporting such issues as union rights as well as developing the human-interest story. In the 1880s, the *World* developed the crusading populism but added a new dimension—"Pulitzer was one of the creators of an American consumer culture" (Steele 1990, 597). While the *Sun* disdained advertising, other than classifieds, the *World* "offered its readers a guide to the abundance of the metropolis" (Steele 1990, 597). In addition to current news and abundant advertising, the paper ran such features as women's pages, etiquette hints, and advice columns. Such material "had no connection to the daily problems of women in the tenements, but it was closely tied to, and constituent of, their dreams" (Schudson 1978, 101). The same could later be said for the weekly tabloid.

Reporters for the "yellow" papers developed the reporting techniques begun by the penny papers, producing stories full of detailed physical description and colloquial dialogue. Francke (1986) describes the writing of a *World* reporter covering a tenement murder in June 23. He "fleshed out his questions with the exaggerated physical description common to court reports in the Penny Press. He first described a young woman with 'a fuzzy growth of light hair over her face that makes her resemble, with the green lustre of her eye, a hard, blighted peach,' and then asked her, in regard to the death of Kate Sweeney, 'What was she doing in the cellar? 'How the _____ should I know. Mabbee she went down there to git some peace.' 'You're a liar,' said another woman who had had her front teeth knocked out and whose voice hissed viciously through the apertures not unlike that of snakes' " (Francke 1986, 7).

Newspapers, through their rich human-interest reporting, still moralized, but by now such comment was less overt, a change linked with the rise of objectivity as a concept (although that term was rarely used at this time). Objectivity as a journalistic concept holds that the facts speak for themselves, whether these facts are observations recorded by a reporter or quotes from sources. Francke (1986) shows that, as stories rich in sensory detail increase throughout the nineteenth century, they are often accompanied by disclaimers as editors justify using gruesome details to expose wrongdoings. Writers disassociate themselves "By portraying the techniques of reporting as something akin to runaway technology. The reporters become as helpless as the Sorcerer's apprentice. . . . They may wash their hands of their sensationalism under such rubrics as 'seeing is believing,' or through that routine act of reportorial disassociation: don't-blame-me attribution which transfers responsibility to documentary and interview sources" (Francke, 2). In much the same way, later tabloid writers use objectivity as a justification for some of their techniques, as we shall see.

Pulitzer's success with the *World* naturally spawned imitators; William Randolph Hearst "began where Pulitzer had the virtue to stop" (Bessie 1938, 51). Hearst started with the San Francisco *Examiner*, copying Pulitzer's style. In 1896 he challenged Pulitzer on his own turf by buying the New York *Journal* and embarked on a "constant series of titillating excursions into the bizarre and the erotic" (Bessie, 55). Hearst's editor Arthur McEwen defined the essential element of journalism as "the gee-whiz emotion" (Bessie, 55), a principle that has been the guiding light of tabloid journalism ever since. In addition to the hardy perennial human-interest stories, the *Journal* included features like comics, sports, and short, pithy editorial content. With the success of the *Journal*, the battle for circulation between Hearst and Pulitzer grew into full swing; by the end of the nineteenth century, "only slight alteration in format and subject matter was needed for the creation of the tabloid" (Bessie 1938, 60).

The first tabloid as such was the *Daily Continent*, founded in 1891 by Frank A. Munsey, "a good merchandiser although a second-rate editor" (Bent 1927, 185). Competing as it was with the Hearst and Pulitzer giants, the venture soon failed, and it was left to Alfred Harmsworth (later Lord Northcliffe) to establish the tabloid as a viable form in Britain. In 1898, Northcliffe was invited by Pulitzer to produce a New Year's Day tabloid edition of the *World*. Although the issue sold over 100,000 more copies than usual, Pulitzer was not convinced.

## The Twentieth-Century Tabloid

Not until 1919 did Northcliffe's ideas prevail, once he had demonstrated the success of tabloids with his British *Daily Mirror* and other papers. Northcliffe advised the *Chicago Tribune*'s Joseph Patterson on the merits of tabloid form, and the first successful tabloid picture paper was the *New York Daily News*, established on June 26, 1919, by Patterson and R. R. McCormick.

The *News* was modeled on Northcliffe's successful British ventures, with short, "personality" stories, and specials like its own beauty contest and detective series. Its first issue featured a half-page photo story on the Prince of Wales, who was scheduled to visit the United States shortly after. In that issue, Patterson pledged: "No story will be continued to another page—that is to save you trouble" (Bessie 1938, 84). Patterson is said to have noted with satisfaction that people could read tabloids easily on crowded subway trains (Emery 1972). Although its beginnings were shaky, within two years the *News* had the largest circulation in New York, at 400,000, and by 1938 its daily circulation was at 1,750,000, with the Sunday edition reaching 3,250,000.

In the 1920s, the paper contained serious, if tersely written, news stories, mixed with human-interest features ("monkey glands give man of 72 youth's health" [Bessie 1938, 88]). The paper covered cooking, fashion, beauty, sports, comics, children's cute sayings: "the subjects covered were almost all within the recognized scope of daily journalism" (Bessie, 94).

By 1924, Hearst, whose morning paper, the *American*, was losing circulation to the *News*, introduced the American *Daily Mirror*. Then as now, tabloids have proclaimed themselves to be the voice of the people, and Hearst's introduction to the *Mirror* was no exception: "And when the tabloid speaks, its language is not dead with the stylism of conventional newspaper wordage but alive with phrases that were spoken. Here is the history of a time as it would have been written by its people" (quoted in Bessie, 99). The *Mirror* promised "90 percent entertainment, 10 percent information—and the information without boring you" (p. 139). Although it began with much the same mix as the *News*, by 1925 the *Mirror* was changing, giving even less space to serious news and more to crime and sport, as another Hearst/Pulitzer circulation war ensued. The years 1919 to 1929 saw the era of "jazz journalism" (Bessie 1938). During that time, three New York tabloids—the *News*, *Mirror*, and *Graphic*—had a combined circulation of more than 1,500,000 without disturbing the circulation of more established dailies (Emery 1972, 553). The postwar "jazz age," with its gangsters, flappers, and apparent affluence "to the tabloid reader was a sensational mixture of sex, crime, conflict, and rags-to-riches stories" (Emery 1972, 557).

The tabloid style was in full flower at this time; it has not changed that much since. The style draws on the same stock of commonplace formulae as nineteenth-century ballads and mass-circulation newspapers. Murder stories continued to use formulae drawn straight from balladry, the classic murder saga always involving the same elements: "Discovery, Chase, Trial, Death Cell, Punishment" (Johnston 1935). "Furthermore, just as in the old ballads there were accepted ways of expressing common facts and conceptions, so now in the tabloids there are certain generic epithets that have become so conventionalized that they too tell their tales. *Banker, clubman, heiress, society leader, brownstone house*—all bring their backgrounds to them. So too do *flapper, crooner, torch singer, sleuth, Red, love thief, love nest, love lure, love charm, love potion, death car . . .*" (p. 119). Some of the words have changed in the last fifty years, but the style continues.

The *News* circulation climbed to one million by March 1926. On August 24, 1926, Rudolph Valentino died. The tabloids gave the event massive coverage and were criticized for virtually ignoring the death of a much more "significant" person, Harvard educator Charles Eliot. Tabloid editors, in the 1920s as in the 1980s, understood that their readership had its own priorities and heroes: "In 1926 the *Daily News* was the instrument of the mass in America's largest city. To this group, as to the masses throughout the nation, Rudolph Valentino was a passionate expression of the glamor and romance so fervently desired and so hopelessly unrealized in their lives" (Bessie 1938, 115).

# Tabloids Past and Present

With the success of the Valentino coverage, the tabloids went all out for "ballyhoo," epitomized in the frenzied 1927 coverage of aviator Charles Lindbergh. Several celebrated murder cases spurred circulation wars; in 1928, the *News* sold a half million extra papers with its retouched photo of murderer Ruth Snyder as the electric current was turned on in the death chamber. The picture was obtained by a news photographer with a camera attached to his ankle (Mott 1963, 671).

As in the 1980s, the interwar tabloids faced a barrage of criticism; they were seen as degrading, demoralizing villains that pandered to the lowest instincts. In *The Independent*, S. T. Moore described tabloids as "an unholy blot on the fourth estate—they carry all the news that isn't fit to print" (Bessie 1938, 19). Bessie also quotes the *Saturday Review of Literature*'s tirade against "Tabloid Poison": "What will the grandchildren of the tabloid readers be like . . . in emotions, ideals, intelligence, either wrought into fantastic shapes or burnt out altogether. Soiled minds, rotten before they are ripe" (p. 213). Bent, however, much as he deplored tabloids, pointed out: "All their characteristics are inherited from their ancestors or acquired from their big brothers. None of their practices but has been sanctified by journalistic tradition or accepted as present-day custom" (1927, 180).

Singled out for particular censure was the third player in the "ballyhoo" war of the 1920s, the *New York Evening Graphic*. It debuted in 1924 under the ownership of Bernarr MacFadden, a devotee of "physical culture" and founder of such successful magazines as *True Story*. Often dubbed the "Porno-Graphic," it was "widely regarded as the worst form of debauchery to which a daily newspaper has ever been subjected" (Bessie, 184).

MacFadden claimed the *Graphic* "would be written by, of, and for its readers" (Bessie, 186), and in his introductory editorial, he proclaimed: "We intend to interest you mightily. We intend to dramatize and sensationalize the news and some stories that are not news. . . . If you read it from first to last and find anything therein that does not interest you, we want you to write and tell us about it" (quoted in Bessie, 187).

The *Graphic*, like today's tabloids, carried no standard news but specialized in crime stories "as told to" its reporters. Vivid pictures, scantily clad women, and bizarre stories were its staple: "My back was broken but I kept on laughing"; "Thousands applaud while woman is tortured for amusement" (Bessie 1938); "Glimpse of slim blonde girl in bed wins Decree for Furrier's Wife"; "Love-crazed Ex-priest shoots Girl, Kills Self," (*Graphic*, June 5, 1929, quoted in Murphy 1984, 64).

The *Graphic* developed the use of the "composograph" for the Kip Rhinelander divorce in 1926, when Rhinelander's wife had stripped to the waist in the courtroom. The paper staged a courtroom scene using *Graphic* reporters and the back view of another young woman, later superimposing the heads of court participants on those of the reporters, providing "an almost invisible note at the bottom of the page" (Bessie 1938). While the device had been used in the old *New York Graphic* in the 1870s, it had always been plainly marked. The new *Graphic* used the technique, along with staged photographs, indiscriminately. Use of the composograph reached ludicrous heights that eventually killed it. "The *Graphic* once even had one of the King of England earnestly scrubbing his back with a brush in the privacy of his royal bath-room" (Spivak 1942, 379).

The precedent was thus set for the fabricated photos and retouched artwork of the later weekly tabloids. The paper also offered advice columns and was the first to print lonely hearts columns for matching couples, now a popular feature in several weekly tabloids. The *Graphic* was apparently in tune with the extravagant climate of the 1920s, and by 1929 its circulation had reached 350,000. However, the more sober atmosphere of the 1930s, coupled with a libel suit and the strain of producing such a paper on a daily basis, proved too much, and the *Graphic* folded in 1932. MacFadden, however, had sown seeds that, while dormant for a while, bore extravagant fruit in the tabloid boom more than thirty years later.

While the *Graphic* went under with the end of the "jazz age," the *News* survived and prospered by becoming respectable. In 1930, Patterson told his staff, "We're off on the wrong foot. The people's major interest is not in the playboy, Broadway, and divorces, but in how they're going to eat; and from this time forward, we'll pay attention to the struggle for existence that's just beginning. All signs point to the prospect of a great economic upheaval, and we'll pay attention to the news of things being done to assure the well-being of the average man and his family" (quoted in Mott 1963, 669).

Although it still featured gossipy stories, advice, and tips, the *News* began covering more serious and foreign news, and the old banner headlines got smaller. As it grew more "respectable," advertisers found it more appealing, and in 1936 the *News* won a Pulitzer Prize for a series on syphilis: "It has truly become an open forum for debate and provides its readers with the materials for intelligent suffrage" (Bessie 1938, 133).

The *Mirror* was not so successful in dealing with the depression. Hearst sold the paper in 1928, then took it back in 1930, when it began its "metamorphosis into a columnist's playground" (Bessie, 147), with celebrity gossip as a mainstay. The paper stole successful Broadway columnist Walter Winchell from the *Graphic*; he "made them feel the delight that comes from intimacy with the great" (Bessie, 150). In 1937, circulation was a respectable 600,000, but the paper never became a very profitable enterprise, and it finally closed in 1963.

By the 1930s, the tabloid form was established as a permanent feature of American journalism. In 1937, there were forty-nine tabloids, with a combined circulation of 3,525,000 (Bessie 1938). The 1920s' vilification and dire warnings about tabloid excesses had died down as tabloids became more respectable. The demise of the *Graphic* seemed to indicate that the most lurid tabloids were a thing of the past; indeed in 1938 Bessie wrote that "the extremely sensational tabloid has disappeared" (p. 218). After World War II, major cities saw a fresh wave of sensational murder cases that kept tabloid circulation wars going (Emery 1972), but generally the "middle-of-the-road" big city daily tabloids continued a tradition of lively, brief reporting of news, features, gossip, and sport.

It would seem that successful daily city tabloids were all that were needed. It was left to Generoso Pope and the *National Enquirer* to set the scene for a new era of national tabloid competition. From 1960 to 1990, Pope and his competitors have at various times picked up on elements of all their predecessors, combining and recombining them to fit new readers.

## The *National Enquirer*:
## From Gore to Grocery Line

The weekly tabloid of the 1980s owes its particular look to the guiding hand of the late Generoso (Gene) Pope, known to his staff as "GP," or simply "The Boss" (Barber 1982). Pope's *National Enquirer* established the format of the family-oriented tabloid, with later competitors moving in to exploit the market he had discovered and tapped. The *Enquirer*'s current incarnation, however, is the latest stage in a series of formats since its inception in the 1920s.

Former Hearst advertising executive William Griffin founded the *Enquirer* in 1926 as a full-size Sunday paper, using a loan from Hearst (*Newsweek* 1969; Klaidman 1975). Hearst used the paper to try out new ideas. "The good ideas carried over into Hearst's own papers; the *Enquirer* was stuck with the bad ones" (*Newsweek* 1969, 79). The paper was never a great success; by 1952 it had a circulation of seven thousand and was primarily devoted to crime stories and racing tips. Generoso Pope bought the paper from Hearst for $75,000 that year and began experimenting with various new formulae. Pope was the son of a New York businessman who had published the Italian language paper *Il Progresso* and owned a radio station. The younger Pope had worked on his father's paper and later spent a year as an intelligence officer for the CIA's psychological warfare unit (Byrne 1983).

Pope tried various formats for the paper before settling on gore. "I noticed how auto accidents drew crowds and I decided that if it was blood that interested people, I'd give it to them" (quoted in *Time* 1972, 64). He credited a 1958 newspaper strike as a catalyst for the success of his new formula, and from then until 1968, the paper built its circulation to one million on stories of horrific murders and accidents, with a sprinkling of unexplained mysteries, unusual human-interest tales, often vicious celebrity gossip, and—somewhat incongruously—occasional pictures of cute animals and children.

A sample issue of the period demonstrates the typical mix. The cover story is headlined "Space Platform Circling Mars—Living Creatures May Be Aboard—U.S. Is Planning Rocket Probes—U.S. Government Scientists Investigating." Inside, gruesome murder stories abound, such as the tersely written, "Murders His Dad for $8." The opening paragraphs read:

> James Lignos crept to the side of his sleeping father and started to go through his pockets.
>
> The father, Robert, awoke, looked at his son, and then said: "What are you doing, Jim?"
>
> In answer, James, 38, grabbed a chunk of wooden board and smashed his father's skull in.
>
> The father was still alive in his blood-soaked bed when James took $8 from his pockets and went to a saloon to drink it up.
>
> But the father died later and James was cold sober when he went on trial. And he cried as he told the judge, "Send me to the electric chair!"

The story was illustrated with photographs of the board used to batter the father and the blood-stained bed he died in (July 28, 1963, 2).

This issue also includes several other murder stories, such as "Stabs Girl 55 Times" (p. 4) and "Terror with High-heeled Shoes," about a woman who killed two men with her shoes. Other typical stories are the "ironic twist" tales: "He Crashes Head on into Another Car and Kills Driver—His Brother" (p. 31); "Drunk Driver Can't Read—Mistakes Prison Camp for a Motel" (p. 28), and "Family Eats Barbecued Meat—Finds It Was Their Dog" (p. 13). This story describes how the Maximo Gomez family of Mexico City bought meat from their butcher next door, only to discover that they were dining on their pet. This tale, like many that appeared (and continue to appear) in tabloids, seems to be a variation of a common legend about a family who are served up their pet dog in a Chinese restaurant (Brunvand 1981, 93).

Another theme is the uncovering of waste or fraud by individuals or government, such as "Child He Claims as a Dependent Is a Cocker

Spaniel" (*Enquirer* July 28, 1963, p. 2), and the UFO coverup story. A two-page photo spread features a bizarre collection of images—a ten-week-old baby "who loves TV," a picture of a Chinese Crested Dog, a bleeding driver being pulled from a car wreck, and June Cooper, "a starlet in England at 35-24-36" (pp. 16–17). There are stories on the John Profumo sex scandal in Britain, Hollywood and TV gossip, and numerous advertisements for products offering readers lovelier bodies, hair-free noses, and the promise of becoming a "mental wizard in one evening." Unlike contemporary tabloids, the 1960s *Enquirer* shows little interest in occult and mystical subjects, either in editorial or advertising material. It does however, offer a racing and boxing supplement that has since disappeared.

Wherever possible, stories of the period featured photos of dead and mutilated bodies, such as a 1963 story headlined "I Cut Out Her Heart and Stomped on It," describing the mutilation murder of Olympic skier Sonja McCaskie. The cover displayed photos of her heart, headless torso, and severed foot (Sept. 8, 1963).

According to Reginald Potterton, who worked for almost a year as an *Enquirer* articles editor in the 1960s, the paper avoided stories that were explicitly sexual, preferring to concentrate on bizarre violence, with such headlines as "Kills Son and Feeds Corpse to Pigs" and "Digs Up Wife's Rotting Corpse and Rips It Apart" (1969, 118). Potterton characterized the *Enquirer*'s signature style as close to "black humor at its blackest," offering a typical opening paragraph: "Eva Fedorchuk battered her husband's face to a bloody pulp with a pop bottle. Then she told police he'd cut himself while shaving" (p. 204).

Under the guise of public interest, the paper published graphic photographs of accident victims, such as a two-page spread featuring a man whose face had been ripped off, his dead wife, and the charred bodies of their children (Sept. 22, 1963). "Don't let it happen to you," blared the headline, pointing out that the family should have worn seat belts. This blend of pious moralizing and reveling in gory detail descends to the *Enquirer* from seventeenth-century ballads and newsbooks and their eighteenth- and nineteenth-century broadside and newspaper offspring.

# Tabloids Past and Present

"Consumer" stories also often incorporated a dire warning while offering such opportunities for sadistic amusement as "Hair Dye Has Made Me Bald for Life" (Potterton, 118). Stories about handicapped people were popular, too: "Accountant Works with Feet Because He Was Born without Arms" (p. 120).

The 1960s gossip columns, which were only a small component in the paper, were far more explicit and vicious than any 1980s tabloid would dare. For instance, on January 3, 1960, a gossip column reported: "Barbara Hutton . . . caused quite a stir in a Tangiers bar when she imbibed far too much and wanted to do a strip for her youngish date. The lad decided Barbara had had enough and half dragged her out of the place. . . . Charles Laughton was so drunk in a London pub the other night that he passed out. . . . Charlie had his face on the barroom floor for almost seven hours before they came to get him out" (p. 7).

Although most of the feature stories were probably fairly accurate, if melodramatic, accounts, "much of the gossip material was virtually pure myth" (Potterton 1969, 120). The *Enquirer* preferred tales of violence and drunkenness to those of sexual indiscretion, although there was often an underlying tone of disapproval for unconventional relationships, as in the Barbara Hutton item. All celebrities were fair game for the *Enquirer* treatment: "Any celebrity who was at one time or another unlucky enough to land in the national press on charges of assault or drunkenness could have his name resurrected and attached to a similar charge for the rest of his life, even if he became senile or joined the temperance society" (p. 120).

Although the gory formula worked well for about ten years, circulation stalled at around one million, and in the late 1960s, Pope decided to try a new approach. Noticing the decline of the newsstands and other conventional news outlets, he turned his attention to supermarkets. These had until recently been an untapped outlet for newspapers and magazines, but Pope took note of the success of *Woman's Day* magazine, the first to be marketed seriously in supermarkets. In order to fit the new outlet, the formula had to be changed, and the new "family-style" tabloid emerged. Pope reportedly based his formula on the *Reader's Digest* of the 1930s, offering "an inspirational version of what the old yellow journalists called 'gee-whiz' journalism" (Rudnitsky 1978, 78). In Pope's words, "We bent over backwards to overcome the image of gore. Anything that has even the slightest inkling of sex or gore is just not used. Initially, we lost a quarter million in circulation but, six months later, we were back at a million—and then up" (quoted in Klaidman 1975, G2).

Two of Pope's decisions were probably the key in the success of the *Enquirer*. The first was the decision to make the paper a weekly that did not cover fast-breaking news. The *Enquirer*, either in its gory or clean phases, did not have to compete with daily newspapers, tabloid or otherwise, so it was not faced with the problem of producing sensational stories every day, as was its predecessor, the *Graphic*. In fact, the "news" in the *Enquirer* and later tabloids rarely pretended to be timely—the appeal lay in the unusual and titillating nature of the stories, whether the events covered happened the previous week or two centuries ago. In addition, the self-proclaimed "national" scope of the paper further placed the *Enquirer* apart from competition with any particular city tabloids.

However, the decision to target supermarkets and drugstores was probably the most important factor in the rise of the weekly tabloids in the 1970s and 1980s, with the new *Enquirer* setting the tone for those that followed. As Radway points out, when discussing the phenomenal growth of romance sales following similar marketing decisions, selling books or other publications can be made profitable and predictable "if one could establish a permanent conduit between a publishing source and a consuming audience and keep that conduit constantly filled with material that would continue to satisfy individual readers" (1984, 24). Pope targeted a new and larger potential readership, astutely realizing that reaching that audience was more direct and consistent through national supermarket and drugstore chains than through conventional newsstands and other publishing outlets.

Pope moved the *Enquirer*'s operation from New York City to Florida in 1971. By this time, he had the *Enquirer* in all major supermarket chains, where it eventually became one of the ten most profitable supermarket items. Indeed, it became "a cash machine" (Byrne 1983, 78–79).

The "new squeaky-clean *Enquirer*" of the 1970s (Peer and Schmidt 1975, 62) abandoned the gore and questionable personal ads in favor of features on household repair, pop psychology, unusual human-interest stories, and frequently flattering celebrity stories. If the *Evening Graphic* was the model for the 1960s, the 1970s version owed more to the middle-of-the-road interwar tabloids, such as the *Mirror*, as well as to Pope's self-proclaimed model, *Reader's Digest*. Around this time, the *Enquirer* and its imitators also picked up an interest in the occult and mystical, interests that continued into the 1980s. Circulation reached four million by 1974 (Peer and Schmidt 1975), with a gross annual revenue of $41 million, up from $17 million in 1973 (Klaidman 1975, G2).

During the 1970s, the paper started to run editorials on such issues as U.S. arms sales to Arab countries. It also featured frequent articles on government waste and bylined pieces by politicians like Representative Les Aspin (Klaidman, G2). It seems that Pope had aspirations for the *Enquirer* to become something of a crusader in the style of yellow journalism or the interwar *Daily News*. "Call it advocacy writing or the old populist theory, . . . we are out to capture some of the old vitality of American journalism" (Peer and Schmidt, 62). However, although the *Enquirer* of the 1980s and 1990s continues its interest in government overspending and "cover-ups," Pope's ambitions have not been realized, and overtly political topics are now largely ignored.

*Murdoch versus Pope*

Australian publisher Rupert Murdoch, after an unsuccessful attempt to buy the *Enquirer*, launched the *Star* in 1974. It drew on Murdoch's proven expertise with the tabloid format in Australia and Britain, with "the same circus-poster layout, garish headlines, and steamy prose of his *Sun* in London" (Welles 1979, 56). The new weekly was in color and was launched with a $5 million TV advertising campaign, propelling circulation quickly to one million (Welles 1979). Circulation then stalled, and a series of editors was unable to raise it. Murdoch had apparently misread American tastes by assuming huge numbers of readers would accept the "sexy" and often self-consciously "working class" British formula: "Most workers in the much more fluid and upwardly mobile American society do not like to think of themselves as part of the working class and tend to avoid publications designed specifically for a downscale, or working class, audience" (Welles, 56).

In 1976, Murdoch changed the *Star*'s format, using the 1970s "clean" *Enquirer* as a model. The new *Star* specialized in celebrity coverage and adopted a somewhat more subdued tone than the Pope paper, characteristics that have since continued. He also belatedly realized the importance of an efficient sales machine, increasing outlets for the *Star* in supermarket and drugstore chains. By 1979, circulation had risen to three million and had become Murdoch's most profitable property in the United States, with an annual net of $5 million (Welles 1979). In that year, Pope counterattacked by changing to a color format and mounting a $30 million national TV campaign, featuring the now-famous "Enquiring Minds Want to Know" slogan. The campaign boosted the circulation to over five million by 1982 with gross revenues at $140 million, up 54 percent in a year (Byrne 1983, 78). In 1980, Pope introduced the *Weekly World News*. Using the *Enquirer's* old one-color presses, the *News's* small staff built a one million circulation on creatively bizarre stories. The debut of the *News* allowed the *Enquirer* to counter the *Star* with a greater concentration on celebrity stories, although it has not abandoned its other specialities. Pope died in 1988, and in April 1989 Peter Callahan of MacFadden Holdings bought the business for $412 million (Rothman and DeGeorge 1989). In mid-1990, G.P. Group, the MacFadden subsidiary that runs the *Enquirer,* bought the *Star* for $400 million (*Wall Street Journal* 1990). According to an *Enquirer* spokesperson, the two papers continue to function separately, "as competitors" (telephone interview with Judy Walsh, May 7, 1991).

## The Globe Tabloids:
## In the Steps of the *Enquirer*

The development of Globe Communications tabloids closely followed that of the *Enquirer*. The tabloid *Midnight* was founded in
1954 by Joe Azaria, under the editorship of current *Sun* editor John
Vader (telephone interview, July 6, 1987). Azaria also bought the
Cleveland, Ohio, *Examiner* name and turned that into the *National
Examiner*. In its early days, the Montreal-based *Midnight* was "little
more than a parochial scandal sheet" (Potterton 1969, 208), with a
circulation of around seventy-five thousand (Rosenbloom 1979).
Later it followed the *Enquirer* into the gore market, but it also devoted more space to bizarre sex stories. This predilection led to it
being condemned by the National Office for Decent Literature, a fate
avoided by the *Enquirer* (Potterton, 118). By the late 1960s, the sex-
and-gore version of *Midnight* "after the *Enquirer*, [was] the best written tabloid and the most professionally produced" (Potterton, 208).

*Midnight* later became the *Midnight Globe,* then simply the *Globe*;
current owner Mike Rosenbloom bought the papers in 1969.
Rosenbloom followed Pope's lead, cleaned up the paper, and began
supermarket distribution. *Midnight* claimed a circulation of 1. 4 million in 1977, and editor Selig Adler, a former managing editor of the
New York *Mirror* and articles editor at the *Enquirer*, offered this advice to potential free-lancers: "Sex and violence are taboo. We want
upbeat human interest material. . . . Stories where fate plays a major
role are always good" (Sandhage and Brohaugh 1977, 27). By 1979,
the *Midnight Globe* was being bought by over 2 million people, an
almost 50 percent circulation growth that Rosenbloom attributed to
an aggressive TV advertising campaign in 1978 (Rosenbloom 1979).

In 1982 the company left Montreal for West Palm Beach, Florida,
and in 1983 founded the *Sun*, the most outlandish of the Globe papers, in response to the success of the *Weekly World News*. As well
as the three tabloids, the company also publishes *Your Health*, a
weekly compilation of health tips, diets, and medical miracles, and
Globe Minimags, small booklets on a variety of topics, also sold in

supermarkets. Globe Communications moved in 1985 to Boca Raton, Florida.

## Tabloid Also-Rans

During the 1960s and 1970s, other tabloids came and went, many modeling themselves on Pope's successful format. According to Potterton, in 1969 there were more than forty weekly tabloids published in the United States and Canada, with a combined circulation of 7 million (1969, 118). Potterton discusses the five largest papers, most of them featuring various combinations of sex and violence: "Ostensibly, the *Enquirer* shuns all contact with sex stories; *Justice Weekly*, on the other hand, boasts an editorial obsession with just about every form of deviation known, short of bestiality and necrophilia; while *Confidential Flash*, the *National Informer* and *Midnight* range over as many bases as possible but incline toward 'straight' sex and horror-violence" (p. 118).

The Chicago-based *National Informer* featured stories "of such blatant flamboyance that none but the most gullible could be expected to believe them" (p. 211). Publisher Vince Sorren told Potterton: "We go after all the sex we can get, although sometimes we have to draw the line," citing a story about a horse and a nymphomaniac as overstepping that line. The *Informer* ran numerous advertisements for sex aids and partners, maintaining a tone of "jovial depravity" (p. 211). In 1969, it claimed a circulation of 500,000 but has since folded.

The now defunct *Confidential Flash* was a "singularly humorless tabloid" (p. 212) published out of Toronto. Its speciality, in addition to the usual sex and violence, was extreme political views. One of its columnists offered this solution to the Vietnam conflict: "Rape the women and burn the men—that's the way to bring these scum into line" (quoted in Potterton, 211–12). Cliff Linedecker, former *National Examiner* associate editor, also remembers the *National Exploiter*, "which they used to print on pink paper. It was terrible, it really had some outrageous stories. . . . I remember one: 'Cement

Mason Finishes Wife' showing the body of the woman and a splash cover headline. . . . We would never get away with that kind of thing now" (interview, Feb. 5, 1986).

The "sex-and-gore" publications do not seem to have survived the tabloids' supermarket metamorphosis, although others adapted and survived longer. In the 1970s, the Florida-based *Modern People*'s content was about 50 percent celebrity oriented (Holden 1977, 19), but a sample issue (June 29, 1975) also contains a two-page color spread headlined "NASA Hiding UFOs from Americans" (pp. 12–13) and self-help features such as "How to 'Win' a Divorce" (p. 14). Other papers that sprung up in this era but did not last included the *National Tattler* and the *National Insider*.

## Tabloids Today

According to Ken Matthews, former *National Examiner* Photo Editor, the "real story" of the tabloids is their phenomenal business success. Referring to the estimated combined readership (not circulation) of about 50 million for the tabloids, he argues, "if a national television show had 50 million viewers it would be regarded as an enormous success. This industry is doing it every week with a relatively small overhead compared to the cost of television production—that to me is the story that hasn't been told" (interview, Feb. 5, 1986). Unfortunately, the financial details of the tabloids' success are difficult to clarify because of the extreme secrecy that both major companies maintain. *Enquirer* personnel are particularly closed-mouthed; as John Engstrom writes, "Like any hugely successful institution, the *National Enquirer* is a creepily self-enclosed cosmos" (1984, 24). Two letters of mine requesting financial information from the offices of the *Enquirer* were unanswered while representatives of the *Star* and of Globe Communications answered but declined to offer such information. (Globe Communications has, however, been extremely helpful with other aspects of the research.)

Nevertheless, from the information that has been available, particularly around the time of the sale of the *Enquirer*, the tabloids are certainly a lucrative business. In 1983, with a circulation of 5.1 million, the *Enquirer* had an estimated net income of around $15 million (*BusinessWeek* 1983) while in 1985 Gene Pope's personal fortune was estimated to be $150 million (Stein 1988). Likewise, the *Star* has continued to be a highly profitable enterprise.

Since the mid 1980s, however, the tabloid business has been characterized by greater segmentation, as more papers have been competing for readers. The *Star*, *Enquirer*, and *Globe*—the three leaders in 1979—have been joined by the *Examiner*, *Sun*, and *Weekly World News*, all of which have developed large audiences, even if these do not rival the original three. The *Examiner* and *Sun*, of course, are designed to complement the *Globe* rather than compete with it, just as the *News* is intended to complement the *Enquirer*.

The problem for the tabloids became how to demonstrate the differences between them so as to solidify reader identification. In addition, increasing worries about legal problems encouraged tabloids to make modifications. Talking about the early to mid 1980s, *Star* publisher Peter Eldredge explained: "There were more tabloids out there, they all cost more and the Carol Burnett lawsuit against the *National Enquirer* cast a cloud over the whole category" (Pfaff 1987, 68).

From 1982 to 1984, the circulation of *Star* was down. In 1985, *Star* management spent $20 million to give the paper a new look, introducing a stapled, more magazine-like format, and raising the price from 55 cents to 69 cents (in 1990 it costs 85 cents). The emphasis on celebrity coverage was reinforced, and mail-order advertising, always a tabloid staple, was cut from about twelve pages to no more than four; no advertisements may promise instant cures or free merchandise (Pfaff 1987). The *Star* then went all out to attract national advertisers like Procter & Gamble, Lever Bros., Philip Morris, General Foods, Heinz, and Campbell's Soup. Circulation rose from 3.2 million to 3.5 million from 1985 to 1986, with advertising revenue up 12.4 percent (Landro 1987). Eldredge has worked hard to distance the *Star* from other tabloids. Referring to the *Enquirer*, he claimed in 1987, "They're still a tabloid newspaper. We're a magazine" (Pfaff, 68). The circulation of the *Star* now stands at 3,562,367 (Boyden and Krol 1990), but with an estimated 3.3 readers per copy, its audience is considerably larger (Brower 1990).

While the *Star* refocused its concentration almost exclusively on celebrities, the *Enquirer* developed an interest in "service" articles and health coverage. While maintaining extensive celebrity coverage, it has tried to differentiate itself from the *Star* by developing a "family atmosphere" with features such as write-in contests and weekly stories seeking adoptive parents for foster children (Pfaff 1987). Meanwhile, the *Enquirer*'s sister paper, the *Weekly World News*, has moved squarely into the "outrageous" market—still offering little sex or gore but covering bizarre and incredible human-interest stories. It features virtually no national advertising, gaining revenue from mail-order products and a circulation that now stands at around 1 million (telephone communication, *National Enquirer*, 1990).

While the *Enquirer* sold 3.8 percent fewer copies in the second half of 1986 than in the second half of 1985, it apparently gained 10 percent in readership, up to an estimated 17.8 million, as more readers pass on copies (Pfaff, 68). However, in the first half of 1988, the *Enquirer*'s circulation fell again by 3.5 percent, and by the end of that year circulation had slipped a further 2.2 percent (Reilly 1989a). Nevertheless, circulation still stood at 4.2 million, and the attractiveness of the business led to a bidding war when the *Enquirer* went on sale after Pope's death.

Peter Callahan of MacFadden Holdings, in partnership with investment group Boston Ventures, bought the Pope holdings for an unexpectedly high $412 million, outbidding British publisher Robert Maxwell by $50 million and French publishing conglomerate Hachette by $100 million (Rothman and DeGeorge 1989). The expected price had been no more than $250 million (Reilly 1989a). At that time, the 1988 operating profit was estimated to be $15–20 million on $140 million in revenues, not a large increase on 1983 figures. At the time, Callahan was not regarded as a major player in the publishing industry. He had founded MacFadden Holdings in 1975 by buying up a group of ailing magazines once owned by the *Evening Graphic*'s Bernarr MacFadden (O'Leary 1989). After a shaky start, the company now publishes a range of magazines such as *True Story, True Confessions, True Romance*, and *Teen Beat*, as well as some more up-market ones. Callahan, commenting that "Elvis bid with us" (Rothman and DeGeorge, 139), explained his interest in the *Enquirer*: "I'm trying to compile a spread of publications that touches every interest. . . . *Chief Executive* is at one end, and the *Enquirer* is on the other" (Rothman and DeGeorge, 140).

There has apparently been some apprehension at the *Enquirer* about possible changes since Callahan's huge bid apparently hurt his cash flow (Kelley 1989). Callahan commented that Pope "ran it [the *Enquirer*] as a hobby" (Rothman and DeGeorge 1989) and that his spending was excessively lavish. *Enquirer* reporters had apparently become used to the availability of large sums of money for pursuing stories (Ressner 1988), the paper spending, for example, $150,000 to cover the death of Princess Grace of Monaco (Byrne 1983). Pope had also become used to spending large sums on projects such as his annual $1 million Christmas tree and party for the town of Lantana, where the *Enquirer* is based. According to *Star* Editor Richard Kaplan, who has worked for both the *Enquirer* and MacFadden Holdings, "They [MacFadden] run a very tight ship. Pope used to throw money around like they were minting it. I think that day and age is over there" (Kelley 1989). Indeed, shortly after the takeover, Callahan announced plans to increase revenue by an estimated $15 million in 1989 (Rothman and DeGeorge 1989).

Since then, the *Enquirer*'s cover price has increased from 75 cents to 85 cents while the number of pages has been reduced from sixty-four to fifty-six. The price of the *Weekly World News* has risen 5 cents to 75 cents. In addition, Callahan has laid off about 60 of the *Enquirer*'s 395 employees and drastically cut the TV advertising budget. The Christmas party will likely become a thing of the past (Reilly 1989b). With money saved, Callahan has talked of introducing a Spanish-language edition of the *Enquirer*, and possibly adding an international edition, a soap opera magazine, and/or a TV show (Rothman and DeGeorge 1989). He has, however, pledged not to reduce salaries, no doubt a great relief in an organization where edi-

# Tabloids Past and Present

tors can earn $150,000 a year. Callahan reportedly will not interfere greatly in editorial decisions, which will be under the control of Pope's right-hand man, editor Iain Calder, whose salary is said to be around $865,000 a year (Kelley 1989). In 1990, the *Enquirer*'s circulation has held steady, now standing at 4,381,242 (Boyden and Krol 1990).

Both the *Star* and the *Enquirer* have been fairly successful in luring major advertisers, although their major source of revenue is still through over-the-counter sales. National companies that had refused to advertise in tabloids because of their image now do so. Campbell Soup Company's Director of Media Services George Mahrlig commented, "There's nothing in those two publications that's socially objectionable in any significant aspect. . . . They round out a print list, delivering the typically non-print target: less educated, not as upscale" (quoted in Pfaff 1987, 73).

"As the two tabloid leaders strive to edit and market their way out of the tabloid category, [Globe Communications papers] are deliberately positioned for the lower-echelon audience that the leaders left behind" (Pfaff, 69). The Globe papers try to differentiate themselves from the *Star* and *Enquirer*, as well as from each other, while trying not to compete among themselves. The *Globe*, the largest, has a circulation of 1.6 million and has the greatest concentration on celebrities; the *Examiner* at 1.1 million is very much like the *Enquirer* of the late 1970s, with a mixture of celebrity stories, human-interest, and "off-beat" stories. Globe's answer to the *News* is the *Sun*, with a circulation of 500,000. The *Sun* is the most bizarre, avoiding celebrity coverage in favor of stories that, as Globe director of corporate development Jack Linder puts it, "you have to stretch your imagination to believe." According to Linder, "We've cornered a certain spot in the market: middle of the road, middle income to rather downscale" (Pfaff, 72). The Globe papers have not been very successful in attracting major advertisers, except for tobacco manufacturers such as R. J. Reynolds, which increasingly find they have to target formerly despised lower economic groups. (Globe's 1990 circulation figures were obtained from the company, and at least some

For Enquiring Minds

may be declining; an *Examiner* staff member in a July 16, 1990, telephone interview stated that circulation of that paper had dipped sharply in recent months).

Although the tabloids' success peaked in the early 1980s, all are doing well enough financially that they can pay staff considerably more than regular newspapers. Ressner profiles an *Enquirer* reporter, Sammy Rubin, who at twenty-eight makes $70,000 a year "and enjoys a lavish expense account" (1988, 54) while even free-lancers can make over $50,000 a year working only for tabloids (Ressner 1988). Under Pope, the *Enquirer* budgeted large sums to pay informants and tipsters, a practice shared by all the tabloids, although others are much less free-spending. At Globe Communications, reporters and writers reportedly earn from about $20,800 to $41,600 a year while editors range from $36,400 to $104,000 per year (anonymous Globe spokesperson, personal communication, 1990). No salary figures for the *Star* are available, although since there is frequent movement of staff among all three tabloid companies, it may be assumed that it offers competitive terms.

Supermarket tabloids of 1990 are still an enormously successful industry, although there is some indication that their popularity peaked in the mid 1980s. Their financial success is not built on an ability to deliver a desirable demographic group to advertisers; tabloid readers are not the upwardly mobile "yuppies" who make advertisers salivate. Rather, it is built on a skill for creating a product that apparently speaks very closely to its readers, who return as faithful buyers week after week. The relationship between today's tabloid texts, their writers, and their readers forms the focus of the rest of this book.

# 2

# Tabloid Content Today

A good "Hey, Martha" would be a story about a body discovered
with no wounds and an autopsy revealing no human heart. Or a story
about a six-month-old Chinese baby who can accurately describe the
physical layout of the Malden, Mass., public library. Something very
weird but compelling. To have The Boss tell you that a story of yours
is a "Hey, Martha" is the local equivalent of winning a Pulitzer Prize.
— P. J. Corkery, 1981

Former *National Examiner* Editor Bill Burt used to hang his walls
with trophies—the covers that sold the most copies, each with its
circulation figure displayed below. For, like all the tabloids, the *Examiner* depends on its cover to sell papers; although subscriptions
are available at substantial savings, most tabloid readers buy their
papers over the counter.

While the covers of tabloids are notorious for promising more
than the stories deliver, the selection of cover features does provide
a suggestion of the contents—the cover is the paper's "shop window," according to a free-lance tabloid writer (Holden 1977). The
cover, "this gamble that we do every week," as *Examiner* staffer Cliff
Linedecker put it, is the one opportunity to snag new readers.

The tabloids are among the most formulaic of publications. Paradoxically, although they aim to startle and titillate, they are absolutely predictable in the way they do this, with the same mix of stories appearing reliably week after week, both on the covers and
inside.

## Tabloid Content

To familiarize myself with tabloid content, I subscribed to four tabloids, the *National Enquirer*, *National Examiner*, *Star*, and *Weekly
World News* for a fourteen-week period in 1985, and since then I
have frequently bought issues of all six papers. In order to demonstrate the consistency of the content, I analyzed specific stories from
one issue of each title, bought in one trip to a convenience store. The
six papers were the March 6, 1990, issue of *Weekly World News* and
the February 27 issues of the other five tabloids. It should be remembered, however, that my discussion of tabloid content is informed
not only by these examples but by a regular reading of the papers
over a five-year period.

The selection of stories displayed on the cover is the first suggestion that the tabloids, though similar in general appearance, are not
interchangeable. The tabloid market, like that of magazines generally, became more specialized during the 1980s. While any of the
stories in any of today's tabloids might have been found in the *National Enquirer* of the late 1970s, the most bizarre tales now appear
mainly in the *Weekly World News*, the *Sun*, and, to a slightly lesser
extent, the *National Examiner*. The *National Enquirer* and the *Star*
are dominated by celebrity stories although their inside pages also
contain human-interest tales of "ordinary people" and occasional
coverage of the bizarre—psychic experiences, for example—particularly if these have a celebrity angle. The sample covers of both the
*Star* and the *Enquirer* feature only celebrities. The cover of the
*Globe*, which has begun identifying itself as more interested in celebrity and "newsy" stories in the last few years, has celebrity features and a "how to" on cutting medical bills. The *Examiner*'s cover
is more eclectic, featuring "love secrets" of the "Knots Landing" TV
cast, but also a picture of a "heartbreak baby," a "medical breakthrough," and spring predictions from psychics. The *Weekly World
News* has no celebrities other than James Dean, who it claims to be
alive. Its main story continues a "mystery" about a World War II
bomber supposedly seen on the moon, and other stories are unusual
human-interest tales. The *Sun* eschews celebrities completely and

## Star

February 27, 1990

85¢

# SINATRA HAS ALZHEIMER'S

## FRIENDS FEAR

At age 74, Frank's memory is failing & he seems to walk around in a daze

**Richard Pryor's son is a drag queen**

Richard Pryor Jr. performs at Peoria club-- to dad's dismay

PLUS: JOE LOUIS' SON TO WED GAY SWEETHEART

**Double love trouble hits Cheers**
- TED DANSON MARRIAGE CRUMBLES AFTER 12 YEARS
- KIRSTIE ALLEY SPLITS WITH HER HUBBY

**EASTWOOD UNVEILS LOVE HE'S KEPT SECRET FOR 4 YEARS**

He gives her 4G a month & plays dad to her kids

**THE HEARTWARMING STORY 60 MINUTES DIDN'T TELL**
## HOW STARSKY'S BRAVE WIFE & SON LIVE WITH THE TIMEBOMB OF AIDS

# COSBY BLOWS TOP AS DAUGHTER, 23, ELOPES WITH LATIN LOVER, 39

**EXCLUSIVE STAR PHOTOS: THE DAY DONALD TRUMP'S ANGRY WIFE CAUGHT HIM WITH HIS OTHER WOMAN**

Cover of the *Star*, Feb. 27, 1990.
Reprinted courtesy of News America Publishing, Inc.

Cover of the *National Enquirer*, Feb. 27, 1990.
Reprinted courtesy of National Enquirer, Inc.

concentrates on bizarre human-interest features, such as its largest headline, "Woman Turns into Wild Dog after Being Forced to Eat Pet Food for 3 Years."

While the covers of the *Weekly World News* and the *Sun* present a world in which ordinary people often grapple with bizarre forces and do incredible things, the world of the *Enquirer* and *Star* is peopled by celebrities, chronicling their everyday bickering and problems. The *Examiner* and *Globe* seem to straddle both worlds quite comfortably. It is clear that the extremely bizarre stories in the *Sun* and *News* would never find space in the *Enquirer* or *Star*, just as most celebrity gossip stories are ignored by the *Sun* and *News*. Yet although the celebrity emphasis and the "that's incredible" emphasis distinguish the tabloids, the similarities of the themes featured inside all the papers are striking. As I shall discuss later, many readers buy all six regularly, and some fail to see any real distinctions between them. Donald Allport Bird, who looked at the *Star*, *Enquirer*, *Globe*, and *Weekly World News*, concluded that, while the tabloids undoubtedly differ in orientation, "I discovered the similarities to outweigh the differences" (undated, 6).

According to Schechter, who studied the *Sun* and *Weekly World News*, "these publications are virtual anthologies of age-old folk themes reincarnated in contemporary terms" (1988, 14). While I shall return to the question of the tabloids as folklore, my initial intention is to discuss the content of the themes that obviously emerge from even a cursory look at the papers. Most striking is that the still popular image of tabloids as gruesome and sexy—"sleazy" is the most ubiquitous adjective that comes to mind—is, with occasional exceptions, no longer true. Schroeder talks about tabloid readers: "What they find beneath the covers is not crime, pornography and distorted news stories, but easy entertainment, non-partisan morality, practical tips about homely concerns, reassurance about anxieties, and hope" (1982, 169). In 1977, tabloid free-lancer Larry Holden characterized the papers for readers of *Writer's Digest*; although the emphasis has changed over the years, his frequently overlapping story categories are still tabloid staples, and I use them to guide my analysis.

# For Enquiring Minds

*Celebrities*

Celebrity stories are obviously a mainstay, although the tabloids vary in the proportion of their space they devote to the life-styles of the rich and famous. As Holden points out, celebrity scandals are valued, and the sample week provided a plum—the impending divorce of Donald and Ivana Trump, a cover story for both the *Enquirer* and the *Star*. The *Enquirer* offers: "War of the Trumps: Sizzling Details of Billionaire's Secret Affair—and How It Wrecked His Marriage" (pp. 28–29, 32). The *Star* counters with exclusive photos of "Fight That Wrecked Billionaire Donald Trump's Marriage—The camera recorded the scene on a ski slope in Aspen, Colo., in January—the very instant when billionaire developer Donald Trump's marriage collapsed" (pp. 2–3).

As Donald Allport Bird points out, the tabloids are often judgmental in their coverage of celebrity scandal, suggesting that "hubris and excess" are deemed punishable: "At the root of much tabloid criticism of unconventional behavior or societal trends is the view that many of these individuals or events who spoil things for the average individual have gone just too far" (undated, 15). Typical is an *Enquirer* story: "Liz in Shock—Her Designer Pal Halston Is Dying of AIDS" (p. 37). The story manages to be positive in its treatment of Elizabeth Taylor, who as a perennial tabloid favorite is almost never maligned. She is portrayed as a warm-hearted woman who stands by her friends, no matter how unsavory they may be. Halston, on the other hand, epitomizes the celebrity who has gone too far, and must pay: "Halston's disease follows a wild life in New York's fastest lane. He skyrocketed to international fame in 1961 after Jackie Kennedy wore one of his pillbox hats to her husband's inauguration. During the 1970s, he also turned into one of New York's top thrill-seekers—gradually destroying himself with a deadly mix of drugs, booze and promiscuous homosexual sex. . . ."

However, although the celebrity scandal is a tabloid favorite, "tab readers are just as concerned about personalities struggling against problems, having occult experiences or being involved in anything that punches through their bigger-than-life images and makes them

# Tabloid Content Today

Cover of the *National Examiner*, Feb. 27, 1990.
Reprinted courtesy of Globe International, Inc.

Cover of the *Weekly World News*, Mar. 6, 1990.
Reprinted courtesy of Weekly World News, Inc.

human" (Holden 1977, 20). Indeed, the popular stereotype of tabloids as endlessly tearing down the reputations of celebrities is no longer very accurate. In the wake of Carol Burnett's successful libel suit, the tabloids are increasingly careful in their celebrity coverage; it may not all be accurate, but relatively little is defamatory. *Examiner* Associate Editor Linedecker explains: "We really try to make our stories upbeat. We think that's what our readers want to read. They like the people they see on television and movies, and they don't want to read bad things about them. . . . If we found something out about a secret romance between a couple of stars, we would run it if we could back it up, but we're really not out to assassinate the character of anybody." He recalled a series of unflattering stories about Elvis Presley that drew an enraged response from readers: "they want to read about the Elvis they wanted Elvis to be."

Levin, Mody-Desbarau, and Arluke (1988), using a sample from the *Enquirer*, *Star*, *Globe* and *Examiner*, concluded that 98 percent of celebrity articles were about mundane or minor events such as shopping sprees, romances, or rumored quarrels between spouses. In addition, the tone of the majority of stories was positive. My sample week had several stories aimed at "making the stars human." The *Enquirer* stressed the positive angle in "Barbara Eden Shedding Tears of Joy—Son Is Winning 4-Year Drug Battle" (p. 3). The *Star* profiled TV star Delta Burke and her struggle with overweight (p. 17), asking readers to send diet suggestions to her in care of the paper. The *Star* also features a story on the marriage breakup of actors Tom Cruise and Mimi Rogers, attributing the couple's problems to his sterility (p. 23). In these two stories the subtext is "that those who are famous, rich and beautiful have their problems too" (Schroeder 1982, 174). As Schroeder points out, photos are often used to belie the image of the famous as always perfect, such as the regular "unflattering candid shots of disheveled beauties, of heroes caught off-guard in a scuffle and of close-ups disclosing warts, wens, wrinkles and overweight" (p. 174).

An increasingly common type of celebrity story is the "inside look" at the life of popular TV shows, with nighttime soap operas and situation comedies the favorites. The tabloids, particularly the

*Star* and the *Enquirer*, spend thousands of dollars every year on inside information about the annual soap cliffhangers and upcoming season's story lines (Ressner 1988), helping to maintain fan interest in the shows during summer hiatus. Throughout the year, the tabloids chronicle feuds and bickering on the sets of popular programs. Thus, "Tony Danza Battles to Keep Peace between Feuding Co-stars" is a typical "insider" story about trouble on the set of the ABC sitcom "Who's the Boss?" Co-stars Judith Light and Alyssa Milano are supposedly at each other's throats because of Light's jealousy of the younger woman (*Star*, 4). Meanwhile, over on the set of NBC's "Cheers," "Ted Danson and Kirstie Alley Console Each Other as Marriages Collapse" (*Star*, 8).

Brower suggests that through such stories "the industry, the tabloids and the fans themselves increasingly are constructing narratives about the industry, its productions, its stars, and their professional but backstage lives" (1990, 227). The focus of these stories, which are a relatively recent addition to the tabloids' repertoire of themes, is no longer only the personal life of celebrities but their lives as they affect their work in the programs that the readers are themselves watching. Brower describes the mutual understanding between Lorimar, producers of "Dallas," and the tabloids: "As a Lorimar publicist remarked, the tabloids' stories about 'Dallas' are 'part of the show's mystique' " (p. 231). The gossip industry, therefore, helps the TV fan achieve a richer and more satisfying reading of the shows, an idea I shall return to in discussing tabloid readers.

*Off-beat Human Interest*

Hardly a category at all, the description of "off-beat human interest" covers any story about people, which in effect means virtually all tabloid stories. The possible range of topics is suggested by Holden: "The fact that Ben Franklin was fired from his postmaster position by the British even though he regularly sent postal profits (amazing, huh?) to London is among my oddity stories for the tabs, plus a conversation with a talking dog, a woman who receives money and prizes almost daily because she knows how to win contests, and an interview with the world champion watermelon-seed spitter" (1977, 20).

The thread that links the tabloid tales is the positive angle; readers should be able to feel good about the story, even if the protagonists are suffering or in pain. Gone are the horrific murders, accidents, and mutilations of the 1960s; tabloid writers always look for the "up" side of even the most heartrending or unusual situation. Unconventional but successful marriages are always popular, as in the *Enquirer*'s "26-Year-Old Marries 'the Perfect Woman'—She's 73!" (p. 2). The *Examiner* offers "Love at First Sight—When the Alligator Man Met the Monkey Woman" (p. 25), about two people who met and married when both worked in a carnival freak show. Although tabloids still have the reputation of celebrating gruesomeness, today's versions go out of their way to avoid the "downer" story, defined as one that will depress readers. While deformity might be considered a "downer, " the "happy marriage" focus of the story saved it. In fact, the story must have been deemed particularly good, because the 1990 version is a rewrite of a 1985 story ("Real Odd Couple: The Alligator Man and the Monkey Woman," *Examiner*, Aug. 13, 1985, 2). The later story uses an updated photograph, in which the "monkey woman" has shaved her beard, but a quote from the husband is used again: "If beauty is skin deep, so is ugliness. When I look at my bride, all I see is the goodness and kindness that shines from her."

Particularly to be avoided are downers about babies and children: "Almost any story about a child being injured is a downer," according to former *Examiner* photo editor Ken Matthews. Matthews points out that "there are babies on almost every cover" on his editor's trophy wall (interview, Feb. 6, 1986), and all the tabloids heavily feature babies and small children. Matthews discussed how the *Examiner* decides on which baby stories can be included, using as an example the paper's use on the cover of a photograph of the "world's oldest baby," a mummified infant. With the help of "some slight enhancement by our art department," the picture was quite attractive, and was deemed a success. "A few weeks later I came up with a picture of a baby born with half its head off, and he was a very ugly child anyway and hadn't lived, but my feeling was, well, the oldest baby worked, so that would work. I showed it to Bill (*Examiner* Editor Bill Burt), he kept it for a couple of days and then he came back and he said no, it's too much and so we didn't run it. I had already paid for the picture and I was confident we were going to repeat the previous success. I thought about it and he was right—the thing was just too gruesome, too awful."

Instead the tabloids concentrate on tales of how babies and children survive and are happy, even if their circumstances are poor. The *Examiner*'s Feb. 27 cover features the "Heartbreak Baby That Can Never Be Cuddled," about a child with a severe genetic skin disorder. While the child's life expectancy is poor, the positive is stressed: "She's such a determined little girl—and she'll always have her family to encourage her!" says her mom (p. 27).

The *Sun*'s contribution is potentially a "downer": "Parents abandon triplets because babies are boys—they wanted girls" (cover and p. 7). The cruel French parents apparently abandoned their babies one at a time in different locations. However, the parents have been arrested and the children placed for adoption, and a social worker declares: "the boys got off to a bad start, but we're confident they'll lead a good life from this point on."

Schechter (1988) noticed the regular appearance of stories about two-headed babies in the *Weekly World News* and *Sun*, offering one practical reason for their popularity: "authentic photos of two-headed babies are exceptionally easy to fake (all you really need are a matching pair of baby pictures, an Exacto knife, and some rubber cement)" (p. 111). He also, however, suggests that "two-headed baby stories are particularly appealing to that strange emotional mix—that unique blend of sideshow prurience and maternal compassion—that the tabloids are designed to exploit" (pp. 111–12). Indeed, the "strange emotional mix" Schechter points to is discernible in many tabloid stories, making them more than the mere freak shows they are often characterized as by detractors.

Throughout the tabloids, the importance of children and good parenting is stressed. The ultimate goal of everyone is to have beau-

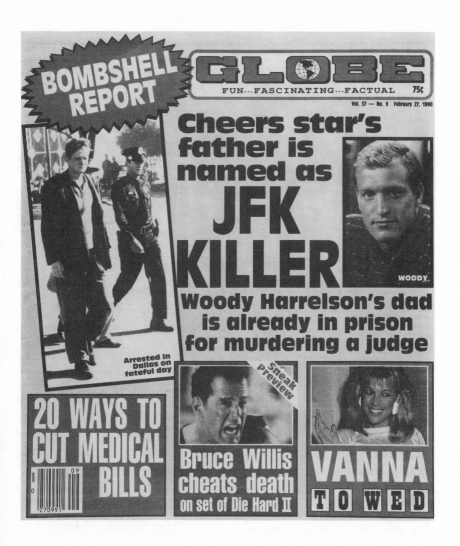

Cover of the *Globe*, Feb. 27, 1990.
Reprinted courtesy of Globe International, Inc.

Cover of the *Sun*, Feb. 27, 1990.
Reprinted courtesy of Globe International, Inc.

tiful and/or courageous children. Infertility is said to have destroyed the marriage of Tom Cruise and Mimi Rogers; another desperate couple mortgaged everything so that a surrogate mother could bear their child, whose birth was "the most wonderful moment of my life," says the new mother (*Globe*, 18). The worst villains are parents who act unnaturally, like the French triplets' parents, or the many parents who have sold, gambled away, or otherwise abused their children, playing the time-honored role of "cruel relative" (Schechter 1988). In the tabloids, all such monsters pay for their sins.

With luck, the cute babies celebrated in tabloid pages will grow into the talented children who also star in the papers. A supreme example is Jordan Ellenberg, "America's top math whiz kid," a seventeen-year-old Harvard genius who won a gold medal in International Mathematical Olympiad, and "taught himself to read at age 2" (*Enquirer*, 5). The story's byline is Paul Einstein. The *Examiner* has its own "whiz kid," a nine-year-old boy who "rocketed from kindergarten to high school in four short years!" (p. 23).

The rule of thumb for human-interest stories, whatever their subject, is that they warm the heart. The *Globe* presents an "in her own words" story of an amazing brush with death: "It's a Miracle We're Alive: Pregnant Teen's Car Plunges Off Bridge—She and Baby are Fine" (p. 9). In another story, the *Globe* combines the "up" side with condemnation of yet another action of the unfeeling bureaucracy: "Free at Last: Innocent Man Gets Out of Jail after 7 Years—But State Fights $1.9 Million Court Award" (p. 27). Cute and courageous animals are also definite "uppers," as in the regular *Examiner* feature "Our Wonderful Lifesaving Pets," including such tales as "Dog Braves Rapids to Save His Master" (pp. 6–7).

Other stories, while hardly heartwarming, also promise retribution for people who flout family values. From the *Examiner*: "Two-timing hubby locks mistress in cellar—while he lives happily with wife and kids upstairs" (p. 2). Italian Carlo Filosa, the "demented lover," apparently kept a woman locked in a dark basement as a "sex slave." Now he faces twenty years in jail. While murder stories are no longer a tabloid staple, they do appear, most often in order to demonstrate the consequences of unnatural behavior that deviates from the family norm. Thus the *Sun* reports on the "revenge of battered wife," a Long Beach, California, woman acquitted of killing her abusive, "sicko" husband (p. 27). Meanwhile, in Germany, "Henpecked hubby Deter Mansberg detested his domineering wife so much that when a blaze tore through their home, he ran to save his precious butterfly collection and left her to die in the inferno" (*Sun*, 9). While allowing one's wife to burn to death might be considered antisocial behavior, in this case it was justified because of the unnatural behavior of the wife, described as "a large-boned, heavy woman with a nasty temper and strong-willed manner." No doubt such a woman was also the victim of a similar choice 250 years earlier, when Benjamin Franklin's *Pennsylvania Gazette* reported: "And sometime last Week, we are informed, that one Piles a Fiddler, with his Wife, were overset in a Canoe near Newtown Creek. The good Man, 'tis said, prudently secured his Fiddle, and let his Wife go to the Bottom" (1729, quoted in Nord 1988, 32).

Other "off-beat" stories are equivalent to those journalists call "brights"—the cheerful tales with pure entertainment value. The *Examiner*, which boasts of having "the week's funniest stories," features a brother and sister in Canada who make clocks from cow dung, which they sell for forty dollars each. The lead: "Quick—What's Brown and Sounds Like Big Ben? DUNGGGG!" (p. 33). The *Weekly World News* reports on Jeffrey Ovellette of Seattle, Washington, who won the Big Burp contest in Copenhagen: "World's Biggest Belch Lasts 3 Minutes and 23 Seconds" (p. 37).

At the other extreme, there are the very few stories that carry on the time-honored tabloid tradition of gore—the morbid stories that appear to have no purpose other than catering to the "accident watchers" that Gene Pope courted in the 1960s. Almost never a feature in the four largest-selling papers, they now surface only in the *Sun* and, occasionally, the *Weekly World News*. Thus the *Sun* breaks the convention of ignoring current news in order to publish a story illustrated with photos of rows of bodies in Romania, as well as photos of executed dictator Nicolae Ceausescu and his wife Elena lying dead (pp. 10–11). The story chronicles in stomach-turning detail the variety of tortures inflicted on Romanian protesters and then suggests that victims who died on the "table of death" might turn into vampires if the table is destroyed. The paper also has a feature on Scotland Yard's Museum of Crime, showing photos of death masks and claiming that the ghost of a murderer haunts the place trying to retrieve his missing head.

Finally, using a gleeful black-humor style straight out of the 1960s, the *Sun* tells a preposterous horror story set in Amsterdam and beginning: "A careless teen who mistook a tube of hemorrhoid ointment for acne medicine no longer has pimples to worry about because the powerful remedy dissolved his face!" Supposedly, the boy's father invented the ointment, which "was designed to actually shrink swelling of inflamed hemorrhoidal tissues." (Any devotee of evening news programs will recognize this direct quote from Preparation H's commercials.) Bylined "Dr. Bruno Grosse," the story quotes "Dr. Morten Sigsweed": "The boy's face is little more than a lifeless lump of pasty white flesh" (p. 5).

Exactly where these stories fit in the overall family-centered orientation of tabloids is a little hard to fathom. Even the Romanian photos are not as grisly as the scattered body parts of the 1960s, but they would definitely appear to be "downers." Yet perhaps this is not quite the case. Unlike the stories of the 1960s, today's gory tales rarely cover people with whom the reader is assumed to feel an easy affinity. Even in the *Sun*, dead bodies are foreign, not American; we never now see the road accident and murder victims that used to be a staple. While this distinction may seem unreal or callous, it is one that is called into play constantly in American journalism generally—we are far more likely to see bodies of war or disaster victims on our TV screens if they are non-American. And in fact, the Romanian pictures were carried by many mainstream media as well, being perceived as genuinely newsworthy. While definitely not "heartwarming," the occasional ventures into gore may be perceived as allowing readers to indulge that "accident-watching" urge while not feeling that their daily lives are threatened.

In addition, grisly stories tend to have closure; murderers are caught, dictators die. The Museum of Crime story concludes with a quote: "Crime gets punished sooner or later—whether by our hands or from a Higher Court" (p. 15). In fact, all crime stories underline this moral point in starkly clear terms, spelling out a moral battle of good versus evil. As Cohen and Young write, "Such news is a main source of information about the normative contours of a society. It informs us about right and wrong, about the parameters beyond which one should not venture and about the shapes that the devil can assume. A gallery of folk types—heroes and saints, as well as fools, villains and devils—is publicized . . ." (1981, 431).

*Rags to Riches*

According to Holden, "The subject of [the rags-to-riches] story should almost always be dirt poor and should struggle to make millions" (Holden 1977, 20). Indeed, the inspirational stories of self-made millionaires have appeared consistently in the tabloids. Blaustein analyzes the "Horatio Alger" myth as one of the most prevalent in the *Enquirer* of the late 1960s, just after the gore period: "The 'rags-to-riches' pattern, in emphasizing the humble origin of the protagonist, establishes ties between him and the common folk. He is down to earth and exalted at the same time. He has not forgotten his poverty and moreover points to it as the stimulus of his success; he embodies and advocates the American ideal of achievement" (1969, 7).

In the 1980s, the appeal of the rags-to-riches story seems to have waned a little, although it still surfaces, as in a *Star* story on writer and radio personality Tom Bodett. Through hard work and talent, "he has gone from blue-collar financial blues to showbiz success" (p. 36). But the inspirational stories about hard work have to a great extent been superseded by stories about luck, where good things happen to people without warning (much as bad things may happen, too). Blaustein had earlier noted this idea of luck as a "semi-magical concept," such as in an *Enquirer* tale: "Another lucky English lad carried a stranger's suitcase and was rewarded with a motorcycle" (p. 6). In 1990, the *Sun* tells of Scotsman Warren Strathdee, who supposedly bought a $5,000 lottery ticket while walking in his sleep (p. 4). The *Star* tops that with its story of New Yorker John Martin, who has won the state lottery jackpot for the second time, adding a share of $4 million to $666,000 he won in 1986. He used the numbers stenciled on his new pair of shoes, beating odds estimated at two billion to one.

*Volunteers and Heroes*

"Volunteers should take in 592 foster children or donate 10,000 gallons of blood, not merely help old ladies cross the street," advises Holden 1977, 21). Meet the *Enquirer*'s "Little Miss Courage," a three-year-old girl who suffered great pain to donate bone marrow to save the life of her six-year-old brother, who has leukemia. "When Lorna McGeown's parents told her that donating her bone marrow in a painful operation could save her brother Joe's life, she didn't think twice" (p. 8). Little Lorna, apparently an unusually articulate three-year-old is quoted: "Would it be awful sore? I am not very good at soreness. I cry. But if it will make Joe well again, and make you and Mommy happy, then I'll have to say lots of prayers so it isn't too sore for me." True to formula, the story concentrates on the heartwarming heroics; the ultimate fate of the brother is unrevealed.

The *Enquirer* also offers a regular hero award, this week's story featuring Carol Dennison: "Gutsy woman jumps into a raging river to save drowning boy" (p. 22). This feature, like much other tabloid material, involves readers by asking them to nominate heroes. The *Globe* combines heroism with the popular "ironic twist" theme: "Fearless hero Michael Wells miraculously lifted the corner of a 50-ft. mobile home to free a little boy trapped underneath during a tornado" (p. 33). Unfortunately, Wells was being sought by police, who promptly arrested him. "Now, he's being rewarded for his selfless bravery—by being thrown in jail." The familiar heartless bureaucracy will bear down on the ordinary person, hero or not.

# For Enquiring Minds

*The Handicapped Overcoming Odds*

Holden's advice to potential writers in the genre of courage among the handicapped is clear and blunt: "The subject should be severely handicapped, yet function as normally as possible. The more handicapped the better" (1977, 21). He explains that such stories should be inspirational and upbeat, and this is almost invariably the case, in sharp contrast to the reveling in gore and freak-show approaches of the 1960s. Some tabloids use such stories to stimulate a fund-raising or letter-writing campaign. In the 1970s an *Enquirer* story on a destitute, sick family raised $164,000 (Holden 1977), and the tabloids continue to raise money in this way.

The *Star* combines handicap (or in this case, the death-sentence of AIDS) with the theme of a celebrity coping with heartbreak in a story about actor Paul Michael Glaser and his family (p. 10). Glaser's wife contracted AIDS through a blood transfusion; his daughter has died from the disease, and his son also has the virus. The story describes their fight against AIDS and how they are "trying to make Jake's life as normal as possible despite the killer within him—and his mom." The story concludes with an address to send money to the Pediatric AIDS Foundation. There is a striking contrast between this account, in which the victims are perceived as innocent, and the story on Halston, which suggests that AIDS is a fitting reward for his dissolute life.

The *Examiner* tells the story of loving parents who watch over their child day and night: "Gutsy Ben McLean cheats death 70 times a night! The spunky four year old has a rare and potentially lethal disorder called Ondine's curse—his brain often forgets to tell his lungs to breathe (p. 15). The *Sun* profiles Madge Bester, the "world's smallest woman" at twenty-seven inches tall. Suffering from a congenital brittle bone condition, she is confined to a wheelchair but hopes to find a man to love her. "While she's still waiting for her knight in shining armor, Madge maintains an upbeat attitude and an unshakable belief in a higher power" (p. 19).

# Tabloid Content Today

*Medical Miracles and Discoveries*

Another popular category includes stories of individuals recovering from illness and disfigurement rather than living heroically with their problem. Thus the *Enquirer* tells of Gwyn Jones of Wales, who had half his face paralyzed by polio as a child (p. 52). "Thanks to incredible skill of plastic surgeons," Jones can now smile again. However, although readers are invited to applaud his recovery, they are also cautioned that beauty is but skin-deep. Happily married before his surgery, Jones declares: "She could see beyond my face to the person inside." The "incredible skill" of doctors was also vital in the recovery of a mother and newborn baby in Union, South Carolina. "Dead Mom Gives Birth to Dead Baby—Then Docs Bring Them Back to Life" (*Weekly World News*, 4–5).

Apart from personal stories, "medical breakthroughs" are always popular. Such a story is the startling announcement from the cover of the *National Examiner*: "Women Can Grow New Breasts." The story inside does not quite live up to this promise, describing an experimental procedure to grow new skin and blood vessels in the laboratory using samples of skin, then sculpting the skin and implanting silicone. The story explains that the procedure may be useful for both breast cancer patients and burn victims.

*Self-Help and How-To*

Although they may be encouraged to hope for good luck, tabloid readers are also offered an array of features designed to help them deal with everyday problems. Holden quotes *Modern People*'s news editor as requiring self-help tips that aid readers in accomplishing something, "especially stories which strike the reader personally, such as how to save money, how to analyze your dreams, how to pin-point your troubled marriage" (Holden 1977, 20). Little has changed since this advice was offered. The *Enquirer* includes "How to Update Your Outfits without Spending a Bundle" (p. 30), "Super Ways to Stay on Your Diet" (p. 9), and "Six Mistakes People Make

# For Enquiring Minds

Again and Again . . . and How to Stop Making Them" (p. 35). The *Star* charges readers $12.95 for a chance to "Discover the Real You—The Secrets to Your Success Are in Your Handwriting" (p. 18). The *Globe* offers "20 Ways to Cut Your Medical Bills" (p. 29) and then ventures into less mundane territory with: "Your Office Space Cadet May Really Be an Alien: Here's How to Tell" (p. 7). In this feature, Brad Steiger, "a renowned paranormal investigator and author of more than 100 books," suggests that aliens will give themselves away with such tell-tale faux pas as wearing a plaid skirt with a striped blouse or using a screwdriver to open a letter.

Supplementing the features are advice columns of all kinds. The *Star* has an astrology hotline with a 900 number, and "expert" Suzy Prudden on weight loss, who offers: "When your buttocks are too big or too small, it usually means you are out of balance with power in your life" (p. 40). Until recently, the paper also had a column interpreting readers' dreams, and it runs "Dear Meg," an advice column in the "Dear Abby" style. The *Globe* and *Examiner* have "Dear Sarah" and "Sheela Wood," respectively, while the *Weekly World News* offers "America's most outspoken advice columnist," known as "Dear Dotti," who when asked what is the stupidest thing she has ever done, responds, "Opened your letter" (p. 23). *News* readers can also "Ask the Countess," who will provide astrological advice based on their charts. The *Examiner* has a medical advice column and counseling from psychic Anthony Leggett while the *Sun* has dream interpretations and a tarot card reader. The *Enquirer* alone runs no advice columns.

## Strange Phenomena

The tabloids vary in the amount of play they give to such "unexplained mysteries" as the occult, psychic phenomena, astrology, ghosts, and UFOs. The *Enquirer* and *Star* tend to be less interested while the *Sun* and *Weekly World News* give this area the most coverage, with the *Examiner* and the *Globe* somewhere in between. However, the *Star* and *Enquirer* are not averse to covering the paranormal, particularly when a celebrity angle can be found. Thus a *Star* story begins: "Beneath actress Michelle Pfeiffer's beautiful exterior lurks a dark secret: She was once totally controlled by a bizarre cult" (p. 39). The *Globe* has virtually the same story, with identical quotes (p. 5), both attributing Pfeiffer's salvation to the love of a good man (her ex-husband, Peter Horton). The *Globe* features a story on actor Donald Sutherland's "dramatic glimpse of life beyond the grave," the near-death experience being a popular tabloid phenomenon: "I Was Dead for 5 Seconds: Donald Sutherland Reveals Amazing Brush with the Beyond" (p. 36).

The *Enquirer* devotes a page to: "Vatican Expert Reveals . . . Most Horrifying Demonic Possessions" (p. 39), featuring an assortment of possessions that are officially recognized by the church. The *Examiner*, in "Psychic's Powers Nab Vicious Killer" (p. 2), carries on a long tradition of credence given to the value of psychics in law enforcement.

The *Weekly World News* is full of paranormal stories, including one on the popular topic of reincarnation: "Georgia Mom's incredible reincarnation miracle: I died in Ohio 76 years ago, and was born again in 1948—to live another life!" (pp. 24–25). It also reports on the feats of two Mexican brothers: "Amazing psychic kids can 'see' with their FINGERS!" (p. 31). The main cover story in the *News* carries on a continuing mystery that the paper has reported before—a World War II bomber that supposedly has been seen on the moon. Now the mystery is explained; the bomber was abducted by aliens and left in a moon crater during the war.

The range of phenomena covered by the tabloids is wide, from UFOs to Bigfoot and mermaids, the lost city of Atlantis, reincarnation, out-of-body experiences, ESP, dream premonitions, witchcraft, astrology, numerology, and other curiosities.

*Bureaucratic Waste and Incompetence*

While Gene Pope's earlier ambitions to make the *Enquirer* a populist crusader have not materialized, the tabloids regularly print stories designed to show the incompetence and nefariousness of government and bureaucracy. A staple is the government waste story, in which Washington bureaucrats are shown to be pouring hardworking taxpayers' money down the drain. At the same time, tabloid writers are advised that "there must be some sort of upbeat angle, with a congressman or consumer group trying to right the wrong" (Holden 1977, 20).

A typical example of the genre is an *Enquirer* story describing a government proposal to force dog breeders to pet or stroke dogs for an hour a day. "'What are they going to do, put undercover men in kennels?' blasted Representative Mel Hancock (R-Missouri). . . . 'I'm speaking about this because I want to let the public know this is the type of thing our government is spending its time on'"(*National Enquirer*, 3). The *Enquirer* also offers: "5 Convicted Ex-Congressmen Still Get Fat Govt. Pensions" (p. 16). The *Star*'s contribution: "Uncle Sam has really taken the taxpayer to the cleaners this time. While Americans were sweating over their IRS forms, the Army spent millions of dollars on a study of women's blouse sizes—then dumped the project!" (p. 22).

Tabloid stories are replete with "bungling officials" and "bleeding heart judges." As D. A. Bird points out, the language is reminiscent of the tirades of former Governor George Wallace against "pointy-headed bureaucrats": "The theme that the public is not well served by individuals on the public payroll, accompanied by numerous exempla, threads its way through a number of tabloid stories" (1986, 18).

Thus *Weekly World News* columnist "Ed Anger" castigates the "nitwit school boss" who suspended a third-grader and notified police in Richmond, Virginia, when the child brought an unopened can of "Billy Beer" to show-and-tell (p. 17). This story was also covered, though less stridently, by the *Star* (p. 5) and by many mainstream media.

Although the sample week does not include any examples, the government coverup story continues the "us-against-them" theme, and appears frequently. Government waste tales often feature the bureaucracy's attempts to cover its tracks, and the government is also

# Tabloid Content Today

accused of covering up facts in such continuing sagas as the Kennedy assassination and UFO landings.

## Current News with a Twist

When Holden discussed the category of current news from an unusual perspective in 1977, the tabloids tended to speculate more about news stories of the day, as in Holden's example of an investigative piece hypothesizing sabotage as the cause of several oil tanker accidents. As celebrity stories have gradually gained more and more space, this kind of feature has declined. The *Enquirer* seems to use more resources on them than the others, such as its two-page "exclusive" coverage of the story behind the firing of CBS commentator Andy Rooney: "The gays finally got me—they set me up, says Andy Rooney" (pp. 20–21). Although hardly current news, the *Globe* also offers a "World Exclusive" that continues the debate on the Kennedy assassination: "Cheers Star's Father Is Named as JFK Killer: Woody Harrelson's Dad Is Already in Prison for Murdering a Judge" (pp. 2–3, 6).

## The "Gee Whiz" Story

The "gee whiz" or simply "whiz" story is the quintessential tabloid tale— the one that helps breaks sales records or graces a cover on Bill Burt's wall. Gene Pope reportedly was fond of quoting Joseph Pulitzer's definition of the "gee-whiz emotion," described as "the offbeat, the dramatic, the curious and the interesting" (Corkery 1981, 19). According to Cliff Linedecker, the "whiz" is "the most difficult of all to keep going" but is the goal tabloid writers strive toward. The "whiz" is recognized not by topic as such but by the sheer impact of the story; it must be "absolutely amazing."

Describing life at the *Enquirer*, Corkery writes that a step above even a "whiz" is a "Hey, Martha." This is the story that makes someone turn and say, "Hey, Martha, did you see this incredible story?"

# For Enquiring Minds

As Corkery describes it, "A good 'Hey, Martha' would be a story about a body discovered with no wounds and an autopsy revealing no human heart. Or a story about a six-month-old Chinese baby who can accurately describe the physical layout of the Malden, Mass., public library. Something very weird but compelling. To have The Boss tell you that a story of yours is a 'Hey, Martha,' is the local equivalent of winning a Pulitzer Prize" (Corkery 1981, 20).

While it is not easy to define exactly what a "whiz" story may be, some examples might be the *Examiner*'s "Curse of the Dwarf Statue": "A bizarre Egyptian curse that causes people to shrink is tormenting a man who accidentally bought a magic statue. 'I've gotten a foot shorter in the year since I laid eyes on that damn thing,' said archaeologist Elmer Finkelstein" (p. 8). The story includes a photograph captioned "an antiquities inspector brushes an ancient Egyptian statue of a dwarf," without identifying the statue as the malevolent one in question. The *Examiner*'s cover story "Women Can Grow New Breasts" might also qualify, as might the *Weekly World News*'s "Bomber on the Moon Mystery Solved." "Whiz" stories, however, cannot be expected every week; "Hey, Marthas" are even more elusive.

## Advertising

No tabloid reader can fail to notice the close relationship between tabloid stories and advertising copy. As Donald Allport Bird points out, "Stories of unexplained cures nudge against patent-medicine advertisements with generous promises of similar cures" (undated, 21). The juxtaposition of "bizarre" and questionable ads with the more outlandish stories is particularly noticeable in the three Globe tabloids and the *Weekly World News*. *Examiner* Editor Bill Burt explains: "It's no secret that we're a platform for all different points of view, like the Atlantis people, the Flat Earth people . . . so naturally we attract the advertisers who want to reach that type of people" (interview, Feb. 5, 1986). Burt and Associate Editor Cliff Linedecker see the refusal of large advertisers to consider tabloids as short-

# Tabloid Content Today

sighted and elitist: "Our people probably part with their money a lot easier than a lot of the others that they focus on—they buy VCRs and all that good stuff" (Linedecker interview, 1986).

Although the Globe papers do carry some national advertising, such as the full-page ads from Michigan Bulb Company on the back covers of the *Examiner* and the *Globe*, much more space is devoted in these papers and the *Weekly World News* to what Burt calls "daft ads." The advertising material picks up the same themes as the "how to" and advice columns—how to improve one's appearance, social skills, and mastery of one's fate. Self-improvement is offered in ads for correspondence study: "Poor English holding you back?— Write and read like a well educated person—even if you never finished high school." The reader can buy products that will conquer gray or thinning hair, wrinkles, ugly scars, inadequate busts, loose dentures. He or she can be taller, more muscled, more attractive: buy the "better sex life formula that also tones and gives overall fat loss." Readers are also offered numerous money-making schemes: "Kansas housewife makes $825 a day with simple answering machine," "How to collect Social Security at any age," "Ex-truck driver gets $421,108 a month doing what you aren't."

If money making does not work, the *News* offers countless short-cuts to fortune: "Danielle Gilbert wants to share the secret that brought her luck—the legendary Ring of Re, an exact reproduction of an ancient piece of Egyptian jewelry. . . . People have won lottery, found love, success in business, everything." (Gilbert, apparently, has served some jail time in France for this particular enterprise [James 1990, 233]). Or you could try "King Solomon's gold "lucky hand" amulet: A waterfall of wealth, money, luck, floods you ($9. 95 + $2.00 postage & handling)." The *Examiner* and *Globe* carry an ad offering to "cancel the evil eye for $6.66," while for $15.50 "Andreika" claims, "I will cast a spell for you!"

Much of the advertising and editorial material in tabloids responds to a perception of luck as a power that somehow can be harnessed if only the key can be found, a perception that belongs in "the ancient mythic class of the *wheel of fortune*." In fact, "there is a subliminal premise that one's poverty is the result of bad luck, but the overwhelming tone is positive: all that we need is a chance for a spin at the wheel of fortune; and here they are, opportunities galore to take the spin and win (not earn) wealth, fame or power" (Schroeder 1982, 177).

The classified ads continue these themes, offering contests, health and beauty aids, inventions, loans and moneymaking opportunities, recipes, astrologers and psychics. One can obtain a degree by mail, or "become legally ordained minister. Credentials sent for $5 offering." Apparently desperate people seek help from fellow readers: "Wife has Alzheimers. Husband heart/arthritis problems. Can't work. Son retarded. Please help." Finally, all three Globe papers run the Sheela Wood "Have a Friend" Club, where men and women advertise for friendship or romance.

Although the tabloids take the "daft ads" willingly, "I'm sure our publisher would sacrifice a few pages of holy relics for a Ford Thunderbird ad or the new Taurus ad," according to Burt. Indeed the tabloids do try to attract national advertisers. The *Star*, *Enquirer*, and to some extent the *Globe* have been most successful in breaking through to "mainstream" advertisers, although even they feature few ads for big-ticket consumer items and appear to be targeted at lower-income groups. The *Star* ads are similar to any found in general-interest and women's magazines, although with a somewhat higher proportion of cigarette ads, such as the full-page spreads for Newport Stripes and Cambridge cigarettes and a smaller ad for Malibu. Other products advertised include Quaker popped corn cakes, Encare spermicide, Wild Musk cologne, and various offers for porcelain dolls and butterfly collections, collector plates, wigs, and clothing. Its one page of classified ads, however, would be at home in any tabloid, with the usual psychics, money-making offers, and recipes.

Of the papers, the *Enquirer* devotes the most advertising space to products like cigarettes, the Whisper 2000 (a surveillance device advertised in full-page spreads in five of the tabloids), collectibles, Bayer aspirin, and so on, but also includes more weight-loss ads. In addition, it gives space to ads familiar from other tabloids—remedies like natural evening primrose oil and cures for puffy eyes, products like an invisible hearing aid, and services like "See the light and talk to God." The *Enquirer* has five pages of classifieds offering the usual products and services.

## Tabloid Content as Conservatism

Unlike the British daily tabloids, with which they are often compared, American weekly tabloids do not take any party political positions and do not run editorials about political issues. In fact they rarely cover "hard news" or political topics at all, except at the personality level. Nevertheless, in spite of their reputation for espousing unusual and nonmainstream viewpoints, they are consistently conservative in a very real sense. In 1977, right-wing commentator D. Keith Mano characterized the *Enquirer* as "straight Wallace social-conservatism" (p. 209), and that description still fits today's tabloids. English (1990) argues that the rise in the popularity of such phenomena as televangelism and "tabloid TV" in the 1980s is at least in part attributable to the reaction of blue-collar, conservative, religious people against what they perceive as the dominance of liberal "hipness."

The tabloid papers, whose surge in popularity in the early 1980s presaged the rise of tabloid TV, are similarly reactionary, constantly rising to the defense of "traditional American values" (in the sense that term is used by the Moral Majority and like-minded groups). Whitby characterizes this New Christian Right: "According to the movement, liberalism (usually equated with communism), science, the public schools, intellectuals of all sorts and stripes, and even the federal government— all are out to destroy traditional American values" (1985, 8). Thus the *Globe* proclaims "Hurrah for Gutsy Co-ed Who Rescued Old Glory" (p. 5). The story describes how Alexandra de Campi, a student at Princeton University, rushed in to save a flag about to be burned by "a pack of punks" (other students) protesting the federal statute banning desecration of the flag. De Campi "watched in horror as two of the creeps doused the flag with lighter fluid and lit a match." The heroine is pictured with the flag draped around her shoulders, and the story concludes: "For her heroic act,

# For Enquiring Minds

Alexandra was honored by the local Marine Corps League and the New Jersey State Council of the Knights of Columbus."

The *Enquirer* uses an article based on a reader survey to help underscore conservative values: "It's a myth that America's parents are too permissive—more than four out of five parents spank their children when they misbehave, an *Enquirer* survey reveals" (p. 25). The key word here, of course, is "too," allowing a careful implication that support of spanking is the correct moral position for parents.

Conservative religious values also pervade the tabloids in spite of the prevalence of off-beat themes that may seem inconsistent with established religion, such as psychic phenomena, reincarnation, and so forth. In all the papers, celebrities regularly ascribe their successes to their faith in God, as do "ordinary" heroes and those who have miracle escapes or even lottery wins. *Examiner* Editor Burt points out that the Bible is always a good draw on the cover: "We've had Bible prophecies, a biblical treatment for arthritis, all good ones." Conversely, sexual explicitness is not a major selling point. Tabloid covers never display photos of even scantily clad women, never mind the seminudes that feature in European papers. Occasional photos of bikini-clad starlets do appear inside, particularly in the *Star*, which even runs a readers' swimsuit contest. Burt contrasts the "more puritanical" American tabloid readers with their British counterparts, who read papers like the Murdoch-owned *Sun*, which features daily bare-breasted women on page 3. The British papers "are bought very blatantly by the Andy Capps of Britain for purely prurient reasons. They're the guys who'll sit beside you on a bus and study that picture for about twenty minutes. Here people would be embarrassed to be seen picking it up—they're much more uninhibited in Britain." Sex is far from absent in the tabloids, of course; the consequences of sexual misconduct are examined regularly. The tabloids were in the forefront of attacks on the various sex scandals involving TV evangelists, who were perceived as badly letting down their constituents.

Even celebrity gossip can be an opportunity to take a swipe at "un-American" attitudes. The *Weekly World News* takes offense at the "Hollywood Bigwigs" who are casting the role of G. I. Joe in an upcoming movie. Actors under consideration are said to include Scotsman Sean Connery, Austrian-born Arnold Schwarzenegger, and "Aussie-accented" Mel Gibson (who is actually an American citizen). "It's enough to make old John Wayne roll over in his grave. Movie moguls are making a flick about our all-American hero G. I. Joe—and they want to give the part to some funny-sounding foreigner!" (p. 13). The *Star* also covers this story, adding American Kevin Costner to the list. More neutral in its coverage, the *Star* simply lists the contenders and invites its readers to vote for their favorite using a 900 telephone number.

At a more general level, one can see conservatism in the choice of stars who appear in the papers. Unlike magazines such as *People*, the tabloids never cover celebrities who might be classed as representing "high" or "elite" culture. "I wouldn't want to try promoting Ravi Shankar on the front cover," comments *Examiner* editor Burt with a smile. Also avoided are celebrities from the worlds of high fashion, art, in fact anything that smacks of "decadence"—perhaps epitomized in the New York club scene peopled by stars like Halston or Bianca Jagger. Burt explains that his paper cannot promote "crazy rockers" except for the occasional "oddity" such as Boy George. Michael Jackson, for instance, has received frequent tabloid coverage, apparently much of it originating from his own publicists (Ressner 1988), largely because his behavior has so often been characterizable as "bizarre." The occasional venerable rock stars, such as Rod Stewart, may make appearances in the gossip columns, but the main characters in feature coverage are the stars of popular TV shows and movies, particularly prime-time soap operas, game shows, and situation comedies, with frequent appearances by country music stars.

English (1990) suggests that celebrities like the ultra-hip David Letterman represent the type of attitude that tabloid TV is reacting to, and indeed people like Letterman are either nowhere to be found or are treated negatively in the tabloid press. "Yuppie" shows like "thirtysomething" are also not popular and receive little coverage. When they do appear, coverage is often unfavorable, for although most celebrity stories are positive in tone, negative comment is often reserved for the celebrities who represent values presumed to be out of step with the tabloid readership. Thus in the sample week, a story on "thirtysomething" concentrates on the alleged tantrums of star Ken Olin, suggesting that the producers are about to "dump" him and his wife Nancy Wettig (*Enquirer*, 24). In an unusual step, the writer finds it necessary to describe the show ("the offbeat series about a group of yuppies") to readers; popular programs like "Dallas" or "Knots Landing" would need no such gloss. Even the *Star*, which tends to cover a wider range of celebrities, including younger ones, draws the line at such people as heavy metal rock musicians. In a montage of celebrity photos, the *Star* includes an extremely unflattering picture with the snide caption: "Fresh from his brilliant discourse at the American Music Awards, Guns 'n' Roses guitarist Slash prepares for his keynote speech at the annual men's springwear collection debut in Paris" (p. 14).

Perhaps most obviously, the tabloids show their conservatism in their representations of ethnic minorities, homosexuals, and women.

*Representation of Minorities*

A glance at all the tabloids suggests that the world they portray is overwhelmingly white, and a closer look confirms this. Levin, Mody-Desbarau, and Arluke (1988), in their four-tabloid sample, found that 98 percent of story protagonists were white. My own reading of the papers also suggests that minorities are significantly under-represented. (One should bear in mind that many stories are not illustrated, and may feature minorities.) Since minorities other than blacks are extremely rare, I shall confine my analysis to the representation of blacks.

Under Gene Pope, the *Enquirer*'s coverage of any stories about blacks was virtually nonexistent. Barber described how Pope monitored all story ideas and marked those rejected with the initials "NG," for "No Good." While his criteria were often mysterious, there were, "however, some totally predictable NG's, chief among them blacks, except when they practice voodoo or are child comic Gary Coleman. I presented Hoy [an editor] with a heart-warming story of a young

# Tabloid Content Today

New Orleans man who had survived a grain elevator explosion and 80 percent burns to become a multimillionaire (a surefire hit under the Rags to Riches category). He immediately asked me what color he was. Black. Kill it" (1982, 48). Barber also pointed out that there were no minority employees at the *Enquirer* under Pope. When it covered "ordinary" blacks at all, the *Enquirer* portrayed them negatively—that is, as murderers or other deviants. The cute babies and heroes were invariably white. Black celebrities were less easily ignored; the Bill Cosby phenomenon could not pass even the *Enquirer* by. However, with the exception of Cosby and his TV "family," even black celebrities were afforded relatively little space, and some, like Eddie Murphy, became favorite "villains."

Since the sale of the *Enquirer*, there has been some speculation that the coverage of blacks might improve, but there has not been much evidence of this so far. In the February 27 issue, there is only one story on a noncelebrity black. "Fat—but Fashionable" (p. 10) features Walter Hudson, a black man who has dieted down from 1,400 to 480 pounds and is now designing clothes for large people. Three of the five heavy models pictured in the story are black, helping to reinforce stereotypes of black women as overweight. Two celebrity stories feature blacks. One portrays heavyweight boxer Mike Tyson as distraught and unstable following his defeat by James "Buster" Douglas: "Lovesick Mike Tyson under suicide watch—depressed over KO and obsessed with his ex . . ." (p. 17). The second is a story on Richard Pryor, Jr., son of the comedian, who has a career as a female impersonator in Peoria, Illinois: "He's Richard Pryor's son—even if he does wear heavy makeup, wigs and sexy dresses" (p. 50). Neither story could be construed as positive.

The *Star* has several stories featuring black celebrities, only one of which is favorable, a story that singer and dancer Lola Falana will become a nun after being cured of multiple sclerosis by a "miracle" (p. 40). The usually positive "family" image of Bill Cosby is dented in "Cosby Blows Top as Rebel Daughter, 23, Runs Off to Wed Latin Lover, 39" (p. 5). A pair of stories on page 20 brings together tabloid attitudes to both race and gays. One tells of Richard Pryor, Jr., "1990 Miss Gay Peoria" and his live-in white lover: "Friends say his dad's lack of affection may have led to Richard's flamboyant lifestyle." On the same page, boxer Joe Louis's son is planning "a bizarre gay, interracial wedding ceremony in Los Angeles," in which he will wed his Australian lover.

The *Weekly World News* has no full stories with black protagonists but has a feature photo of two bouncers who work in a British disco, one 4 feet tall and 77 pounds, the other 6 feet 4 and 364 pounds—the larger man is black (p. 29). It also runs a photo of pop singer Janet Jackson in the gossip column, reporting that she collapsed on stage (p. 12).

The *Globe* and *Examiner* feature minorities more prominently. In particular, they more often run stories about "ordinary" blacks, which the *Enquirer*, *News*, and *Star* rarely do. In the sample week, all the protagonists in the *Globe*'s "hero" story, "Ex-con Lifts Trailer to Save Trapped Boy," are black (p. 33). The story has photos of the hero, Michael Wells, and of the rescued boy and his mother; even though the photo of Wells is a police "mug-shot," the overall tone of the story is very positive. In addition, the paper has a group shot of celebrities, many of them black, saluting entertainer Sammy Davis, Jr. (p. 14), and a photo of a "Mighty Strongman" performing one of his amazing feats (p. 15). Finally, the *Globe* has a full-page story on Miss America Debbye Turner answering criticisms that she belongs to a religious cult (p. 19). Although the story could easily have been written as another "bizarre cult" exposé, it actually presents Turner's religious faith in a very favorable light: "I'm being crucified for the way I worship God and for living like a real Christian!"

The *Examiner* also tends to cover minorities more often, although the sample week is poor in this respect. The *Examiner*'s only story is about the love life of "Knots Landing" stars, including Shari Belafonte. The *Sun*'s sample issue has no stories with photos of blacks, and this does seem to be fairly representative of its lack of coverage.

All the tabloids underrepresent blacks significantly. Perhaps more important than the actual space devoted to them is the tone of the coverage. Tabloid stories always take a point a view, either explicitly or implicitly: "The universe depicted is a bright, uncomplicated, unambiguous place where things either are (in this category we may include . . . UFOs and psychic fork-bending) or are not (unhappy endings, celibate celebrities, wise government)" (Barber 1982, 48). The Mike Tyson and Richard Pryor, Jr., stories could have been written to cast the protagonists in a favorable light—Tyson struggling to regain his confidence after a setback, or Pryor making his own way out from under the shadow of a famous father. Conversely, the *Globe* could have played up the prison record of its black "hero" or, more likely, killed the story altogether. The implicit racism of many of the tabloids does indeed bear out their characterization as the last bastion of George Wallace–style conservatism.

*Representation of Gays*

If the racism of at least some of the tabloids is implicit, their attitude toward gays and lesbians is decidedly explicit. According to Barber, at the *Enquirer* gays "may be beaten up at will" (1982, 48). The *Enquirer* story on Halston (who has since died of AIDS) has already been discussed; the stories on Richard Pryor, Jr., in the *Star* and *Enquirer* and the "wedding" of Joe Louis's gay son are replete with words like "bizarre," "outrageous," and "drag queen." The *Enquirer* also has an exclusive on the Andy Rooney story (Rooney was suspended by CBS for allegedly making racist remarks in an interview with a gay magazine). The paper accuses the magazine, the *Advocate*, of mounting a "gay plot" against Rooney because he has repeatedly made homophobic remarks. While the *Enquirer* accepts that racist remarks, if proved, might be grounds for dismissal, Rooney's proven attitude to gays is perfectly acceptable; they are responsible for his predicament.

Perhaps the most irresponsible story of all graces page 3 of the *Sun*. "Miracle Shrine Cured My AIDS" tells of a young man's supposed complete cure as a result of praying to the Virgin Mary at a shrine in his parents' home in Arizona. The only direct reference to homosexuality is a damning one—the man, Ricardo Vasquez, is described as a "former homosexual" who has now repented and vowed "to make her proud of me by living righteously until the day I die." Homosexuality is unambiguously represented as a sinful choice that can be repudiated while repentance will cure the punishment for deviance, AIDS. This attitude is most explicit in the *Sun* and the *Weekly World News*, which frequently indulges in "gay-bashing" stories. A most unusual exception was a 1985 story in the *News*, which reported in remarkably straight-faced style on a "Gay Teen's Heartbreak," the story of how a nineteen-year-old self-proclaimed gay was ejected from his high-school prom in Trenton, Ohio, because he arrived wearing "a ruffled chiffon tea-length dress, sexy satin slippers and his mother's musk-rat cape" (*News*, July 9, 1985). The story, illustrated with a photo of Warren Harper in the offending outfit, claims that he was humiliated and is suing the school district for assault and violation of his civil rights. While one would expect the angle of the story, particularly in the *News*, to be the "outrageous" or "sicko" behavior of the young man, the paper seems instead to have chosen the "bullying behavior by petty officials" approach—an unexpected and isolated aberration, it seems.

However, although the tabloids are profoundly homophobic, until recently they preferred not to "expose" popular celebrities as being gay or having AIDS, in keeping with their general policy of giving positive coverage to favored celebrities. Designer Halston was an obvious exception—undoubtedly the decision was made that he was not a personality who was viewed with affection by tabloid readers, and thus he could be portrayed as the epitome of gay self-indulgence. Other celebrities who have died of AIDS have been protected until after their deaths, or until they publicly announce their illness, as Rock Hudson did. According to *Examiner* editors, the paper had several AIDS-related stories about Hudson "waiting to go" once he died or his condition became known: "Nobody would do a Rock Hudson is a flaming fag thing until he got his AIDS. Everybody knew it that covers Hollywood, but people don't want to believe that—Rock Hudson is a wonderful lover, he's all male, all man" (interview with Cliff Linedecker 1986).

Beginning in 1990, the tabloids seem to have become less reticent about naming celebrities as possibly being gay, although they still wait for an allegation to be made elsewhere before covering the story. A number of tabloid stories in early 1990 appear to be related to the practice of forced "outing"—in which the gay community has named prominent people as gay without the celebrities' consent. Industrialist Malcolm Forbes, for example, was "outed" after his death, the revelations being taken up by the tabloids. Likewise, the April 24, 1990, issues of the *Star, Enquirer,* and *Globe* all gave front-page coverage to accounts in gay magazines that actor Richard Chamberlain had declared himself to be gay. The *Star* covers the story in a very neutral tone, reporting on two articles in French and American gay publications and providing additional information about Chamberlain's relationship with his alleged lover. The tone of the story suggests that the paper assumes the allegations are true, with the headline "Richard Chamberlain Is Gay" on the cover. Surprisingly, the paper makes little comment, apart from pointing out the supposed irony that Chamberlain is a "TV Casanova" and listing the famous actresses with whom he has starred. The *Globe* leads on Chamberlain's denials, headlining the cover story "Richard Chamberlain: I Am Not Gay" and stressing his anger and hurt at the allegations. The *Enquirer* returns to the "gay plot" theme: "Chamberlain believes the reports are the work of gay activists who think that having celebrities admit they're gay will help get more sympathy for homosexuals with AIDS—and more money for AIDS research" (p. 21). While the *Star* quotes neighbors and acquaintances who tend to confirm the reports, the *Enquirer* focuses on the opinion of Chamberlain's "pals" that his relationship with the alleged lover is "strictly business."

Thus the tabloids, while picking up stories covered by other media, are still reluctant to break "gay exposure" stories, particularly on well-liked stars. And the more popular the star, the less negative the reports—the *Globe* and *Enquirer* actually seem to try hard to give credibility to Chamberlain's denials while the *Star* is careful to point out that he has tested negative for AIDS.

Stories about lesbians are less frequent, although more have begun to appear recently, such as the *Enquirer*'s "Roseanne Delighted as Her Lesbian Sister 'Marries' Another Woman," a headline that editor Iain Calder is quoted as saying would probably not have run under Gene Pope, who was as hostile to homosexuality as he was to minorities (Kelley 1989). Other tabloids have recently reported on the alleged lesbian relationship of Cher's daughter, Chastity. The *Star* presented the lesbian as crazed fan (threatening fans who "stalk" stars are frequently featured) in a story headlined "Cagney and Looney," describing how "Cagney and Lacey" star Sharon Gless is being terrorized by a "rifle-wielding lesbian" (Apr. 17, 1990). In general, however, lesbianism, if covered at all, is seen as less threatening than male homosexuality, with its connections to AIDS.

*Representation of Women*

Tabloid representations of women are a little more complex, and more open to variations in reading. Undoubtedly, feminism in any articulated political sense is the antithesis of tabloid perceptions of women. The word "feminist" itself might as well never have been coined; to tabloids, "women's libbers" are eroding society, much as gays are. As *Examiner* Associate Editor Linedecker says, "we can use stories that are very definitely anti–women's lib. . . . Other people are scared to death to say anything about the gays and women's libbers anymore because they come down on you so hard" (Engstrom 1984, 22).

Schechter assumes that tabloid readers are predominantly women who are untouched by feminism, their main concerns being marriage and parenthood—"a fact which accounts for the tabloids' high concentration of horror stories, tearjerkers, and wondertales concerning pregnancy, childbirth, offspring, and husbands (or 'hubbies' as they are invariably called in the *Weekly World News* and the *Sun*)" (1988, 107–8). Although his perception of tabloid audiences is overly simplistic, tabloid representations of women do to some extent bear this out. We have seen already that marriage and children are of prime importance—tabloid heroines are not successful career women but women who make unusual marriages and succeed as mothers. Villains, on the other hand, are women (and men) who disrupt the family ideal. Celebrities are often seen as hopelessly pursuing the quest for a perfect marriage and family; perennial favorites like Elizabeth Taylor will never be truly happy until they find the perfect mate.

Nevertheless, there is another side to this representation. Female celebrities may spend a great deal of energy on marriage and children, but they also are unmistakably career women leading exciting, glamorous lives. Women like Roseanne Barr are pictured as running the show on the TV set; tabloid role models toss lovers aside: "*Dallas* Beauty [Linda Gray] Splits with Beau—Loves Being Single and Free" (*Enquirer*, 11). In spite of the advertising and editorial material that pictures aging as a terrible fate, many popular tabloid celebrities are women like Taylor, Linda Evans, Joan Collins, or Linda Gray, who are in their forties, fifties, or older.

Perhaps most significantly, women are simply very much present in tabloids in a way they often are not in mainstream news. Levin, Mody-Desbarau, and Arluke (1988) found that 47 percent of subjects in tabloid stories were female; although this does not accurately reflect reality, it comes much closer than many media (Tuchman, Daniels, and Benet 1978). Women's heroics may often be directed toward preservation of the family, but they are recorded and praised. Tabloid content does indeed present a distinctly conservative picture of women but also leaves space for celebration of a limited range of active, achieving role models.

The most striking aspect of tabloid content is its predictability. The categories of story that Holden described in 1977 still apply to the tabloid of 1990, with minor variations. Furthermore, all of these categories can be found without any difficulty in a single issue of each tabloid. Indeed, regular tabloid reading leaves one with an impression of timelessness—just wait a couple of weeks and the same story, or one very much like it, will appear once again. The names of the individuals featured may change, but the themes are reiterated with each retelling.

While those at the "high-literate" end of the spectrum find this formulaic predictability wearisome, tabloid devotees relish it, and tabloid writers learn quickly to provide it. In the oral tradition, "praise goes with the highly polarized, agonistic, oral world of good and evil, virtues and vice, villains and heroes" (Ong 1982, 45), and tabloids retain countless characteristics of their oral ancestry. Of course, the predictable themes, the definitions of virtues and vice, are not ideologically neutral. While sensational in any usual sense of the word, tabloids are also distinctly conservative and puritanical, a trait inherited from their ancestors, both folkloric and journalistic. Steele recognized the parallels when discussing the Pulitzer papers of a century earlier: "Like twentieth-century supermarket tabloids, the *World* used sensationalism as bait; the underlying message was prim enough to satisfy rigid Victorian mores" (1990, 596).

Tabloid content today presents a picture of decent folk standing siege against an army bearing the standard of humanism, liberalism, and loose morals. And as we shall see, the content is the product of an ongoing collaboration between readers and writers about how the world is or should be constructed.

# 3

# Writing the Tabloid

It's wonderful. I love talking to witches and Satanists and vampire hunters, and people who've been kidnapped by UFOs—it sure beats covering zoning board meetings.

—Cliff Linedecker, former associate editor
of the *National Examiner*

## Who Writes the Tabloids

For the checkout counter browser, perhaps the most common response to tabloid headlines is incredulity: who are these people, and where do they get this stuff? The very words "tabloid reporter" conjure up images of "sleaze" personified—the slimy, pushy nuisance working in shabby offices who will do anything to dig up dirt and invent preposterous stories. In this chapter, I aim to answer some of the questions, looking at who writes tabloids, where stories come from, and what relationship tabloid practices have to mainstream journalism.

A visit to the offices of Globe Communications reveals a prosperous operation doing business from a spacious office block on the outskirts of Boca Raton, Florida. Tabloids are now a multimillion-dollar industry, and the working conditions for their staff are more attractive than those of most newspaper journalists. Tabloid writers tend to be secretive about their day-to-day operations, citing intense

# For Enquiring Minds

competition among the various publications as well as irritation at having constantly to defend the way they work. The *National Enquirer* is particularly secretive: "the tab is run with the fervor, secrecy and determination of an efficient intelligence agency. . ." (Ressner 1988, 56).

Globe Communications, especially the staff of the *National Examiner*, has been the most open in allowing access to outsiders. Members of the staff have appeared on several television news shows, and they seem well rehearsed and eager to state the point of view of the tabloid writer. After requesting permission to visit and observe the operations of the tabloid, I was originally invited to visit the *Examiner* offices for one day in February 1986. After I had interviewed several members of the editorial staff, I was then permitted to return for a second day of interviews. I was not, however, allowed to attend editorial meetings or watch staff at work for extended periods. During the two days, I interviewed *Examiner* Editor Bill Burt, Associate Editor Cliff Linedecker, Photo Editor Ken Matthews (Burt, Linedecker, and Matthews have since left the paper), Staff Writer and Advice Columnist Sheila O'Donovan ("Sheela Wood"), and Psychic Adviser Anthony Leggett. In addition, I spoke casually with other staff members who happened to be present. All formal interviews were tape-recorded; any information attributed to *Examiner* staff was obtained from transcripts of these recordings.

The writers were extremely cooperative, spending several hours discussing their work with me. After some initial suspicion, as it was established that a "hatchet job" was not my intention, rapport developed easily. I believe a more complete picture would have been obtained through some prolonged observation; writers were obviously aiming to promote the most positive account possible of tabloid journalism. The interview, while a useful methodological tool, provides information made up from the self-reflexive accounts of participants. As Bruner points out, "There may be a correspondence between a life as lived, a life as experienced, and a life as told, but the anthropologist should never assume the correspondence nor fail to make the distinction" (1984, 7). I quickly gained the impression, for example, that tabloid life as told by my informants was a rather more noble and altruistic enterprise than it might have appeared to a fly on the wall. In addition to my interviews, several "inside" accounts of tabloid life have appeared (Barber 1982; Corkery 1981; Gourley 1981; Ressner 1988), and these helped provide some useful corrective to the accounts I obtained.

Although the tabloids proclaim themselves to be highly competitive with each other, they often cover the same stories in very similar styles, occasionally using the same sources and identical quotes. At least in part this is because the papers share, in effect, a constantly circulating pool of writers and editors, who move between the papers often and tend to know each other. *Examiner* Editor Burt, for instance, is a longtime friend of *Enquirer* Editor Iain Calder, a fellow Scotsman.

The careers of writers on any one paper can be short, and many move from paper to paper or free-lance for any of them between jobs. The *Enquirer* under Pope was notorious for the pressure placed on writers to produce a constant stream of good stories; Gourley (1981) writes of how Pope pitted teams of writers against each other, firing those who failed. Since my 1986 interviews at the *Examiner*, Linedecker, Matthews, and Burt have all been fired—Burt after five years of apparent success as editor (Linedecker now works at the *Sun*). Mike Nevard, formerly editorial director for all three Globe papers, was also fired, and now works at the *Enquirer* (having at various times also worked for the *Star* and the *Enquirer* under Pope). The *Examiner*'s new associate editor, Joe West, was formerly with the *Weekly World News*. As Ken Matthews put it, "What's happened all these years is we've just traded people up and down the East Coast from the Globe papers to the *Star* to the *Enquirer*—we need new blood badly."

*Examiner* staff bemoan the small number of young American journalists who want to work for tabloids, in spite of the lucrative salaries. Rather than rely on American journalists, all the papers have a core of writers whose backgrounds are in British or Commonwealth daily tabloids which, though more "newsy" than American weeklies, provide training in the desired style. At the *Examiner*, Burt, Senior Editor Harold Lewis, O'Donovan, Leggett, and others are British.

# For Enquiring Minds

British staff at all the Florida tabloids tend to know each other and socialize together as part of the now large expatriate community in the Lantana area. "The Fleet Streeters began arriving in droves during the 1970s, enough of them to field cricket teams, fill dart rooms and prompt some local eateries to include bangers and mash on their menus" (Smilgis 1988, 13).

Scottish-born Burt, who worked for local and national papers in Britain, later for the *Enquirer*, "prefers places that are a bit scrungy" to his palatial *Examiner* office. He explained his preparation for tabloids: "I've been told to bug off so many times that I'm totally insensitive to it. . . . I spent too many years going up and down tenement buildings and getting punched in the mouth and hit over the head and getting involved in car chases —I was brought up in a really good school."

When available, American journalists are in demand, and many have worked for several tabloids. Associate Editor Linedecker's background seems fairly typical of American tabloid writers; he has considerable experience of "straight" journalism, including many years with the Philadelphia *Inquirer*. Matthews's credentials include the Washington *Star* as well as papers in Connecticut and California and six years as a correspondent in the Far East: "I didn't come to this because I was not acquainted with ordinary journalism. I did come to work for the *National Enquirer* when I came back from Asia and they were offering me much more money than anybody else was." While salaries were an incentive for both, they, like Burt, find tabloids a respite from the "burn-out" of regular journalism. Matthews explains: "When you've been in the business a few years, you feel like you've done everything and written every story. When it stops being exciting it's pretty much a dull job, I think."

Tabloid writers not only enjoy pleasant working conditions and large salaries, they rarely have to venture outside the newsroom—unless they are celebrity "stake-out" specialists. As Burt sees it, the successful tabloid writer is one who is not ashamed of the particular techniques he or she must use but who can revel in the "fun" of tabloids without being cynical. A tabloid writer has to be able to adapt: "We couldn't hire a Bob Woodward or Carl Bernstein here. Number one, they'd think they were too good for tabloids; number two, they'd be no good for tabs; and number three, you've got to enjoy it, you've got to get into the fun and excitement the paper can be. . . . If you're a total cynic and don't have a sense of humor, you'll never get on in a tabloid." The key to tabloid writing? "Let's flag it, let's do a bit of Barnum and Bailey. . . . If you don't get a chuckle yourself, the reader's not going to get a chuckle out of it." And most of the *Examiner* staff do indeed seem to "get a chuckle" out of their work, seeing it as a welcome change of pace from daily journalism.

## Getting the Story: Celebrity Legwork

Celebrity reporting is the main area in which there is real "legwork"— interviewing, chasing contacts, trying to beat the competition. Tabloid reporters track down the "untold story" of celebrity spats and dalliances with the tenacity of investigative journalists on the trail of a political exposé. Ressner describes tabloid reporters and photographers swinging through trees, dangling from helicopters, and staking out celebrity homes. Describing paparazzo Phil Ramey, he comments, "it's Ramey's abnormally boorish behavior and persistence that have landed him hundreds of exclusive snapshots" (1988, 53).

Audrey Lavin, a full-time free-lancer who has worked on the *Star*, the *Globe*, and the London *Sun*, is described as "a natural stake-out queen." She "has nailed stories by sliding into Prince Rainier's limousine in New York to ask about his personal relationships; by bargaining with John McEnroe for an interview after watching him publicly bawl out his pregnant wife, Tatum O'Neal; by sweating out a three-week Liberace deathwatch in Las Vegas" (Ressner, 54). Corkery describes the *Enquirer* operation that swung into action with the death of Elvis Presley, culminating in a front-page photo of the singer in his coffin, taken by a family member who was paid by the tabloid. The issue was the paper's biggest ever, selling out the press run, and starting "a new *Enquirer* tradition . . . the dead celeb in his box on page one" (1981, 21). *Enquirer* reporters began to go to great lengths to get such pictures: "When Bing Crosby died, the religion reporter disguised himself as a priest and helped get a picture of Bingo in his box. On the way out of the chapel, still dressed in clerical black, he granted an interview to Geraldo Rivera, cautioning the ABC reporter against intruding on the privacy of the mourning family" (Corkery, 21).

Celebrity specialists make it their business to know as much as possible about their subjects' lives; even if the most damaging information may not surface in the paper, it can be used. According to Ressner, "One of the most powerful weapons in a tabloid's arsenal is leverage—quashing an item on a celebrity's deep secrets in exchange for cooperation on another, less sensitive story." Of course, such threats may be hollow: "the *Enquirer* would probably not use the more explosive information anyway, since it thinks of itself as a wholesome family paper that shies away from sick sex or depressing drug stories" (Ressner, 64).

Obviously, then, the relationship between tabloids and celebrities is often confrontational, with many celebrities spending a great deal of energy avoiding such people as the "stake-out queen." The Carol Burnett libel suit, along with actual or threatened action by other celebrities, does reflect the hostility felt by some stars (Schardt 1980; Levin and Arluke 1987). The other side of the coin is that the entertainment industry and the tabloids often work symbiotically in keeping celebrities in the public eye. As mentioned already, the majority of celebrity stories are favorable, even if not all were given willingly. According to a study by Levin and Arluke, 46 percent of *Enquirer* celebrity stories are "upfront" interviews. Many tabloid stories do come direct from celebrities' publicists, who will sometimes offer a story on a major star in return for tabloid coverage of a less well-known personality (1987, 85). In addition, certain stars maintain good relationships with the tabloids and are accorded the status of "friends" (Ressner 1988). Reporters may read back quotes to "friends"; some may even be allowed full copy approval. Michael Jackson, who received extensive tabloid coverage for some of his eccentricities, apparently had his representative give photos of him in his "hyperbaric chamber" to the *Enquirer*. "One of his people called up and said, 'You can do me a favor—would you please call this bizarre? He wants the word bizarre used" (Ressner 1988, 64).

Similarly, the tabloids have been largely responsible for hyping the excitement about "cliff-hanger" episodes of prime-time TV soap operas. Over the last few years, a tabloid staple has been the "exclusive" on the forthcoming season's story lines, appearing during the summer hiatus. Thus it suits program makers to maintain interest in their shows, and tabloids oblige, often paying large sums to get inside information. The *Star* and *Enquirer* are the main competitors for this information, using specialists with connections, like the *Enquirer*'s Sammy Rubin: "I may buy the material from the janitor, but the producer gave him the scripts and my phone number" (Ressner, 54).

For these and other show business stories, people like Rubin rely on their connections and a large expense account: "We don't rummage through people's garbage anymore. . . . We don't have to. I haven't done a formal stakeout in three years. I can call" (Ressner, 56). Rubin reportedly spent $7,000 in cash in one evening on inside tips, the end result being the scripts to the cliff-hanger episodes of three major soap operas (Ressner, 54).

Celebrity reporters' networks of contacts may be huge, including such people as relatives, lawyers, hairdressers, and secretaries— "anyone and everyone with information to peddle" (Ressner, 64). On the *Enquirer*, payment for information is routine, with fees ranging from $50 for a small gossip item to $1,600 for information that leads to a front-page story. "For really explosive stories, payoffs can soar into the high five figures" (Ressner, 64).

## Getting the Story: Newsroom Creativity

While the high-profile celebrity stories may require investigation and supplies of cash, most tabloid stories, including those on celebrities, are considerably more routine. The popular image of a tabloid writer may be the sleazy nuisance who relies on eavesdropping, intrusion, and harassment as basic research methods, but in fact most of the staff rarely leave the newsroom; their days of "legwork" are behind them. For some, that in itself is a central attraction of tabloid work. For tabloid stories, wherever they might originate, are made in the newsroom. Although they admit the existence of "top-of-the-head" stories, tabloid writers publicly deny they "make up" most of the material. So where do those stories come from and how are they written?

The key to tabloid technique is the recognition and transformation of run-of-the-mill news filler into the kind of gripping narratives whose headlines can produce an irresistible cover—the bait that turns the mildly interested browser into the buyer. To achieve the perfect mix, the staff spends hours sifting through other publications from the United States and abroad, ready to take a story "nugget" and mine it into a tabloid narrative. Freed from the constraints of timeliness that a news reporter works with, they see their role as more similar to that of a feature writer, who may develop the human-interest angle of a news story. Some stories are simply rewritten in tabloid style while others may involve some follow-up research: "We take that story nugget and then we have a reporter who will call authorities, individuals, police or whatever, get some more quotes, and then develop it in our style. We'll take a story that is two paragraphs in some paper and through phone calls and our kind of questioning, we'll have the story," says Linedecker.

Editor Burt is unabashed as to what "our kind of questioning" entails. "You've got to put words into their mouths. Say you get somebody who can only speak about ten words of English and you want to get a first-person account of what it was like floating for twenty-four hours with sharks circling their rubber dinghy or whatever. Not just the tabloids, but *Reader's Digest* or anybody. . . . Are they going to sit down and say, 'My God, it was hell' (point, new paragraph) 'The black fin of the shark spun around mercilessly and I thought it was only a matter of time. I dreamed of my little village back in blah blah blah. . . .' No! They don't talk like that, of course they don't." So instead, "you ask them a question phrased that way. I make no apologies for it, I think it's fair journalism."

Linedecker elaborates: "If we have a story line, of course we'll try to get comments that will back it up if it's a good one, but if it's just absolutely not true then you drop the story." Dropping the story is a last resort, however, and sometimes a little persuasion helps: "Just because they're a little hesitant at first to give you that good-money quote doesn't mean that you give up, because a lot of people maybe do agree with you but don't want to be quoted right away, and if you're persistent you can usually come up with that good-money quote unless your whole story is just absolutely wrong and then there's no place to go."

Questioning the participants in the story is just one way to come up with the "good-money quote." Like all journalists, tabloid writers have stables of sources who can be contacted to provide expert opinion on any issue. Like other reporters' sources, these may be doctors, psychologists, or university professors, but they may also be psychics, seers, or students of alien life forms.

In a more conventional story, reference sources and medical experts might provide background and additional details, as in a story Burt recalls about an eleven-year-old girl who gave birth to twins: "We thought it was quite remarkable—but we were way off. You know, it was a true story but there've been cases of girls of eight giving birth to triplets." According to Burt, "we go to a doctor and find out how rare it is—that's interesting—then we go into our own files for case histories of other unusual or extremely young births and in the course of which we might find out there's a much younger one, and we develop that one, hold it for a later date."

Except for more fast-breaking celebrity stories, timeliness is not a major tabloid news value. Indeed, human-interest features in regular newspapers are also frequently timeless; all journalists are familiar with the profiles and "soft" features that get printed when space is available. Tabloids are almost all "soft" news; human-interest stories that first appeared in daily newspapers may surface in tabloids weeks, months, or even years later. As Burt explains, "People don't care. . . . Take our story on girl, 5, has baby, one of our first over the 1 million mark. It did happen in 1939, and it was the youngest recorded then." Many tabloid stories are generated from such file material, from medical reports in magazines and newspapers, census and other demographic data—much of the same background material as any feature writer might use.

Less familiar to the conventional reporter might be the "expert" in the occult and paranormal. The tabloids have their source files for these stories, too. A perennial favorite is the UFO story: "Every province in Brazil, for example, has got a UFO society, so you go and phone up the chairman. He'll give you anything you want, and if you can't find the local UFO buff there's always somebody who knows. To find out about UFOs in Caracas, for instance, I can get you a contact in five minutes," says Burt.

According to Linedecker, the paper's "specialist" in the paranormal, experts can always be found to back up his stories. Discussing several stories dealing with reincarnation, Linedecker asserts that the experts quoted do exist: "We frequently interview Indian authorities. . . . Reincarnation of course is a big part of the Hindu religion and they're aware of these cases when they occur. The universities over there seem to be far more likely to take them seriously and investigate them, so a lot of our reincarnation stories come from India."

However the story is generated, the particular stamp of the tabloid is given to a story in the writing, and *Examiner* staff members are quick to describe this as a creative process. According to Matthews, "we're constantly looking for these kernels, nuggets, and it's very satisfying when you make one grow, so it's a much more creative process than most people are engaged in."

This creativity follows well-defined lines, of course. All tabloid stories are reshaped in the newsroom, and they show the mark of a formulaic pattern of storytelling. Reporters, though they work on a story alone, must follow those formulae. Sheila O'Donovan, a reporter who doubles as advice columnist "Sheela Wood," explains that ideas go through an editor before being written up. "A lead sheet comes back and he'll write the lead or the angle that he wants you to follow on it, and then you just sort of evolve the story around that. But you basically have to follow his guidelines."

Once a tabloid story's characteristically clear point of view has been established, information is used to tell that story rather than any other that may be generated from the same sources. Corkery explained how stories were generated at the *Enquirer*, with different teams of editors and reporters bringing them to Gene Pope for review. "If he approves an idea, it gets typed up on a special form, is given a file number and becomes an entity. Once an idea is approved, you must turn in a story. It is very hard to kill an idea once it's okayed by The Boss" (1981, 20). Barber agrees, writing that stories often have less to do with what is really happening and more to do with what "the editor wishes to have happen" (1982, 49). At the *Examiner*, the same basic process operates, although apparently without the cutthroat competition that prevails at the *Enquirer*. As Matthews puts it, "you approach these things with a certain point of view, a frame of mind, and then you fashion it to fit that formula."

The formula for writing style is easily recognizable, characterized by Burt as "short and pithy" and by Linedecker as "plenty of drama and pathos." Matthews adds, "all of our stories are rewritten no matter where they come from—it's just a matter of style, you have to put in a lot of amazings and startlings and incredibles." The "brand loyalty" of the reader is constantly solicited. As Matthews puts it, "Whenever I could use the phrase 'the vast family of *Examiner* readers' you can be sure I stuck it in somewhere, because we encourage that identification." The language and style of tabloids has not changed greatly since the 1930s. As D. A. Bird writes, "each tabloid article normally is limited to a single theme or metaphor. Elaboration usually repeats the same point in different ways" (1986, 4). Stock clichés, some of them part of a larger "journalese" common in other newspapers, give tabloid writing a consistently familiar look. Apart from the torrent of adjectives—all the stories that are amazing, baffling, untold, secret, incredible, startling, etc.—certain story types generate the same words over and over again. Heroes are always "spunky," "gutsy" and/or "plucky"; a male celebrity may have a "gal pal" or "cutie"; females may have a "toy boy," or possibly a "hunk." Small children are always "tots," often "heartbreak tots," dogs are "pooches," husbands are "hubbies." Unsavory, un-American types are "punks," "creeps," or "sickos." And so it goes on. The "creativity" employed by tabloid writers often entails little more than combining and recombining information in familiar patterns, a point to which I shall return.

The creative freedom enjoyed by tabloid writers shows in other ways, too. For instance, all the staff deny that photos are ever staged and then misrepresented as an actual event, a practice that apparently was not uncommon in tabloids twenty years ago. But they are free to produce "creative" photos in a way other papers would not be. Burt recalls an extremely successful "whiz" cover story that reported on the possibility of Nazi war criminal Josef Mengele living as a woman in South America. According to Burt, the story came from AP or UPI agency reports about a group of Nazi hunters and one member's theory that Mengele is still alive: "That's been his theory for years, and that's not a new story. . . . He takes his theory one step further and he says Mengele is living as a woman. . . . We took the picture issued by the agency that says this is how he looks now, superimposed it with a woman's hair and got the art department to soften the features and from the picture of Mengele issued by all the news services, we explained that's how he would look today if he were a woman."

However, not all artwork is unambiguously labeled. Illustrations of UFOs, aliens, and similar phenomena are often obviously line drawings, but occasionally pictures are used that appear to be photographs, such as an apparent photo of the Mount Everest "Abominable Snowman" (*National Examiner* July 2, 1985, 17). Although the photo is not actually identified as the Yeti supposedly seen by an "expedition of crack mountaineers," neither is it labeled as an artist's conception or composite, as it must be.

## Tabloids and Journalism

Bill Burt is proud of his success in building the *Examiner's* weekly circulation to over one million in less than three years, and he resents what he sees as elitist criticism that "sneers at the tastes of millions of people." He and his staff maintain that critics misunderstand the nature of tabloids in comparing them unfavorably with "straight" newspapers. Rather, Burt argues, they should be considered an entertainment medium comparable to television shows like "Entertainment Tonight," "Lifestyles of the Rich and Famous," or "Ripley's Believe It or Not." Tabloids, says Burt, are primarily for fun and should not be taken too seriously. The staff agree that, above all, tabloids are in the entertainment business, even though they also publish informational articles. According to Matthews, the tabloids' competition is not newspapers but fellow tabloids, magazines like *People* and *Us*, and even all the other items competing for consumer dollars in the supermarket: "It's also the chewing gum and the dogfood, and there probably are people who say, I can buy the premium dogfood for Mitzi if I don't buy the tabloid. That's the competition, not the *New York Times*, not the *Miami Herald*."

Burt, probably more than anyone else on the staff, celebrates the "fun" of tabloids, which seek only to amuse and intrigue their readers: "We're fun, we're fascinating. When you don't want to be bored, you turn to your tabloid. . . . We're providing them with an alternative, relieving them from the barrage of boredom that hits them every day. The magazines that scoff at us, like *People* magazine, like *Us* magazine, they're doing exactly what we're doing, only they're trying to disguise it. We yell it, they whisper it."

Yet at the same time, he and his staff frequently compare tabloid reporting methods with those used in newspaper journalism, arguing that the differences are less than might be imagined. They contend that "respectable" journalism has little relevance to the lives of many Americans, and that their product offers an alternative view of the world that intellectuals might prefer to think does not exist. They argue that tabloids print many informational articles on diet, self-help, and other topics familiar from any newspaper's life-style pages. *Examiner* writers maintain that the clear line journalists like to draw between "real" journalism and "sleaze" simply does not exist. Tabloids are entertainment that also informs; newspapers are informational, according to traditional journalistic standards, but they must also entertain to survive. While asserting that their product is basically entertaining fantasy, tabloid journalists are not prepared to call themselves fiction writers, and they are eager to show that in many respects they have not abandoned the methods of objective journalism. And indeed, the end product owes much to the basic philosophy of objective, "detached" reporting, albeit strongly laced with a dose of "creativity" that gives the tabloids the flamboyant style that is their pride and their critics' despair.

*Objectivity*

A standard constantly invoked by *Examiner* staff is the journalistic tenet of objectivity. As so many scholars have noted (Schiller 1981; Schudson 1978, 1982; Tuchman 1978), objectivity has become a central "strategic ritual" of journalism, which, although increasingly under fire, is still a cornerstone of the profession. As Jensen (1986) puts it, the news genre incorporates a stance that stresses the role of the journalist as an independent observer, gathering information to be presented to the audience as fact. Typically, that information takes the form of quotes from sources, which the journalist assembles in recognizable generic form, offering information aimed at proving the source's credibility.

Tabloid writers, most of whom have training or experience in regular journalism, claim to apply the same basic strategy. Ken Matthews, photo editor at the *Examiner*, uses the philosophy of objectivity to explain stories that many people would find incredible or ludicrous. He stresses that whether the reporter believes the "expert," who may be a psychic or UFO hunter, is irrelevant. "I've said the same thing about covering the White House. You ask the secretary of state if he has done or intends to do something and you record his answer. You don't say, I've established on my own that there are no American troops in El Salvador, you ask the secretary of state and if he says there aren't, that's the news today. We do the same thing."

As Roshco writes, "Giving sources the responsibility for supplying content freed reporters from the need for extensive knowledge about subject matter" (1975, 42). A story is "accurate" if it faithfully reports what was said or written by sources. By this standard, much of what is written in tabloids can claim to be accurate. In fact, the *National Enquirer* has been touted in *Editor & Publisher* as "the most accurate paper in the country" (Barber 1982, 49). The paper maintains a research department headed by Ruth Annan, a sixteen-year veteran of *Time* magazine. According to Annan, "We police the copy. We verify the quotes that are in the stories, the background information" (Levin and Arluke 1987, 119). Levin and Arluke, who spent time interviewing at the *Enquirer*, mention the paper's verification procedures approvingly, in contrast to other newspapers: "They [newspapers] do not ask their reporters to use tape recorders, to verify the accuracy of quotations, or to check the veracity of credentials," (1987, 120). Indeed, it was an absence of any systematic verification procedures that allowed Janet Cooke's infamous "Jimmy's World" story to end up winning a Pulitzer Prize (Goldstein 1985). In general, reporters' honesty and accuracy are simply taken for granted.

However, accounts by former tabloid writers show how the much-touted "accuracy" sometimes worked. Jeff Wells, writing about the "nightmare" experience of covering a celebrated UFO sighting, describes how information was selected and organized: "The polygraph man said it was the plainest case of lying he'd seen in 20 years, but the office was yelling for another expert and a different result" (1981, 51). Even after Wells produced a memo detailing why the case was obviously fraudulent, the *Enquirer* filtered enough "facts" from the data gathered to run a major feature on the Travis Walton UFO abduction (Dec. 16, 1975).

As Barber writes, the research department does indeed check facts, "And yet it regularly lets through palpable inanities. . . . If the tapes and copy jibe, and sources when contacted agree to what has been reported, the story must, however reluctantly, be granted the imprimatur of accuracy" (1982, 49). Furthermore, evidence collected in a recent "60 Minutes" broadcast (Sept. 30, 1990) suggested that at least some *Enquirer* sources are unlikely to confirm stories—they may never have actually worked on them. The "60 Minutes" team found people listed as sources who knew nothing about the stories but had received checks anyway. The suggestion was that the rules requiring three sources for a celebrity story were being bent, to say the least.

One problem of course is that, even if every quote included may be "accurate," the research department can only confirm that this "fact" was said by someone. They cannot discover what else a source said, what was left out, what sources who were not consulted would have said, what the context was, and so on. Former *Enquirer* staffers have explained how some reporters deal with the tape rule by "feeding" a source with appropriate quotes that are then given back to the reporter on tape (Corkery 1981; Schardt 1980). Barber mentions a Gene Pope memo instructing reporters to "ask leading questions," using much the same method as that described by *Examiner* Editor Burt. Thus the wording of the questions, coupled with yes/no answers, suffices to provide the quotes. Pope's memo elaborates how these questions should be phrased: "Quotes should not only be appropriate but believable. A Japanese carpenter should not sound like Ernest Hemingway, or vice versa" (1982, 49).

Burt, however, compares this type of questioning to that done by other journalists: "It's like: 'President Reagan denied last night that he was contemplating taking military action against Libya.' Now that would infer that President Reagan stood up and said, 'I am not contemplating taking any military action against Libya.' They asked a question, and all he said was 'no.'"

Getting the "good-money quote," the one that confirms the premise of the story, is the central aim. While Cliff Linedecker argues that the *Examiner* occasionally drops stories if the quote is impossible to obtain, Barber writes that, at the *Enquirer*, this virtually never happened once Pope had approved a story. He describes how Pope wished to run a story on the Three Mile Island nuclear plant leak asking "Was it sabotage?" The story eventually ran, using some quotes about a "suspicious couple" in a motel, with a can opener and a radio characterized as "weaponry" and "sophisticated communications equipment" (1982).

This type of questioning was behind one story whose subject challenged two tabloids in the courts. Henry Dempsey, a commuter airline pilot, was sucked out of his plane when a door popped open as he was checking a noise. After clinging to the plane for fifteen minutes, Dempsey managed to climb back in and survived with only minor injuries. Some time afterwards, the *Enquirer* and the *Star* ran stories about the incident, even though Dempsey had refused interviews to both (Bailey 1989). Both stories were filled with quotes attributed to Dempsey; the *Star* even gave him the byline.

Both headlines were written in typical tabloidese. From the *Star*: "The sky grabbed hold of me like a sharp cold hand—and pulled me out of the plane"; from the *Enquirer*: "My back burned . . . the wind tore at my face . . . I was trapped in a wild, wailing hurricane" (quoted in Bailey 1989, 10). The *Star* quoted Dempsey: "The urge to survive is the strongest sense of all, and I held on to that rail with all my strength, just kind of praying or at least saying 'God' a whole lot, and bracing myself against this great force trying to pitch me into the sky." The *Enquirer*'s quotes are equally colorful; many " fail the straight-face test and make Dempsey sound a bit like Sergeant Fury." Dempsey reportedly said he "stared death in the face," and "I knew that I was the luckiest man in the world at that moment" (Bailey, 10–11).

Dempsey sued both papers for invasion of privacy, claiming he had been placed in a false light and commercially exploited. In court papers, *Star* Editor Richard Kaplan acknowledged that the paper was wrong to give the byline to Dempsey and said that the quotes were pieced together from interviews with Dempsey's friends and conversations with the reporter who covered the story for the Murdoch-owned *Boston Herald*. Dempsey's suit was settled out of court for an undisclosed sum in January 1989 (Bailey 1989). However, the suit against the *Enquirer*, which had also spoken to unnamed friends, was dismissed in June 1988. The judge ruled that, although the account was fictionalized, it could not be considered "highly objectionable to a reasonable person" (Bailey, 10).

The outcome of the case suggests that, while the *Star*'s false byline went too far, tabloids—and other papers—can get away with leading questions and other "creative" interviewing practices as long as the resulting story is not defamatory. *Enquirer* lawyer Gerson A. Zweifach argued that the story accurately portrayed Dempsey's feelings, and "I thought it made him look appropriately courageous for hanging on and getting through it" (Bailey, 11).

This guiding principle also seems to be behind the tabloids' coverage of celebrity stories, following the 1981 Carol Burnett libel suit, in which Burnett was initially awarded $1.6 million (later reduced to $800,000 on appeal). Ressner (1988) confirms that the *Enquirer* now is more careful with celebrity stories, employing an attorney from the influential Washington, D.C., law firm of Williams and Connolly to go through stories every week searching for problems with libel and invasion of privacy. Other tabloids also retain lawyers for this purpose, and the generally "upbeat" coverage of both celebrities and "ordinary people" stories probably protects them, as well as pleasing their readers.

The tabloid writers are the first to agree that their story styles are formulaic, that they gather quotes and facts to construct a story with the intended structure and content. But again they compare this kind of storytelling to that used by other journalists. They argue that tabloid writers are not unique in pursuing a particular "angle" to a story, that angle in the end defining what questions are asked, which sources are interviewed, and which story is ultimately presented as "the truth." Increasingly, journalism researchers argue essentially the same point— journalism of whatever kind is storytelling that owes as much to established codes and conventions as to a relationship with "the real world out there" (see Bird and Dardenne 1988 on news and storytelling). Darnton (1975) recalls constructing quotes that were appropriate to particular types of news genre, such as bereavement stories, while Cohen writes that media descriptions of "mods and rockers" in Britain owed a great deal to the reporters' "conception of how anyone labelled as a thug or a hooligan should speak, dress and act" (1981, 275; I shall return to this point in chapter 6).

Tabloid staff defend their style as simply a variant on other kinds of journalistic writing—finding "the story" within an event and shaping it to fit a particular construction of reality. According to Matthews, "American journalists do the same thing. I've been at it nearly twenty-five years in all facets and you do the same thing. You go to a speech, you go to a meeting of the town council and you sit there and it's mostly boring, and then all of a sudden someone says something and you say, that's the story. And you begin writing the story in your head. . . . It's just that we take a different view of what we want to extract from the situation." Burt agrees: "Any story— let's say, 'Mum Gives Birth to 50-lb. Baby'—I could write it in such a way that it would be acceptable in the *New York Times*, and then I would write it properly, and it would go into the tabloids." Matthews readily admits that tabloid writing is stereotyped and predictable but argues that it is essentially just one such style among many: "Tabloids are a formula just as the *Washington Post* is. Every morning they sit around a table like this and decide how they're going to fashion a product and each department reports on what they've got available to fit in and then somebody decides how we'll stir it all up together so we'll come out with the proper mixture. And we do the same thing."

Indeed, the process of creating "stories" is structurally very similar in both kinds of publication. Tabloids, working on a two- or three-week lead time, do not cover "hard news" at all. But feature writers on any newspaper would be familiar with the practice of developing "enterprise" stories—the features that spring from perceived social trends, government statistics, and so on. Reporters bring their ideas to editors, who decide which ones to pursue. Although there is tremendous competitiveness among tabloid reporters to generate the blockbuster "whiz" stories (Corkery 1981), many more run-of-the-mill tabloid stories spring from medical reports in magazines and newspapers, census and other demographic data, and much of the same background material as any feature writer might use. Other ideas are more intangible, stemming from such "life-style" issues as the endless stories in mainstream media about yuppies, "DINKS," and other "baby boomers." Their tabloid counterparts may be the stories that develop ideas that are similarly "in the air" among their readership—UFOs have landed, garlic will cure everything, people win the lottery all the time. Stories that seem to make sense according to the folklore of one part of the population may seem irrelevant or ludicrous to another.

The argument that tabloid journalism is simply one genre of reporting among many is persuasive up to a point—surely only the most naive journalist would cling to the idea that newspapers simply transmit "reality" to the printed page, unaffected by preconceptions, formulaic story patterns, and other considerations. Yet at the same time, tabloid writers continue to maintain that, above all, they are in the entertainment business. Unfettered by any need to "inform" their readers, they are able to exercise their creativity in, to say the least, more flamboyant directions, and thus they can afford to neglect such journalistic concepts as "balance." After all, the best and most vivid stories are consistent and clear in their point of view; competing interpretations are anathema to a good tabloid tale.

*Credibility*

The concept of "credibility" is another important journalistic credo. Once the reporter has abdicated factual responsibility to sources, the problem becomes whether the reader should believe what the source says. Thus journalistic stories are peppered with attribution, listing of sources' credentials, and so forth. The idea is that the qualifications of sources will ensure their credibility, and at the same time, anyone reading the story should be able independently to verify the existence and credibility of the source. How do tabloids fare in this department? As already mentioned, tabloid writers have stables of sources who may be contacted, much as other journalists do. Experts who would be consulted by mainstream reporters—physicians, psychologists, academics, politicians—are also regularly used by tabloids. Shorn of their adjectives, many feature stories in tabloids would be interchangeable with those in other newspapers. Rather less interchangeable are the stories whose attribution rests on the word of more unconventional sources.

As the *Examiner* staff sees it, quoting psychics or "UFO freaks" is essentially the same as quoting doctors and politicians, given that the world view of their readers may be different from those of, say, the *New York Times*. "Credibility" is still important, but its meaning shifts according to the context. In presenting the views of an "expert," newswriters are careful to provide credentials and qualifications that effectively absolve them from responsibility for the expert's opinions. Tabloid writers claim to do the same, except that in their audience's view of reality, "qualified" faith healers and ghost hunters may be as credible as doctors or scientists. "We don't believe everything that comes in, but if we have legitimate people we can quote who will back up the story, then we'll present their case and you let the readers decide for themselves how credible these individuals are," says Linedecker. He goes on to explain, "I think people accept science, but they hold on to a lot of old beliefs too. It gives them comfort to think that there's something else up there. . . ." Burt echoes these points: "There's a lot more people believe in the paranormal than will admit to it. . . . I'm not saying they're all daft, I'm just saying they have a different, nonconservative point of view." Resident psychic Tony Leggett agrees. "This stuff is sensational if you don't believe it; if you do believe it, it's the norm, it's natural."

Journalists might argue that the very fact that such sources are used at all shows that the tabloids have no real concept of credibility, and that there is a clear distinction to be made between the "true" scientific world view and the "crazy" view of the psychics and UFOlogists. Yet straight newspapers regularly run stories on the strange and unusual, often quoting "experts" in nontraditional fields. And, as Frazier (1984) notes, mainstream media often produce stories that are as credulous as anything in the tabloids.

Klare (1990) studied coverage of psychic phenomena in two regional newspapers, the *Cleveland Plain Dealer* and the *Columbus Dispatch*, and two "papers of record," the *New York Times* and the *Washington Post*. He concluded that all the papers were likely to cover paranormal topics from a "credulous," or at best "neutral," point of view (although the *Times* was the most inclined to offer a skeptical viewpoint). Stories relied overwhelmingly on the testimony of believers in psychic phenomena, either those who claimed to have experienced them or "experts" who were avowed supporters. Skeptical sources were ignored or given minimal coverage. Indeed, "experts" with all the right academic credentials also happen to believe in creationism, Bigfoot, the Loch Ness Monster, and other such phenomena, and are all quoted by tabloids and newspapers alike. Once again, the tenet of objectivity allows all journalists, tabloid or mainstream, to abdicate responsibility for their stories. As Klare comments, "it appears that the problem of uncritical stories is inherent in the reporting process itself" (1990, 363).

And when social trends happen to be those lived by journalists themselves, credibility standards apparently shift happily. Gans (1979) writes that the world view that is perceived as "common sense" by mainstream media tends to be that of the upper middle class. Journalists often write about what interests them: "Many of their ideas for features or investigations grow out of conversations on the patio, over white wine, after tennis" (Stephens 1988, 268). Thus we see columns filled with stories about that quintessentially upper-middle-class "yuppie" phenomenon, "the New Age," such as a *Time* cover story that quotes all manner of gurus in sympathetic style (Friedrich 1987). To a trendy journalist, "New Age" experts make perfect sense while the more flamboyant, but not dissimilar, tabloid stories may be dismissed as loony. As Hofstadter writes, "It would seem that your concept of truth is closely tied in with your way of evaluating the 'style' of a channel of communication, surely quite an intangible notion," (1982, 18).

Perhaps most important, the objective practices of journalism leave journalists open to manipulation by sources who wish a particular story to be told. Tabloid sources successfully get their stories about UFOs or ghosts across to the public, and so do State Department officials and others with a point to make. Porter (1989), in a profile of public relations expert John Scanlon, points out how professionals like Scanlon teach companies how to feed the media favorable information and quotes. Sibbison writes on how the *New York Times* and other media wrote reassuring stories about pollution, "relaying to readers self-serving statements by EPA officials as truth" (1988b, 26). Underwood (1988) concluded that regional newspapers in the home area of the Boeing Company gave the company overwhelmingly favorable press even when problems were being documented elsewhere. Uncritical journalistic reliance on sources can allow those sources to construct the story, whether the article appears in the *National Examiner* or the *New York Times*.

In addition, any journalist knows that a story can be written very differently depending on which sources are used; the reporter may use the standards of objectivity selectively, quoting sources to obtain a particular story. Tabloid writers do this all the time, as we have seen, but part of all reporters' routine of "finding the story" within events involves finding the right people to back the story. In researching stories, journalists often consult the same sources repeatedly, at least in part because they know what such people will say. MacDougall (1989), for example, has written of selecting his sources to provide quotes confirming a certain angle to his stories; the strategy of objectively quoting sources has at least the potential of allowing reporters to write the particular story they want.

Of course there are times when the practices of tabloids quite simply cross the line that any journalist would find acceptable. Although Corkery (1981) reports that an *Enquirer* journalist was fired for misrepresenting an expert source, tabloids are obviously very creative with their sources. The *Sun* and *Weekly World News*, which specialize in "top-of-the-head" stories, undoubtedly attribute information to sources that do not exist. Greenwell (1987) offers "tips" for proving that many tabloid stories on anomalous creatures, such as living dinosaurs, are false. Experts are named, but their affiliation and location is omitted. Verification is made impossible because the location or fate of the animal involved is not given. The concept of objectively quoting a source is stretched to its limits in these tales, with a "stringer" or tipster in some other country being taken as sufficient evidence, and no possibility of verification. Thorn (1989) tried to track down and verify three sample stories that appeared in the *Weekly World News*, concluding that two, both set in foreign countries, were complete fiction. The third, like the majority of stories originating from the United States or Britain, was verifiable, even if the style was flamboyant.

Tabloid staffers argue that they simply do not have the resources to research all their stories, particularly those originating outside the

United States. As Matthews wryly comments, "A lot of these phenomenal stories occur in rather hard-to-reach countries; it's surprising the number of phenomenal things that happen in Bulgaria, for instance." Eddie Clontz, managing editor of the *Weekly World News*, told Thorn, "We do not investigate these or report on these in the way we would a story in the U. S." (Thorn 1989, D5). The primary concern of a tabloid is a good story, and while the best stories are enhanced by some verification, the lack of it rarely stands in the way.

*Information vs. Entertainment*

The worst excesses of tabloids are easily dismissed as bearing little relationship to mainstream journalism. The tabloids are often characterized by distorted quotes, pure fabrication of information and sources, absence of any balancing point of view, and the use of paid tipsters and informants. But tabloids also cover much of the same ground as newspapers do, and they use similar methods. They frequently write about science, medicine, and self-help; their advice columnists are virtually indistinguishable from Dear Abby or Ann Landers.

Indeed, the tabloids can be a source of useful and accurate information. Hinkle and Elliot compared science coverage in the *Star*, *Enquirer*, and *Weekly World News* with the *New York Times*, the *Philadelphia Inquirer*, and *USA Today*. The *Star* and *Enquirer* devoted the highest percentage of their news hole to science (although the *Times* gave it more actual space). Although the *Weekly World News* covered a significant amount of pseudoscience, the other tabloids covered far less than the researchers expected. "All three tabloids featured a fair amount of short, but legitimate, medical/health stories. Some science articles would have been acceptable in the mainstream press" (1989, 358). Evans et al. (1990) compared science coverage in the *New York Times*, the *Philadelphia Inquirer*, the *National Enquirer*, and the *Star*, concluding that the four papers covered science in roughly equal proportions. The tabloids were actually more likely than the "prestige" press to report stories derived from academic journals and conferences. While the "prestige" papers' stories were more comprehensive, they, like the tabloids, often omitted important contextual and methodological information. Once again, the reporting process itself seems to lead to particular emphases in story construction.

While undoubtedly the the *Sun* and *Weekly World News* still occasionally run miracle cure stories that may raise false hope, other tabloids have "evolved out of that," according to the *Examiner*'s Matthews. The *Enquirer* has recently been developing associations with organizations like the American Cancer Society and arthritis foundations "which check out all of the tabloid's articles on related subjects" (Pfaff 1987).

Similarly, Fred Schroeder, looking at four sample issues of the *Enquirer*, concluded that the papers contained many helpful features: "The articles, needless to say, are all commonsense. The quoted sources include five physicians, three marriage counselors, one business counselor, one professor of mechanical engineering and one woman journalist (a successful businesswoman)" (1982, 170). After all, a major source of tabloid news is daily journalism—stories that merit a column or two in the *New York Times* are picked up, dressed up, and spread over half a page in a tabloid. The difference lies in the style of presentation, not the subject matter. "Thus, much of the misunderstanding about the *Enquirer* and its imitators is the result of equating its vulgar style with its presumed content" (Schroeder, 170).

Certainly the tabloids stress entertainment over information, if we understand these terms in the traditional journalistic sense. As John Pauly writes, American journalists like to draw a distinction between "information" and "entertainment," placing media like tabloids firmly in the camp of the trivial. "Forgotten in such an analysis, of course, are the many assignments that require 'serious' journalists to interview the Chamber of Commerce's Miss Teen Personality, document the annual Christmas rush at the airport, or promote the newspaper-sponsored boat show or charity marathon." (1988, 254). Pauly argues that the distinction between "information" and "entertainment" is "intellectually feeble" but still valued greatly by journalists because it helps to define boundaries and justify the value of what they are doing. And while the *New York Times* may consider its straight news "important information," to many people it is information that bears no relationship to their lives; it is not information they can use. On the other hand, tabloids may provide a great deal of "trivia" that is regarded by their audiences as "important information," such as human-interest and celebrity stories that have offer lessons for their lives, or medical information. Tabloid writers and readers argue that "respectable" journalism has little relevance to the lives of many Americans and that their product offers an alternative view of the world that intellectuals might prefer to think does not exist.

And of course the boundary between subject matter classed as "information," regarded as important and serious, and "entertainment," regarded as trivial and perhaps even morally suspect, changes all the time. In the 1960s, President John F. Kennedy's undoubted "womanizing" was not reported by the mainstream press, although tabloids started writing about it not long after his death (Bird 1990). In the 1980s, "respectable" journalists broke the story of Gary Hart and Donna Rice after apparently staking out his residence; the *Enquirer* then published the damning photos that were reproduced in newspapers and TV screens nationwide (*National Enquirer*, June 2, 1987).

Tabloids do not claim to be fiction, even if they do claim primarily to be entertainment. They do report on real people and events, and their staff members are journalists. Although their emphases are different, newspapers and tabloids are unavoidably related along the same storytelling continuum. Maybe one reason newspaper people despise tabloids so vehemently is precisely because the line separating them from "real" newspapers is not as clear-cut as they would like to believe. Whether they compete with newspapers or not, their very existence raises some questions that may be troubling to journalists. Many stories that appear in tabloids are virtually indistinguishable from feature stories in other publications; many use the same sources as other journalistic stories; the bizarre, the unusual, and the rich and famous are valued in regular newspapers as well.

Newspaper journalists may resort to questionable tactics to get a story, and, although verification attempts are usually less perfunctory than those at the *Weekly World News*, they often rely on anonymous sources and tipsters. Levin and Arluke (1987), for example, found that 70 percent of *New York Times* front-page stories used at least one anonymous source. Anonymous "informed sources" may in reality be no more than unsubstantiated rumor, as in the 1975 coverage of Soviet leader Leonid Brezhnev's health problems: "In various accounts, 'informed sources' stated he was suffering from no fewer than 21 ailments ranging in seriousness from a bad toothache to leukemia" (Rosnow and Fine 1976, 108). As historian Charles Beard wrote in 1927, "it could hardly be said that the patterns created by tabloid pictures were less authentic or—more inimical to intelligent citizens than the substance of the more reputable papers—the vast flood of political speeches and innumerable Associated Press dispatches masquerading as 'news' on the basis of 'it is said' or no foundation at all except the secret inspiration of some interested official or powerful individual, unnamed in the text, or of some partisan reporter" (quoted in Bessie 1938, 21). In addition, any journalist knows that a story can be written very differently depending on which sources are used. In researching many stories, journalists often consult the same sources repeatedly, at least in part because they know what such people will say.

Each taken as a whole, the *New York Times* and the *National Examiner* may be poles apart, and recognizably very different. But where do many other newspaper stories fit along the line that separates them? It may be easy to identify the tabloid stories that are completely fabricated, but how easy is it to detect the moment at which vivid, perhaps melodramatic, human-interest writing becomes hackneyed, dishonest "sensationalism"? If the use of the same basic journalistic techniques can produce tabloids, how effective are those techniques at producing the "truth" that journalists seek so avidly? Indeed, how is it that experienced newspaper journalists can so readily adapt to a tabloid setting, even continuing to use many of the same techniques they have learned on daily papers?

Tabloid writers themselves are keenly aware of the questions surrounding their work, and their simultaneous arguments coexist uneasily and often unconvincingly—they just do what other journalists do, but really they're only in the entertainment business and therefore should not be criticized. Straight journalists are also torn; they are in the "important information" business, yet unavoidably they have to be entertaining or they will lose their audience altogether. Perhaps they see some truth in *Examiner* Editor Burt's comment that "newspapers think they've got a sacred duty to put people to sleep." But just how far can they go in entertaining before they go over the edge into the "sleaze" that the tabloids represent?

Perhaps, in the end, journalists do not want to look too closely at the parallels between tabloids and "real newspapers," or to think that even some tabloid storytelling is little different from what "real journalists" do. What matters is the image that tabloids convey, and the role they play in journalists' world view. Like Rupert Murdoch as an individual (Pauly 1988), they represent a collective "demon" that tells the journalistic profession that what journalists do is a distinctly different and inherently more noble enterprise. Better to consign the tabloids to the incinerator, along with Janet Cooke and other sinners, rather than confront the more subtle questions their existence may pose.

# 4

# Reading the Tabloid

It's like waiting for each paper like a juicy steak dinner. I lay on my
waterbed, and munch on a bag of California fruit mix, and then
I enter into the world of the *Examiner*.

—a tabloid reader (letter 67)

Although we know that millions of people buy the tabloids every
week, and that millions more read them, there is surprisingly little
information about who tabloid readers are and how reading tabloids
fits into their lives. In the place of real understanding, we see stereotypes—images of tabloid readers that are generally so unfavorable
that the people they portray can be easily dismissed. As defined by
the elite, tabloids are the epitome of "trash" reading, as described by
Brown (1989): "First, trash connotes that which ought to be dis-
carded, a sort of instant garbage; second, it connotes cheapness,
shoddiness, the overflow of the capitalist commodity system. Third,
it connotes a superficial glitter designed to appeal to those whose
tastes are ill-formed according to the dominant perspective. . . .
Fourth, trash is excessive: it has more vulgarity, more tastelessness,
more offensiveness than is necessary for its function as a cheap commodity." And if tabloids are trash, so are their readers.

The stereotype of tabloid readers has evolved over the years,
though it is invariably negative. Potterton, writing in 1969 of the
"blood and guts" era when tabloids were usually bought by men, offers his image: "I pictured such a person as a roller-derby fan who

owned several Lugers, voted straight lunatic fringe and cruised around the neighborhood in a 1955 Mercury sedan, hoping to come across fatal accidents" (p. 212). In 1977, as the family tabloid moved into the supermarket and was bought more by women, Mano provides a new picture: "America is a 300-pound woman. This woman has two dogs, two TVs, hypochondria, and no secondary education. Also she's broke, bored to tears, over 40 (her husband was once alcoholic, unfaithful, crippled, or laid off), and yet, despite all, she still believes in life after death. Got to be. She's the only person who'd buy *National Enquirer*" (p. 209). Schechter's 1988 opinion of *Weekly World News* readers is kinder, though somewhat patronizing: "it seems safe to assume . . . that its regular readers are, by and large, people of distinctly narrow means and limited education" (p. 101). Finally, in 1985, unconventional filmmaker John Waters echoes right-wing critic Mano: "I'm convinced that typical *Enquirer* readers move their lips when they read, are physically unattractive, badly dressed, lonely and overweight. Especially overweight" (p. 44).

The tabloid companies themselves have done little research into who their readers are. At the *Examiner*, staff prefer to rely on the immediate feedback of letters and circulation figures, which can be charted week by week. According to Pfaff (1987), however, the *Globe* and *Examiner* appeal to poorer and less-educated readers than the *Star* or *Enquirer*. He describes an advertising agency's profile of these readers as being 65 percent female, with a median age of thirty-five, and 51 percent having household incomes under $20,000. Sixty percent never graduated from high school.

The *Star* has carried out some audience research, but Editor Richard Kaplan would share only a few details: "We appeal to a predominantly female (75 percent) audience with a joint household income in the high twenties. Median age high thirties. Percentage of working women conforms to national figures. Married. Families. Mrs. America, to be candid" (personal communication, 1990). An *Enquirer* spokesperson told Lehnert and Perpich, "We never really asked our readers what they like or dislike about the paper" (1982, 105). Instead, Gene Pope used to monitor audience reaction through the million or more letters a year the paper received (Lehnert and

Perpich 1982). The paper's image of its typical reader, however, is similar to that of the *Star*: "We are writing for Mrs. Smith in Kansas City, but she could be in Queens, New York, or a suburb of Chicago. Mrs. Smith is Middle America" (*Enquirer* Editor-in-Chief Iain Calder, quoted in Levin and Arluke 1987, 96).

*Examiner* staff are reluctant to categorize their readers, pointing out that they receive mail from people of both genders, all ages, and a range of educational levels. The "typical" buyer they imagined, however, was a middle-aged woman who worked, or whose husband worked, in a blue-collar or clerical occupation. From the evidence of readers' letters, however, they assume that, while women may usually buy the papers, their husbands and families read them, too.

## The Reader Study

Two previous academic studies of tabloid readers have been carried out. Salwen and Anderson (1984) used a fairly large sample for a uses-and-gratifications study while Lehnert and Perpich (1982) employed a more subtle Q-methodology to classify readers into three categories. Their categories were based on the way people read the papers—for instance, whether they believed what they read. While both studies yielded some insights, I found they were unable to say a great deal about the actual context and experience of reading tabloids. Salwen and Anderson, for example, concluded that all readers use tabloids for "entertainment"—a predictable conclusion that says nothing about what "entertainment" actually is or how that "entertainment" fits into readers' lives.

My intent, therefore, was to go beyond predetermined research categories in order to reach a deeper understanding of the process of reader reception. Jensen discusses the need for qualitative audience research: "What goes on in the reception situation should be understood with constant reference to the social and cultural networks that situate the individual viewer, and these networks do not necessarily coincide with the income brackets or segments of market research" (1987, 25). In this kind of research, we look at how media viewing or reading fits into the lives of the consumer. Lull (1982), for example, looked at how television viewing provided conversation material for families, while Morley (1986) also studied the role of TV in the daily dynamic of family life. Studies of soap opera, such as Hobson (1982) and Brown (1989), showed how women use the programs as focal points for discussion of social issues and private, personal problems. Jensen, discussing audience reception of news programming, argues that approaches like uses and gratifications can yield usable correlations, "but neither the responses nor the correlations will bear witness to the experiential qualities of concrete news programs as received daily by the viewers" (1987, 27).

It is the "experiential qualities" of tabloid reading that I wanted to explore, concluding that a qualitative approach was the only way to do this effectively. One of the crucial criticisms of much audience research is that its linear approach tends to assume the "audience" as an objective mass of people, differentiated perhaps by socioeconomic categories such as age, sex, and income. That is, the audience is viewed as if it actually exists as such—that "tabloid readers," for example, are a unified, identifiable body of people. It is easy for the researcher to slip into the perception of people who read tabloids as "tabloid readers" first and foremost. In reality, according to Martin Allor, "The audience exists nowhere; it inhabits no real space, only positions within analytic discourses" (1988, 228). The point Allor makes is not that readers or viewers do not exist but that "the audience" is not the objective reality that researchers often assume—rather the moment of reading or viewing is one moment among endless "articulations" among an individual's daily practices and identities. In any given context, "tabloid readers" might see themselves primarily as mother, worker, UFO enthusiast, baker, Sylvester Stallone fan, or any number of countless identities—"tabloid reader" probably only comes to mind when talking to me. As John Fiske reminds us, "the audience precedes the text"; it is important to see the audience outside our definition of its role as audience. Writing about television, Fiske argues that media researchers have been too eager to put the text first: "the viewer makes meanings and pleasures from television that are relevant to his or her social allegiances at the mo-

ment of viewing; the criteria for relevance precede the viewing moment. If this account of watching television is acceptable, we must
recognize that it has collapsed the category of audience" (1988, 247).

I have argued elsewhere (Bird 1990) that a grasp of the fluid, shift-
ing nature of "audience" can have the effect of paralyzing audience
research. If the audience as we know it does not exist, how is it possible to study it? I think we must accept that a complete understanding of the media role in social life is forever elusive. Even the kind
of large-scale ethnographic projects envisaged by Radway (1988)
must at least focus on specific questions of interest to the particular
researcher, just as anthropologists, even as they look at an entire culture, concentrate on particular elements of that culture. The important point is that the role of media must be seen ethnographically, as
one element in a complex interconnected mesh that constitutes culture and the individual's experience of culture.

A crucial element in such research is described by Jensen: "Qualitative analysis attaches primary importance to those categories that
can be derived internally from the respondent's own conceptual
framework" (1987, 31). One way to do this is to undertake what
Fiske (1987) has called an "ethnography of discourse"—an analysis
of talk about experience rather than an observation of experience itself. This is, essentially, the approach I have taken in discussing both
tabloid writers and readers. While ethnography in the classic sense
entails fieldwork and observation of behavior, the point Fiske makes
is that ethnography always strives to understand experience from the
point of view of those involved. While debate rages in anthropology
and related disciplines as to whether it is ever really possible to
"speak for the other," (see Bird 1990 for fuller discussion of this issue), I believe that an ethnographic approach is the best possible way
at least to strive for a reader-centered rather than researcher-centered
picture of the tabloid-reading experience. Michael Agar, discussing
the minimal requirements for research defined as ethnographic,
writes: "The assumption here is that whatever the interests of the ethnographer, he must understand the way that group members interpret the flow of events in their lives" (1980, 194). An "ethnography

of discourse," aimed at allowing readers to define the experience as far as possible, was my intention.

Ang (1985) solicited letters from regular viewers for her analysis of the experience of watching "Dallas." Initially, I followed her approach to obtaining the kind of reader-oriented material I needed. The *National Examiner* agreed to place a staff-written announcement in the paper, asking readers to write to me. The brief notice read: "Readers, tell us about yourselves: Researcher Elizabeth Bird wants to know all about you— why you like to read the *Examiner*, whether you read any other weeklies, and what your favorite kinds of stories are—celebrity, occult, crime, human interest, etc. She also needs to know your age, sex, occupation, and any other information about yourself that you care to share." The notice ran once in the *Examiner* of August 25, 1987.

I had requested that the notice be kept as open as possible and would have preferred to omit the story type request, which I felt reflected the staff's categories rather than readers' definitions. I received 114 letters, from seventy-seven women, thirty-two men (one man wrote five separate letters), and one organization. The responses ranged from scrawled, barely legible notes to neatly typed, carefully presented letters. Although most letters arrived within two or three weeks, responses continued to trickle in until January 1988 as readers received their passed-along copies from friends and relatives. While Ang used only letters, I wished to allow at least some readers to explore their reading more fully. I followed up with phone interviews with fifteen readers (ten women and five men) from around the country, selecting the readers to give a range of ages (see Appendix). I added these to one face-to-face interview I had carried out in Iowa City, Iowa, after a largely unsuccessful attempt to locate readers through a classified advertisement in a shopper paper. The interviews averaged around one hour each.

I make no claims that those people who responded are a scientifically representative sample. Indeed, they were a self-selected group who not only were interested enough to write but had the time to do so. Writing letters is a task that many people rarely do, and I think it is safe to assume that the respondents were more enthusiastic about writing than many other readers would be. I believe also that those who wrote may have been disproportionately older and/or working at home—many were retired or were self-described housewives, who are likely to have a more flexible schedule in which to write. The average age of the 69 women who gave their ages was 52.7; the youngest was 14, the oldest 94. Only 4 women in their twenties wrote—all divorced single mothers of at least 3 children. The average age of the 27 men who gave their ages was 50.1; the youngest was 21, the oldest 90. Fifteen, or just over half of the men, were 50 or under, while only 25, or about one-third of the women, were 50 or under. The great majority of those who specified an occupation outside the home were in skilled or clerical positions. The notice had not asked readers to specify race; only 3 (1 man and 2 women) identified themselves as black, of whom 1 woman was among those interviewed (interview 15); 2 had Hispanic names. Minorities obviously do read the tabloids. For example, in the sample week of the *Examiner*'s "Have a Friend Club," 14 out of the 87 women advertising were black, 4 were Filipino, and 2 "Oriental." Of the 59 men, 9 were black, 1 East Indian, and 1 Mexican. In Salwen and Anderson's (1984) sample of 132 readers (98 women and 34 men), 15 were black.

The group of readers who responded to my announcement, therefore, were fairly close to the "typical buyer" the *Examiner* staff envisioned—mostly white, predominantly female, and middle-aged or older. In discussing their reading experiences, I use their words as much as possible to illustrate my analysis. When quoting from letters, I have made no changes in spelling or grammar, in order to convey the tone of the letters as accurately as possible.

## Reader Definitions of Tabloids

Spradley and McCurdy discuss the understanding of native categories and definitions in achieving an ethnographic perspective: "The label we search for in order to get a handle on the category is the one our informants use most frequently in casual conversation" (1988,

76). I quickly found, for example, that the very term "tabloid" was not one employed by most readers. The announcement had used the word "weekly" to describe the papers; *Examiner* staff had told me this was the term used by readers generally. Indeed, this usage was most common both in letters and in interviews, along with "paper," "magazine," and even "book." When an interviewee occasionally used the word "tabloid" in conversation, it was almost invariably after I had introduced it, usually inadvertently. The letter writers who did use the word consistently were those I have labeled "self-conscious" readers. In fact, it seems that "tabloid" is essentially an "outsider's" term carrying negative connotations not generally felt by regular readers. Tabloid staffers themselves seem to prefer the somewhat affectionate "tabs" to distinguish their publications from newspapers.

"Native" perceptions of the papers also emerged during discussions of whether readers ever felt embarrassed about buying them. "Self-conscious" tabloid readers, as well as critics, tend to assume that reading the papers is universally a kind of guilty secret, and that anybody would naturally be embarrassed to be seen buying one. The intellectual reader tends to enjoy the papers alone or share them with others in a determinedly "ironic" way. Like Brown (1989), when she was buying soap opera fan magazines, I have found myself looking furtively around while loading a grocery cart with six tabloids, ready to justify my purchases to anyone who queried them. The "elite" perception of tabloids is largely irrelevant to their loyal readers, who find it hard to see what the fuss is about. Towards the end of each interview, I asked readers whether they ever felt embarrassed about purchasing or reading a weekly. A typical response was slightly baffled— why should anyone be embarrassed to read such harmless material? Reader definitions of tabloids are not the definitions of the dominant ideology. While the critics' favorite descriptive adjectives may be "sleazy," "vulgar," "sensational," or "clichéd," readers never used these terms. They characterized the style of the tabloids as instead "fun," "exciting" "newsy," or "interesting." Several readers described them as "well-written" precisely because they used the kind of direct, stereotyped language they enjoyed. Likewise the im-

# Reading the Tabloid

age of tabloid reporters was positive—"they have exciting lives . . . to travel and to meet all the interesting people—they've got to have fun" (interview 2).

Male readers, in particular, contrasted tabloids favorably with "girlie" magazines. "If I was going to buy a *Playboy* or a *Penthouse* or something I might be embarrassed, but a weekly paper, I mean that's just open news" (interview 10). "I wouldn't mind being seen reading either one of the magazines on a bus, or in a city park, or anywhere, no it doesn't bother me at all—if it was a girlie magazine, then, well, ha, I might feel a little ashamed, I might want a little more privacy" (interview 14).

The complete lack of male embarrassment may be connected to the way the men seem to define the tabloids as "information," a point to which I shall return. The women, on the other hand, were more likely to acknowledge that some people do not approve of the papers, but they attribute that disapproval either to the tabloid's "gossipy" qualities or sometimes to a feeling that women should not waste grocery money on frivolity. "Sleaziness" is not really a factor.

Either way, they happily ignore any disapproval: "If they don't like it, well, that's their problem . . . they don't have to watch me pick 'em out" (interview 2). "I take 'em to the counter and those girls start reading 'em and forget what they're doing . . . I think, buy your own and let me go" (interview 3). "People they sneak it into their groceries and I say, why, it's an American paper, and it's got all these different kind of things in there" (interview 11). If people stare, "I always laugh. I say I'm getting my daily papers, my daily medicine, it's my tonic. I don't drink, I don't smoke, that's my upper, is the paper. I read that, and get high on other people's lives and that makes me happy" (interview 15). Another woman echoes these sentiments: "I don't go to movies, I don't take the other papers. This is just a little bit of juicy gossip here and there. I don't know if it's true, I don't care how they got it, that's their business . . . as I said to someone, I don't drink, I don't smoke, I buy this paper, so it costs me 59, 69 cents and the *TV Guide*, now that's my two sins" (interview 11). Brown observes that "trash" consumers derive pleasures from their reading "that are formed partly in the knowledge that they are devalued by the dominant value system" (1989, 174), and a certain defiance is apparent in some women's comments.

## The Self-conscious Reader

Before addressing the reading experiences of the majority of my respondents, I should describe a different kind of tabloid reading, one that exists within the dominant perception of tabloids, and of which the papers' staffs are aware. Although he works with a middle-aged, low-to-middle-income woman in mind as his reader, *Examiner* Photo Editor Ken Matthews has a picture of another kind of tabloid reader: "I sort of have a vision in my head of a swank apartment in Nob Hill in San Francisco, and there's people in there wearing elegant gowns and fancy kimonos. And along with the $25 four-color books on the coffee table there's a copy of the *National Examiner*, and people are peeing themselves with laughter saying, 'look at this, isn't this crazy, who did that, what sort of mind is at work there.' There are the people who are just flummoxed by what they see as these preposterous ideas that are presented there, and laughing, and not being offended, and not even worrying for a minute over whether it's true, or whether the people who wrote it think it's true—it doesn't matter."

This kind of reader, kimono-clad or not, certainly does exist. Apparently they buy tabloids as a type of self-conscious joke, making absolutely sure that no one could think they are taking them seriously. The self-conscious reader is epitomized by Richard Wolkomir. He writes of shunning tabloids in the checkout line until, while vacationing in Barbados, he met a Boston electronics firm's "high voltage president" who revealed "his secret for relaxing after a turbocharged day in the corporate cockpit. 'It's a fire in the fireplace, a glass of vintage chablis from the wine cellar and a stack of tabloids,' he said. 'Zip! You're in another world!'" (1987, 240). Frequently these kind of readers carefully distance themselves from the people they perceive as "typical" readers—note the Chablis, the wine cellar, and the Barbados vacation. Filmmaker John Waters, for instance, writing on "Why I Love the *National Enquirer*," claims that reading the paper is "one of the few chances I have to participate in something so genuinely mainstream. For once, I feel normal" (1985, 44). Normal, perhaps, but not typical; recall his description of the overweight tabloid reader.

Tabloids, of course, are not the only popular media that attract the "self-conscious" or "ironic" fan. Ang (1985) referred to ironic readings of "Dallas"; probably most forms of popular culture have a band of fans who enjoy them with the fervor of a gourmet lunching in a "greasy spoon" diner. As Schechter (1988) puts it, tabloids are "the archetypes of schlock," and determined enjoyment of schlock is what this kind of reading is all about. Underlying this ironic attachment is Ong's distinction between the residually oral and the literate. Self-conscious connoisseurs of schlock are invariably closely identified with a literate tradition. They identify tabloids as trash because they are familiar with literary conventions and concepts of originality. The stereotyped and "excessive" character of tabloids is about as far removed from literary ideals as one could imagine. Ong describes the discomfort of "far-gone literates" with the clichéd style of residually oral cultures, "which strikes persons from a high-literacy culture as insincere, flatulent, and comically pretentious" (1982, 22, 45). One response to that discomfort is to deride the style, as critics of tabloids often do. Another response is to incorporate it, treat it as "camp" or schlock, and enjoy it, as do the self-conscious readers.

Press (1990) found a difference in the way middle-class and working-class women responded to the prime-time soap opera "Dynasty." Working-class women took the program at face value, relating directly to the characters, while middle-class women, while still fans, took a more detached stance, discussing the unreality of the situations the characters were in. Although Press did not interpret her findings in these terms, it seems that middle-class women were exhibiting all the characteristics of a high-literacy response, seeing "Dynasty" in relation to other genres, interpreting it as one text among many. The working-class women, on the other hand, showed the more concrete, less abstract response typical of residual orality because, in our culture, the continuum from orality to high literacy inescapably coincides with the class structure. Ong cites the work done by Bernstein (1973) on the difference between the essentially oral "restricted linguistic code" of the working class and the highly literate "elaborated linguistic code" used by the middle and upper classes.

A few "self-conscious" readers, all male, responded to my notice; all their letters reflected their need to put distance between themselves and "real" readers. A forty-six-year-old Canadian male scientist reads the *Examiner* and the *Weekly World News* "for relaxation and amusement." He was quick to point out his other favorite magazines—the *New Yorker*, *Psychology Today*, *Nature*, *Science*, *New Scientist*, *Science News* (letter 43).

A male geologist from Pennsylvania, who enclosed his professional resumé, writes: "My interest is mostly humor—the outrageous stories." He mentions that his wife buys several tabloids; "I think the wife takes it more to heart." This reader advised me: "I assume you realize that this kind of readership survey will draw a disproportionate share of writing-oriented people such as myself and (I assume) very few of the poorly educated, inarticulate types who (I also assume) are the majority of readers" (letter 55).

Finally, the editor of a literary humor magazine writes that he uses tabloids in a regular column: "There is an amusing world out there, beyond the groves of academe, that is vastly hilarious and outrageously ridiculous. Let us face it: the world is made up of imbeciles who cannot cope with the modern world . . . their crime being that they are too stupid to cope with the growing complexity of the world around them" (letter 104). Indeed, there seems to be a minor literary industry in satirical articles about tabloids. In addition to Wolkomir and Waters, William Glenn satirizes the many tabloid stories about children raised by animals: "The non-refereed weekly supermarket tabloids . . . have proven to be a rich source of illustrative case studies" (1989, 32). McDonald (1987) offers satirical comments on "*Enquirer* stories worth thinking about."

The "self-conscious" reading accepts the view that tabloids are "sleazy" and "vulgar," but reading them is an enjoyable kind of "slumming." Some of these readers may claim to be trying to share a culture to which they do not belong; all mock the "genuine" readers, who they perceive as being gullible and stupid, swallowing completely the absurdities through which they, as superior people, can see.

## The Question of Belief

Perhaps the most common question asked about tabloids is whether readers indeed "actually believe all that stuff" about UFOs, psychic powers, ghosts, and the rest. Lehnert and Perpich (1982) were interested in this question, concluding that at least some readers—the "selfish believers"—did find everything in the tabloids credible. Certainly, my respondents did express a great deal of interest in all kinds of paranormal phenomena. I found, for example, that each of the sixteen people interviewed explicitly believed in one or more of such phenomena as astrology, numerology, UFOs, ESP, reincarnation, biofeedback, near-death experiences, and others, even though most had not specifically mentioned these in their letters. Many other letter writers did connect their tabloid reading at least in part to their interest in the paranormal, which was sometimes deeply felt, such as this reader's interest in reincarnation: "I know that's true, I've read a whole book after I started reading about it in the paper, where they actually come back and remember places that they've never been, you know, and they're 4 or 5 years old, these things are weird, I mean it makes you think, doesn't it?" (interview 13).

Many *Examiner* readers, especially women, singled out the column of psychic adviser Anthony Leggett as a highlight of the paper, and many had written to him: "Tony Leggett is a wonderful person. I've always believed some of the things he writes about and he's the only person I've read that seems to feel about people as I do" (letter 114). "I like Tony Leggett—I sometimes wonder is he as good a person as he comes across to me. I think he must be" (letter 75). Another goes even further: "I know Tony isn't a Saint in the beatified sense of the word, but he is one of God's chosen. I use his column as a learning tool and as a haven. . . . I trust him!" (letter 81). Men tended to be more skeptical: "I don't feel any humanoid can control your destiny. . . . Writing to Tony and getting put on his list is not going to get you money tomorrow for groceries" (interview 4). One man expressed the kind of ambivalent maybe–maybe not attitude that so often characterizes "belief," explaining that he had written to Leggett to ask whether he should start a business. Leggett answered that he should, "but if he said I wouldn't be too good a success at it, I think I'd want to try it anyway, but then again, maybe I wouldn't" (interview 14). Leggett, a "consulting editor" not employed on staff, had received 250,000 letters from readers in the three years prior to my visit to Boca Raton, which does suggest a high level of hopefulness, if not unconditional belief.

Indeed, readers were quite selective about the particular phenomena they chose to believe in. Skeptics might tend to classify all such beliefs as pseudoscience and assume that people who believed in UFOs might also believe in Bigfoot or ESP. Many readers' classifications of the world were plainly different. A twenty-eight-year-old Ohio woman was skeptical about UFOs: "You know some of these stories, I don't know if they're really true. I'd have to see one." Yet she was convinced that psychics can predict the future, claiming to have had several psychic experiences herself and reading tabloids' regular annual predictions in order to "be prepared" (interview 2). Another woman believed in UFOs, describing how one "followed him [her husband] all the way to the garage and over the garage— we both believe in that." She also believed in psychic powers but has a lot of trouble believing some of the "unusual birth" stories: "Like now, this little boy, what is he, eight years old and this woman, 37, she had twins by him. My husband says, hey, I don't believe this, they made it up" (interview 3). This reader refused to read the *Sun*, because it is "too weird" but regularly reads the other five tabloids.

A Minnesota woman scoffed at UFOs, saying that only those people who had lived a "duller life" than hers (she was a former circus acrobat) could possibly believe in such ridiculous ideas. Yet she was an avid astrologer, doing readings for friends and saving articles on astrology in a scrapbook. A Florida woman believed deeply in psychic powers, citing personal experience: "I can identify myself with them, they've had the same kind of experiences as I've had and it's really good to read." One of her own psychic experiences had been the basis of a story in the *Globe*, when the paper asked readers to send in personal accounts. She also claimed to have seen evidence of a UFO in Wisconsin: "I believe we, as people, were probably placed on this earth from outer space people years ago when they were experimenting, and so they're still checking up on us to see how we're doing." However, she did not believe in astrology at all and dismissed phenomena that to some people might seem more plausible: "It hits you right away, like some woman in Russia had given birth to babies with two heads you know." Finally, she had little interest in celebrity stories because she did not believe any of the gossip could be true (interview 5).

Another woman, who described herself as a "gifted medium," also believed in ESP, numerology, astrology, and biorhythms, attributing her successful recovery from surgery to her expertise in these areas: "The doctors were really amazed." Yet she was skeptical of UFOs, basing her opinion on personal experience, as did virtually all other readers: "You know, those stories have to be verified, like people that have been captured by 'em or not. Well, I think it's a bit far-fetched myself, because how come I've been in this work since my early teens, I'm a gifted person since the age of three, and I want to tell you, I haven't come into contact with any of them flying saucers" (interview 11).

Apparently, readers are allowing tabloids to reinforce their already existing beliefs while finding no inconsistency in dismissing stories about subjects they did not have faith in, confirming Fiske's (1988) insight that the "relevance" of a media message is what gains readers' interest. As Rosnow and Fine write, "truth is only accepted when it is consistent with one's frame of reference. Information is processed in light of the assumptions one holds about the nature of the world, for knowledge is culturally determined" (1975, 18). Readers generally said that they found tabloid stories well researched and verified. One man speaks for many: "made-up stories are very disappointing and disgusting. You know, I like to read about things that are true and actually happened" (interview 14). He scoffed at the idea of UFOs; stories about them were indeed "made-up." Yet this did not shake his belief that tabloids as a whole are well researched.

Thus the relationship between "belief" and tabloid reading is more subtle and complex than the image of totally gullible readers would allow. None of the readers I spoke to would fit the category of "selfish believer," accepting everything they read as true. Many readers were able to describe their reading more subtly, illuminating the playful dimension in the reading. A Wisconsin woman explained that she did believe in UFOs, describing government coverups of landings. On psychic powers she was more ambivalent: "I sometimes think so, but I'd never tell anyone." Others she dismissed, such as any stories from England: "Most of the stories that come out of there are all, they're just too strange to believe. Oh, when they tell me an 80-year-old woman just gave birth to two babies, you know, I have my doubts." Finally, she explained her reading this way: "You know, you gotta read it and absorb what you want to absorb and say the rest, oh boy, this is too much—that's the way we read it" (interview 6).

Another woman seemed at first completely credulous: "I believe just about anything nowadays." After further discussion, she seemed more skeptical, explaining that, while her husband believed in UFOs, she did not, although she enjoys and puts some faith in psychic powers and predictions. Of some of the more bizarre birth stories, she said, "It's difficult, but yeah, I believe it could happen, I sure do, stranger things are going on all over the world right now. . . . It's kind of intriguing, you know, it's like a lot of people let their imagination run wild" (interview 7).

In fact, some readers seem to enjoy reading tabloids *as if* they are true, playing with the definitions of reality, wondering if it could be so. Said this twenty-eight-year-old woman: "A lot of people claim it is a lot of bull. But I find it very intrested. . . . Sometimes it seems so real and sometimes I don't know what to think" (letter 27). A Virginia man says, "I think everybody needs, you know, a sense of laughter, I think it's so zany and stuff. . . . You know that there's no such thing, but in a sense you wish that there was, you know" (interview 9).

# Reading the Tabloid

The Oregon man explains his enjoyment of bizarre human-interest stories: "I don't believe them because they're never any in the United States, they're always in some God-forsaken part of the world where people are half ape and half people, you know. . . . But it stymies my imagination, where they could dig up something like that, like they dug up a tomb in Egypt and found two slaves chained together that died of starvation, that kind of stuff, that kind of makes you wonder you know, what the hell is this? But I don't take 'em all serious, I don't worry about 'em at all" (interview 4).

Many others expressed a similar lack of seriousness about the tabloids: "I wasn't quite born yesterday with some of that stuff. I take a lot of it with a grain of salt, but it's amusing" (interview 8). A reader writes: "Every week I buy all the papers, then I tell my friends and sisters I read so and so and they tell me I'm nuts to believe everything they put in. But I don't care what they say, I enjoy myself" (letter 90). A Georgia woman describes the anticipation of enjoyment each week: "It's like waiting for each paper like a juicy steak dinner. I lay on my waterbed, and munch on a bag of California fruit mix, and then I enter into the world of the *Examiner*" (letter 67).

One woman expressed a "desire to believe" that is shared by many: "My grandchildren laugh when I tell them I believe in the UFO stories and aliens that might be among us. I would like to believe everything that I read but I know that's silly" (letter 31). A sixty-five-year-old woman explicitly equates tabloid reading with play: "I sometimes play a game with myself, asking myself what stories are true and what is just a bunch of bull—I notice that all the outrageous storys (good for a laugh) usually claim to be from some place in Africa, Bornio or someplace like that" (letter 75). According to Fiske, "the power of play involves the power to play with the boundary between the representation and the real, to insert oneself into the process of representation so that one is not subjected by it, but, conversely, is empowered by it" (1987, 236). Later, I will discuss how readers not only "play" by simply reading the stories but also how, taking an "as if" stance, they play with the ideas and possibilities through gossip about the papers.

Few tabloid readers are skeptical, critical readers, in the sense that they weigh up evidence and research a subject. Once again, that kind of response would be more likely from a "high-literate" person. Among readers there is undoubtedly a widespread belief or interest in paranormal or unusual phenomena, which the tabloids are able to feed from and into. At the same time, few tabloid readers are completely credulous, swallowing everything the tabloids produce. In some senses, many take the tabloids less seriously than the critics who worry about the effect of the papers. "Self-conscious" readers are not the only ones who use the tabloids for amusement and play, however much some of them may try to distance themselves from the people they imagine to be "typical" readers.

## Tabloid Reading and Alienation

Interest and belief in various kinds of paranormal phenomena are certainly not confined to people who read tabloids. Study after study shows that such beliefs are widespread in this country and elsewhere, and among all ages and education levels (Mendez-Acosta et al. 1984; Wagner and Monnet 1979). Singer and Benassi, for example, found some level of belief in ESP among 80 to 90 percent of the population (1981). The surge in popularity of books about such things as alien encounters must respond to some need in many people (Ben-Yehuda 1985). Interest in the paranormal certainly does not define a person as unusual or "weird." As *Examiner* Editor Bill Burt comments, "You'd imagine our readers might be like a scene from 'One Flew Over the Cuckoo's Nest,' but surprisingly these people are very respectable, very sane."

Although there is some overlap with the recent "New Age" movement, the paranormal phenomena explored in tabloids do not tend to be the central ones of New Age beliefs, which are "most popular among white-collar workers and those of high educational achievement" (Ben-Yehuda, 76). Crystals, channeling, and past-life regression are rarely covered in the tabloids. Instead, we see older and less trendy beliefs—astrology, numerology, palm-reading, ghosts, Bigfoot, psychic predictions, communicating with the dead, witchcraft, and ancient curses. New Age phenomena tend to be concerned with the inner self; practitioners are looking for spiritual fulfillment, and they often reject traditional religions, moving from one hoped-for spiritual solution to another (Ben-Yehuda 1985). The tabloid phenomena are concerned more with material survival and control over one's environment, and exist alongside traditional religion; readers cited the Bible as a source of information on witchcraft and the occult. Interest in psychic predictions centers on the possibility of controlling or at least anticipating future events, as do astrology, numerology, communicating with the dead, and all kinds of fortune-telling. A perennial favorite is the story about or advertisement for lucky numbers that will win the lottery, or lucky charms that will bring fortune and fame. These stories seem to appeal to the same desires as game shows, with their enticements of gambling and easy money (Fiske 1987). Indeed, many readers named game shows, such as "Wheel of Fortune," among their favorite TV programs.

Several readers mentioned their hopes, even expectations, of one day striking it lucky. One woman enjoys reading about lottery winners: "It makes me feel like I'm not the only one that really hasn't got all the money and the riches, you know, but some day I might get there too" (interview 5). Another, who reads all six tabloids, writes: "I am very much interested in the Lottery and I know that some day I will win, I am winning small amounts but looking forward to the big win" (letter 54). Another optimistic woman, who is also interested in astrology, writes: "I have no doubts that I will win the Ohio Lotto and when I do, I will travel these United States and see and smell everything!" (letter 34). Another woman pinned her hopes on a songwriting career, writing to me for help in getting started: "I never never drove a car but some day I will sing my two patriotic songs for the Statue of Liberty and become famous and never be poor again and I'm sure destiny will have it that I succeed and I amount to something great (letter 20).

This interest in luck and the whims of fortune is, I believe, connected to a class-based feeling of powerlessness and alienation from the mainstream—a sense that "Chance, fate and luck basically deal the cards in any game" (Willis 1977, 165). As Willis describes this, working-class people may not perceive themselves to be systematically oppressed, but they do see themselves as disadvantaged, apart from the forces that control their lives. Young sees this alienation as "evident, for example in the language of those newspapers directed to the working class involving the distinctly non-bourgeois world of fate, luck, inequality and cynicism" (1981b, 411). People in this position have little ability to influence the system directly, and they may maintain a sense of control by trying to track the forces of luck and destiny. Cross-culturally, superstitions thrive in situations where control seems to be lacking (Malinowski 1954; Jahoda 1971); for the relatively poor, fate may seem to offer the only realistic key to possible affluence or success.

Complementary with the element of control that paranormal beliefs may offer, there is pleasure to be gained from feeling superior to establishment figures. The sense of alienation from the establishment emerged during discussions of what might broadly be defined as scientific topics. Tabloids exhibit a dual attitude to science and scientists that is reflected in the variety of readings of scientific stories. On the one hand, as Schroeder writes, there is a deferential attitude toward doctors and scientists: "Authoritative beyond mere humans, they are agents of progress, ministers of hope" (1982, 177). Readers agreed that expert testimony is considered vital, explaining that they find a story convincing because doctors or scientists were quoted.

However, while this faith is very apparent, it is complicated by other factors, one of which is a distrust of science as representing "them"—the faceless people who control the country. Some readers, in comparing their tabloids with other news sources, complained that scientists, politicians, and experts talk in language they do not identify with, and dismiss experiences they consider important. A Georgia woman illustrates the "common sense" view that anecdotal, "eyewitness" accounts negate the necessity for scientific confirmation: "There's a lot of fictitious stuff going on out there, but when it comes to something as real as UFOs and for people to sight those things . . . I believe it when they say they've had an experience, I truly believe that, and for a person to say, I've seen a UFO, I don't believe any further research is needed. No amount of LSD or drugs can make a person trip out so bad—if they see a UFO they know what they've seen, because believe me it'll make your hair stand up on end and it will sober you up, that's so true . . . these things are reality, and people need to deal more with reality" (interview 15).

The tabloids cater to this attitude, with stories often glorying in the "bafflement" of supposed scientists and experts. Blaustein describes an *Enquirer* story in which actor Glenn Ford talks about his belief in reincarnation: "In the Glenn Ford story, we find a respected and famous man confirming a belief unacceptable to 'official culture'" (1969, 8). For the scientifically untrained, one person's individual experience can "prove" that the experts are wrong. Once again, readers may find no inconsistency in dismissing, say, UFOs, because they believe there is no scientific proof while accepting ESP purely on the basis of personal experience. Scientists may be used to confirm one's existing beliefs, but they can be disregarded as remote "pointy-heads" when they question those same beliefs.

Tabloids are indeed "agents of the fetish of science, technology, and sciencism" (Schroeder 1982, 178). Their writers know that the scientific seal of approval is important to many readers, so they pepper their stories with quotes from scientists, real and imaginary. For some readers, that is enough: "I don't think they'd print ones that were wildly improbable. One that came out this week—somewhere in the Mexican desert zoologists had found a dinosaur egg and they said that one of them was fertile—a bunch of fossilized eggs, one of them was fertile, and they'd hatched out this baby dinosaur, you know, the eggs were a thousand years old and they didn't actually have a picture of the dinosaur, but, you know I can't see why they would print a thing like that if it hadn't actually occurred, and it's a scientist that was doing it, somewhere down near Mexico City" (interview 12).

But tabloid writers also know about a parallel strain of fear and distrust of science. People may indeed buy into the "fetish" of science, but they often do not understand it, as the above quote amply illustrates. This lack of understanding may result in acceptance of preposterous claims because of "scientific" attribution, but it may also encourage a rejection of science as remote, dangerous, and uncontrollable by the individual. Carl Sagan discusses this fear: "We live in a society exquisitely dependent on science and technology, in which hardly anyone knows anything about science and technology. ... I know that science and technology are not just cornucopias pouring good deeds into the world. . . . There's a reason people are nervous. . . . And so the image of the mad scientist haunts our world—from Dr. Faust to Dr. Frankenstein to Dr. Strangelove to the white-coated loonies of Saturday morning children's television" (1990, 264). It is this image of scientists that is held up and knocked down in the stories of phenomena that baffle experts and, in effect, make them throw up their hands and give up, acknowledging that there are, indeed "stranger things in Heaven and Earth than we can ever dream of," as one reader paraphrased Shakespeare (interview 13).

These two "readings" of science as supremely authoritative and remotely "pointy-headed" can and are reconciled in an accommodative interpretation that many readers seem to employ. This reading accepts the authority of "experts," buying into the fetish of sciencism. But it is also able to accommodate psychics, UFOlogists, and others into that picture. If a person recasts a psychic as a scientist, much as creationists recast their faith as "creation science," the two readings—faith in science and distrust of mainstream science—can co-exist comfortably. Each may come into play to interpret different stories, and the elevation of dubious experts to scientific status, often in opposition to established scientists, helps resist the feeling of alienation many readers experience.

## Political Readings of Tabloids

Distrust of and alienation from the establishment were also very apparent in the political attitudes of readers. Although I rarely asked overtly political questions in interviews, some sense of political views did emerge. Most readers I interviewed, especially women, claimed to be uninterested in politics and national issues—after all,

# Reading the Tabloid

that was one reason they preferred tabloids to newspapers. Even they, however, would often make comments that showed a particular political attitude.

*Examiner* staff were clear in their perception that tabloid readers tend to be politically conservative, and this was generally borne out. I should stress, however, that this conservatism is not obviously party-affiliated; rather it is a tendency to be "traditional," "family-oriented," religious, and patriotic in a nostalgic, flag-waving sense. Readers often expressed the view that America is declining because of liberal attitudes, immorality, and godlessness. A thirty-eight-year-old Tennessee woman writes: "I'd love to see the U.S.A. arise from her disgrace, with more grace than she's ever had before . . . God Bless America . . . God Bless You Liz!" (letter 2). She elaborates in her interview: "They're destroying us fast. Everything that's going on, the world is being destroyed and I don't think it'll be long before, you know, Jesus comes back and that'll cause the rapture" (interview 7).

Many of those who discussed politics expressed a strong belief that the government, media, big business, and scientists are hiding information from the American people. Lehnert and Perpich (1982) had found only one issue that united all the participants in their study—the importance of the stories about government waste and misuse of tax dollars. These stories, and related ones about coverups, have a central place in the tabloids and apparently do represent their readers' concerns. This concern often goes hand in hand with conservatism; the Tennessee woman believed tabloids should cover more political topics: "I do think we have a right to know what's going on in our government. . . . If we could all stand together we could bring it back" (interview 7). A fifty-seven-year-old woman expressed her support for Iran-contra defendant Oliver North: "Please make this your next subject of research: Congress of the United States and the mistreatments of patriotic, anti-Communist Americans." She adds, "Found the conservative movement a refreshing wind in the brain-washed academic circles—like Sisiphus rising from the ashes" (letter 91).

An eighty-year-old farmer, on behalf of himself and his wife,

# For Enquiring Minds

writes: "We are very much concerned with what is done in our Government we are very much concerned about the news media seemed to lean very much to Socelisom or Communism and a great number of Politicians seems to lean that way also. We are very much Conservitive" (letter 42). Another typical comment: "I believe in the government for the people by the people, and we're getting away from it, and it worries me" (interview 6).

Overt racism was rare. One overtly racist letter was interesting in its demonstration that people's attitudes do not necessarily come packaged the way we might assume. This woman, who wrote what amounted to a thirteen-page tirade of personal and political grievances, has basically right-wing views, but they are combined with a hatred of President Reagan and opposition to contra funding: "Our Gov't is rotten for letting in all these Damn Foreigners and giving them jobs and saying to hell with the Americans who voted them in. I think Pres. Ronald Reagan is a Tyrant Mad Man who loves killing our young Servicemen. I say impeach the bastard!!! . . . I haven't been able to get a job! First the Blacks took them all. Now the Gov't is! Our nation is in a mess. Only Jesus's 2nd Coming can help America! God Bless America, Again." She continues: "I am still laughing at how we Bombed Hiroshima and Nagasaki and put those Japs in their place. I think our Pres. is crazy for sending Millions and Millions of dollars to the Contras so they can shoot some farmer in a field" (letter 87).

Many comments reflect a sense of alienation from mainstream politics, the sense that the government—"they" up in Washington—has its own agenda and is conspiring against the people. (A view not necessarily confined to tabloid readers!) They welcome stories that reveal the "truth" about events the establishment is trying to hide. Thus a Wisconsin woman has this to say about UFOs: "I think there's censorship in the local papers, actually, I've thought that for years. . . . I was just reading an article in one of my papers just a couple of days ago and they said that very definitely the government has censored a lot of stuff because they don't want to alarm, so-called people, which I don't think that's what's at back of it, but you never know. . . . It seems like they have found various, like this one that

- 130 -

crashed in New Mexico, and various things, but they've never disclosed it—that one in Texas, back in 1888 or something like that and they found, the townspeople did that, they found the guy and buried him, and lost him, now they don't know where they've put him" (interview 8).

A Florida man agrees: "I think our government, I think Russia, I think some of your big governments know all about 'em, and they're just keeping it covered up, it might even belong to some of the governments or all the governments together . . . you just had a case of that with this Iran-contra affair, that's just one of the little ones, no telling how many more were covered up" (interview 6).

Another reader talks about the "us-against-them" theme that is taken up in many tabloid stories: "I like to see the big guy get it once in a while because the poor guy, if he was to be in that position, like, in jail, the big guy gets a carpeted floor, he gets to go home on weekends . . . the poor guy gets bread and water inside of a jail cell with rats in it" (interview 9).

Schroeder has pointed out what he calls the "element of class warfare" in tabloids: "Government and its bureaucracy is the corrupt, inefficient and (by implication) ineffective class enemy." He suggests that this alienation stems partly from tabloid readers' presumed regular struggles against the powers that be: "*Enquirer* readers meet the government in an endless cycle of baffling faces, words and forms: taxes, welfare departments, social security, medicare, foodstamps, employment and unemployment, licenses, veterans' benefits, the military, police and courts. All without power or powerful agents such as lawyers and accountants" (1982, 175).

Indeed, tabloids do seem to allow for an element of resistance against what is seen as the all-pervasive power of government, media, and other forces. One route of resistance is fate—the chance to beat the system by finding the key that will unlock the secrets of luck. Another route is through knowledge—tabloid readers can hear about the "little guys" succeeding, or at least they can direct their anger at the bureaucracy that grinds them down. They can find out what is "really" going on in the world; they are privy to secrets that "they" do not wish people to know. As Levin and Arluke write, "Having some understanding gives everybody a sense of control over her or his life" (1987, 53).

In addition, tabloids offer ammunition against what is seen as a liberal establishment that denigrates the "traditional" values of many readers. Schroeder's comments about tabloid readers and their battles with bureaucracy tend to assume that they are at the bottom of the class heap, an under class living on welfare. While his picture of a power battle may be accurate, the frustration felt by tabloid readers does not stem from their position in some kind of under class. Most tabloid readers actually seem to be positioned such that they are fairly well educated and interested in the world around them, yet they perceive themselves as unable to do anything significant about events. But there is pleasure in the knowing and a sort of empowerment in their resistance. Once again, some readers may believe tabloid "secrets" implicitly while others may be more playful—either way, storytelling about overcoming "them" can be pleasurable.

## Unusual Readings

Tabloids, in which most of the stories have a clear-cut point of view, seem to offer a relatively narrow range of possible interpretations. Yet one letter did suggest a possibly very different reading; I have no way of knowing if it is idiosyncratic or if it may speak for others. The writer, a thirty-seven-year-old man who works in a jewelry store, gave only a first name and no address: "I must remain socially secret." While most readers see tabloids as confirming their conservative views about such issues as women's roles ("women's libbers" being frequent targets in some tabs), this reader saw things differently: "I enjoy reading about how Women are changing their lifestyles to fulfill their needs as well as their desires. Along with the articles that display the changes in Women: I also prey for articles about changing Men. Men who are bold enough to expand their ridgid guidlines. . . . I'm somewhat dissappointed as the Media tends to ignore any trends for Men that may be non-traditional and label it as deviant. For example; Men wearing skirts or doing anything that may be viewed as sissy or of the feminine gender. . . . for a hobby I like to write articles that give an honest opinion of how people really feel about themselves and how they are kept by the rules of what I call the 'Mouthy Majority'" (letter 97).

Though not completely happy with tabloid attention to his areas of interest, the writer does perceive the papers as occasionally offering some kind of radical alternative to mainstream media. This reading may derive from the many portrayals of active, independent female celebrities. While for most women (see chapter 5), these portrayals are tempered by the supposed failure of such stars to find personal happiness, this reader may see them as positive role models. Although the reader does not explicitly identify himself as gay, his letter does suggest the intriguing possibility of a gay, perhaps "campy" reading of tabloids, similar to gay readings of prime-time soap operas (Fiske 1987). Indeed, some of the most popular female celebrities in tabloids are the very stars that have enthusiastic gay followings, such as Elizabeth Taylor, Joan Collins, and Linda Evans.

In addition, the nonmainstream nature of the tabloids does attract at least a small number of people who by almost any definition might be described as mentally disturbed. The tabloids, with their eclectic acceptance of all kinds of phenomena, do seem to feed the fantasies of some individuals in ways I feel ill-equipped to explore.

Thus one letter came illustrated with drawings of crystals and UFOs the writer had seen, together with a plea that her visions were real, even though she had been hospitalized as a mental patient several times (letter 99). Another woman, describing her life as a "shambles," explains that she has had three breakdowns and suffers from hallucinations: "I had to stop working in the nursery with babies because thoughts came into my mind to take them by their feet and lam 'em against the floor" (letter 56). She reads the tabloids "because I hope to find my problems are solve in them." Another letter describes the writer's visions: "I have six guardian angels that sing to me when God speaks to me in white words" (letter 64). Five letters from a Kentucky man, each several pages long, consisted of apparently disconnected stream-of-consciousness thoughts (letters 107–11). Finally, there is letter 106: "I am 51, a Paranoid Schizo-

phrenic . . . I have had sex with 120 women, most of them prostitutes. . . . According to psychologists I am the smartest man ever to
walk the earth. . . . I would like to personally impregnate hundreds
of bright single women in order to produce a crop of great geniuses
to improve the world."

## Tabloids and Other Reading

"Self-conscious" readers and critics seem to make the assumption
that tabloid readers obtain their complete world view from the papers, reading little else. Waters comments on the *Weekly World News*:
"this fanatical, right-wing prime example of hepatitis-yellow journalism seems to be popular with illiterates . . ." (1987, 44). A basic
point seems to escape many critics—"illiterates" would hardly be
reading tabloids or any other printed material. The tabloids, whatever else they may be, do contain many written pages, and to get
pleasure from them, a person does have to be functionally literate
enough to derive enjoyment from reading, a standard of literacy that
millions of Americans do not reach. Tabloid readers may not be the
most highly educated people, but they are not the most poorly educated, either.

The readers who responded to my request may indeed enjoy writing and reading more than the average person, but they are also
among the most avid tabloid buyers—almost all mentioned that they
read several tabloids; many read all six. While some letters were difficult to read and were certainly written by people who were not used
to writing, most were not. Not infrequently, the spelling and writing
style were at least as good as many student term papers I have received.

It may seem contradictory to stress the "literacy" of many readers
while at the same time discussing the "residual orality" of tabloids.
However, as Ong (1982) emphasizes, in a literate culture, orality is
relative. Many people are literate, and may read a great deal, but they
are not interested in the "high-literate" end of the spectrum—their
tastes lie more with genres that indeed bear such hallmarks of orality

as formula and "excess." For others, there is pleasure to be gained from both formulaic and "artistic" literature. Tabloid readers, like any other collection of individuals, cannot be categorized neatly.

While few tabloid readers had "high-brow" or "literary" tastes, many counted reading as a major pleasure in their lives. One woman, who buys "about four" tabloids every week, explains: "I grew up in a house with books and when I go into a house and see no magazines I'm upset. Now if you read only tabloids and you don't read anything else, then I think you're in trouble." She is particularly interested in astrology but enjoys all the tabloids: "I read everything and I clip for friends" (interview 1). A former circus acrobat, she now writes a column for a circus newsletter.

Another reader, who buys several tabloids every week, writes: "I love to read, I read all kinds of books, magazines that gets in front of my eyes" (letter 34), while a reader of all six tabs agrees: "When I run out of reading material, I read the Dictionary!" (letter 36). Her other regular reading includes *True Story*, *California Magazine*, and *Time*. Like some other readers, this woman confounds stereotypes in her categorization of enjoyable TV shows, mentioning game shows and "films on UFOs and *National Geographic*, also J. Cousteau's water and land films." A twenty-eight-year-old man also has eclectic tastes, reading newspapers, books, and the Bible, and mentioning his favorite writers—Erma Bombeck and Edgar Allan Poe (interview 9). For this reader, as for others, tabloids are just one source of enjoyment among many.

Most frequently, readers mentioned romances, science fiction, westerns, all kinds of magazines, and frequently the Bible. Enthusiastic readers often mentioned that they read daily newspapers regularly in addition to tabloids, feeling that the weeklies supplemented the information they received elsewhere. A woman whose other "weekly" is *Newsweek*, writes that the *Examiner* provides light relief and conversation material in contrast to the crime news she sees everywhere else: "The *Examiner* is amusing, entertaining and sometimes informative—although not bought for the latter" (letter 72). Some made the distinction between the kind of news they obtained in newspapers and the more enjoyable stories in tabloids: "I get sick and tired of reading nothing but bad news, you know" (interview 14). As one reader puts it: "I think the tabloids want to look at it from the way a person would want to look at it, but I think the newspaper wants to look at it just to give you the information there" (interview 9). Another reader, who does subscribe to a daily newspaper, speaks for many others in saying that news is depressing: "In your weekly papers you have more human-interest stories, things people are doing, things people accomplish, things like that, I enjoy that" (interview 10).

Some readers, however, do reject the idea of reading newspapers at all. A few see the tabloids as serving their informational needs: "We don't get a newspaper so this serves the purpose of reading it" (letter 1). "The *National Examiner* tells me more than most daily papers, which I don't have time to read" (letter 26). More common, however, is a sense of frustration at what they see as a constant flow of "bad news," and a feeling that "the news" is about events that do not impinge upon their lives and over which they have little control. A divorced mother of three young children, working two jobs, says: "I work at McDonalds, and I work from 5 in the evening till 12.30 at night so I usually don't get to catch the news. And you know, most of the news on TV any more is about, you know, killings and stuff like that, and I don't want to hear that, I want to hear interesting stories, about people" (interview 2). Another woman watches TV news but does not read newspapers, preferring tabloids: "They go into more human-interest stuff whereas your newspaper, it's just crime, and I get enough of that in my own neighborhood without reading about it" (interview 8).

Tabloids, then, are most often one among many sources of information and enjoyment, and their significance in readers' lives is very variable. Some people see them as roughly equivalent to news, others as a source of laughs. For many, they find a niche as sources of conversation, tools with which to "read" other media more enjoyably, a point to which I shall return. Readers generally are interested in the world around them and make efforts to find out about it—they are not the self-absorbed misfits the stereotypes portray. In fact, one letter stood out as as very different from most, in that it was the only

# Reading the Tabloid

one that did come close to that stereotype. The writer was a fifty-seven-year-old divorcée, who has seen a UFO and thinks "nothing is more fun than watching cute kids do cute things." She writes: "I dont love to read. And these papers have a lot of pictures in them. And short articals that dont take so long to read. . . . Sometime it sounds like they have found americal for loosing wieght. I weigh 273 lbs, I'm not interested in movie stars and celebrity's I'm more interested in my own improvement and survival" (letter 86).

All in all, tabloids do not replace newspapers, magazines, television, or other media, but they seem to provide an added dimension. The tabloid is the one forum where, in addition to stories that could be found elsewhere, the whole gamut of nonmainstream, nonrational ways of seeing the world is offered. What the reader does with these ways of seeing the world is variable, picking and choosing according to her or his existing interests and beliefs. As one reader put it: "It has a variety. It's just like when you go into a good restaurant; you're eating at the salad bar and you have all your other side orders, and then you get to dessert, and that's what I call all the juicy stuff, is dessert. Sometimes, I'll read all the stories that have human interest, and then I'll save the celebrities for last; I always go back to them last" (interview 15). While readers vary in their definitions of side orders and dessert, few if any simply consume the whole meal without variations in taste and enjoyment.

# 5

# Gendered Readings

We're people, and so we're naturally interested in what everybody
else is doing. If you live in a house, don't you want to know
what your neighbors are doing?

—interview 1 (female)

I like to read short true stories. . . . I do not read gossip.

—letter 19 (male)

Although their tabloid readings vary, regular readers share some
common experiences, defined at least in part by class and a subse-
quent feeling of alienation from dominant ways of thinking. Tabloids
are seen as an alternative, a way of knowing about the world that is
not offered in other media. However, a crucial point that emerged in
my "ethnography of discourse" was that women and men read the
tabloids differently. A useful way of defining that difference is suggested in the work of Nancy Chodorow (1974; 1978) and Carol
Gilligan (1982), who suggest that in our culture men and women follow different paths of moral development. The socialization of
women tends to produce an attitude that values interpersonal relationships and places most importance on how events affect people.
Men, on the other hand, are encouraged to develop a sense of au-
tonomy and an awareness of the importance of abstract principles.
As Chodorow puts it, "feminine personality comes to define itself in
relation to a connection with other people more than masculine per-

sonality does" (1974, 44). Gilligan explains the female ethic of caring: "Thus women not only define themselves in a context of human relationship but also judge themselves in terms of their ability to care. Women's place in man's life cycle has been that of nurturer, caretaker and helpmate, the weaver of those networks of relationships on which she in turn relies" (1982, 17).

Women do seem to read the tabloids very much in terms of this role as care givers and maintainers of personal relationships. The personal dimension was best illustrated in the letters from readers in my study, who had been asked to give "any other information about yourself that you care to share." Much of what they wrote had little direct bearing on the act of reading tabloids, but it provided some rich illumination of the experiential context of that reading. (Once again, letters are quoted exactly as written.) Women, for instance, often described themselves physically, giving height, weight, hair color, and whether they considered themselves attractive. They discussed their diets and health regimens, or their looking younger than their years. An aspiring songwriter, for example, wrote: "I am 5 ft 4", 98 lbs most grey hair green eyes a pretty nose 34B breast" (letter 20). From another reader: "I'm 48 years old but men tell me I have the body of a star. If they think so what can I do to be a star. I am 40-32-40. God must have given it to me for some good reason" (letter 70). Part of one woman's self-description read: "age 47, oval face, high arched brows, almond shaped eyes, full lips an average size nose, small ears, wavy light hair" (letter 101), while another woman gives a detailed description ending in the comment, "my hair is Platinum Blonde, it's my real color not dyed" (letter 90). Only one man gave his height and weight—the self-described paranoid schizophrenic who believed himself to be the smartest man on earth (see chapter 4).

The personal descriptions were striking in the way they suggested how much many women's sense of self is tied up in physical appearance—how they look to others, and what others think of them. Only women, for example, seemed surprised and even grateful for the opportunity to tell about themselves. A thirty-three-year-old, "dark brown hair, blue eyes, 5 ft 5, 115 lbs," ended her letter, "thank you for wanting to know about me" (letter 40). Another woman concluded: "Thank you for the opportunity to write to someone and sharing my thoughts and dreams of Life and the AfterLife—God Bless You" (letter 41), while yet another commented: "when I got your letter I was so thrilled, I said, I can't believe this is happening, I couldn't believe it, I mean, wow, this is unreal" (interview 15).

The difference between men and women in the central importance of relationships was very clear. Men tended to describe their jobs, whether they were married, how many children they had, and other factual matters. Only two comments in the men's letters touched on the personal dimension of their relationships. A sixty-nine-year-old Florida man wrote: "I recently lost a very dear woman friend we were very close for 3 years. I miss her" (letter 9). A forty-five-year-old Kentucky man described himself as "married for 26 years to same wonderful woman!" (letter 79).

Women, however, not only listed their husbands and children but described their relationships with them, their pride in their achievements, their satisfaction or otherwise with their own lives, and a great deal of other personal information. In telling about their lives, many gave the names and details about not only their husbands and children but also their parents, siblings, and even grandparents. The sense of "family" as a central concept pervades the letters. Thus a woman with thirty-eight grandchildren and six great-grandchildren described how she loves baking because it is one way she can stretch her limited budget to cover her whole family: "Try to get a few goodies to each one on their birthdays. Sometimes pretty hard if I don't have money to buy what I need" (letter 1). A self-described homemaker also gave details of her family, explaining that she likes "family stories with a happy ending." She describes herself: "I am a giver. I think the world is made up of two types of people givers and takers. There are more takers than givers. I came from a family of takers, I've raised a family of takers. My husband is a taker so I decided to give so people can be happy" (letter 114).

A seventy-four-year-old who reads all six tabloids writes: "I'm a housewife, have been all my life and wouldn't trade places with Queen Elizabeth." She continues: "I love most people, if one looks deep enough one can find good in all of them. . . . Sometimes when I feel low on the totem pole, I think of all those who are lame or in wheelchairs or maybe not completely mentally bright. So much we have to thank our Lord for. Right?" (letter 62).

An element in the stereotype of tabloid readers is that they are lonely misfits, "shut-ins," or other people who lead sad lives. Some readers indeed did not sound happy, such as this fifty-two-year-old divorcée: "I lead a rather lonely life. . . . I like to go to amusement parks and fairs and really enjoy being around other people. Thank you for running this poll" (letter 58).

Many more, however, expressed great satisfaction with their lives, even those who had plainly had difficult lives. Most often, that satisfaction was tied up in the success they had made of their role as wife and mother, such as this fifty-three-year-old mother of two sons: "I love my children very much and have been a good mother trying to teach them right from wrong, trying to instill in them the values of things, to be kind and care for others, not to make fun of others. Tought them love and understanding and to try to help others and to love everyone no matter what the color or anything. . . . our kids are our pride and joy and why people can be cruel to children I'll never understand." She describes telling her sons about sex, and how to look after themselves: "I told them they might marry someday and their wife could get real sick and noone to help." Although she stresses the value of mothers staying at home, she stresses the importance of women's values in the world at large: "Too much killing and hate in the world. . . . We should have a woman president." Her letter concludes with a postscript: "My boys think I'm a terrific mom and not an older lady" (letter 100).

Another woman tells of her struggles to maintain a family identity through many hardships, including life with an alcoholic, abusive husband: "Oh yes, I'm 84 I've been married four times and three of them are dead. . . . I've lived a full exciting life. . . . I find one can fall into problems and then get up and try again. Sure its hard and a lot of work but one has to do something and I love being alive and able to see to my own home and drive" (letter 103). An eighty-nine-year-old widow expresses satisfaction with her life and the family she has raised, writing that she "had a beautiful life" and now spends her time writing letters and reminiscing with friends: "writting these letters, sometimes I smile and enjoy daydreaming, pictureing of long ago. letters can be a great passing times at such age. . . . I'd love to be younger, in to-days, life theres such wonders happening" (letter 82).

Widows and divorcées told me how they were looking for a man by corresponding through the Sheela Wood "Have a Friend" Club, and they shared their specifications for the perfect man. A seventy-five-year-old, widowed after fifty "wee bit dull" years of marriage, discussed whether she should marry a man who had proposed: "he has the foulding stuff but I am saying no, as a good marriage cannot be built on that, as, I'm sure you know! I deeply long for romance but few American men know anything about it and very few know the joy of sex with love" (letter 78). A "good marriage" often seemed to be viewed as elusive, but an ideal nevertheless. A sixty-two-year-old woman, for instance, explained that she reads Sheela Wood's columns "because I've got a daughter that's been divorced for three years and I've been thinking awful hard about getting her acquainted with someone" (interview 3). A fifty-seven-year-old widow is happy with her daughters' lives—"I have two daughters both married fine husbands. educated, good jobs"—and she is now "looking for that very special (active) man" through the Sheela Wood club (letter 10). Only one man mentioned the "Have a Friend" column, explaining that his wife was ailing: "I also look at at least part of the lonely-hearts ads and 'advice' column. Maybe because I anticipate being single again in a few years, and I want to know who's out there that I can afford?" (letter 55).

Many women described how they combed the papers for information that would be useful to friends and family, clipping out and saving relevant articles, something men did not mention. The sharing and distribution of specific articles and entire papers is a task taken on by women, even when men are some of the readers. Readers' comments contradicted yet another stereotype—of tabloid reading as a solitary, guilty pleasure. D. Keith Mano writes: "I doubt if any newspaper has lower per-copy readership. You don't save *Na-*

*tional Enquirer"* (1977, 209). Indeed you do; readers saved whole issues, collected scrapbooks of particular kinds of articles, pointed out helpful stories to neighbors and work mates. According to Brower (1990), the *Star* works on the assumption that each copy is shared by an average of 3. 3 readers; the *Enquirer's* late-1980s advertising campaign claiming 18 million readers seems to be based on the same kind of estimates.

Typical is a fifty-six-year-old woman's description of picking up her five tabloids every Tuesday: "It takes me 3 or 4 hours to read all five. I cut out and save the horoscopes which come in 4 out of 5. . . . When I am through with the magazines I pass them all along to a friend who also passes them along" (letter 15). A twenty-four-year-old graduate student describes how her parents, siblings, and a "neighbor lady" shared the tabloids: "We'd all pass it around and read it and it got to the point that we'd all expect to read it, and every week we'd pick up the *TV Guide* and the *Enquirer* at the newsstand. Then after I left home my mother stacked them up for me so I may not read them every Saturday evening but I read every week eventually. . . . I guess the perfect example is my neighbor at my parents' home. She gets two of them in the mail, her sister who lives three miles away gets two of them, different ones, and then they trade, so they each get four" (interview 16).

## Male Readings and "Information"

Although tabloids are often associated with women, who do comprise the majority of their readers, men certainly read them too. Unlike romance novels or soap operas, tabloids are not exclusively identified as a women's genre. Tabloid reading is complex; as already discussed, there is an element of resistance in the readings of both men and women, in accordance with their shared class experience. Yet the different emphasis in the readings of men and women definitely emerged both in the background information of the letters and in more direct discussions of tabloid articles. Both women and men enjoy reading the "human interest" stories about family crises, freak births, handicapped people who succeed, and strange phenomena. As already described, people of both sexes explained that such stories were uplifting, made them feel good about their own lives, and were a welcome change from all the depressing news in regular newspapers. But their explanations often differed.

While women use the tabloids to negotiate their personal world, a central male reading strategy seems to be a positioning of the tabloids as "news" or "information" that helps them find out about the world outside them. Significantly, Lehnert and Perpich (1982) also found that their category of "distracted information seekers" consisted mostly of men. Men appear to relate less personally to the stories, treating them as "interesting information" that, while fascinating, has little relevance to their personal life. Morley (1986) writes that, in choosing television programs, men claimed to prefer programs that increased their knowledge of the world and things around them. Male tabloid readers explain their preferences similarly, such as a forty-four-year-old Mississippi man: "I seen several Siamese twins stories here lately, girls with their heads grown together. . . . I like those kinds of stories, this is what I call life stories, these are real . . . it's something that's really happening, it's real interesting because it's unusual. When I was a small kid, you know, I went to a fair, we have a traveling fair, I saw a guy that had two bodies, that was unusual because he had one coming out of his chest almost like a extra body growing out of him . . . then I saw this other guy had three legs, which was unusual" (interview 10).

Similarly, a twenty-one-year-old premedical student reads the *Examiner* and the *Sun* because "I seem to get a lot of information from them which I would not get otherwise" (letter 5) while another reader likes tabloids "because of the well written articles" which he finds "extremely interesting to read" (letter 7). A forty-year-old prison inmate stresses the "informational" value of the *Examiner*: "the most source information their is for a person of my caliber. . . . Thus, it gives me past history(ies) and present events, and the possibility(ies) of future events to avert a future shock. Therefore, it enhance my wide knowledge of the many things that I, have learned, and reinforce 'their are nothing under the sun, new.'" The *Examiner*, along with *Jet* magazine, "make a powerful informed person, against half-truths and double-talk which a firm grip on the real story (ies) behind the headlines of the events that shape our's world" (letter 18).

A thirty-one-year-old reads all six tabloids for the "research in medicine, such as cancer. The information in hazzard products, waste that can cause disease and death. The scientific articles are very well put together, that add new insight. It's ahead of the New York and Chicago Times, in reporting, current events" (letter 88). A forty-five-year-old Kentucky man also reads all six papers: "I like to compare, all the stories, to see who has the best, and most unusual items" (letter 79).

Several men mentioned that they read the tabloids because of stories about specific subjects that interested them as hobbies. Thus a thirty-nine-year-old man wrote that he liked stories on aliens, UFOs, and scientific discoveries because his hobbies are parapsychology, vitamin therapy, and physical fitness (letter 12). Another vitamin and natural healing enthusiast writes that in the tabloids "I learn alot about health and what to eat and what not to eat" (letter 39). A thirty-six-year-old who runs a vacation business in Britain writes, "I read it because I like to see how some people are making money and sometimes I can adopt their ideas over here" (letter 74).

In keeping with this "informational" orientation, men were much more likely than women to express an interest in stories defined as being about science. Many of these stories concern mainstream science, but many others do not. Topics that a highly educated person would dismiss as pseudoscience or bizarre can and are perceived by a reader as informational and scientific. For instance, the *Sun*, the least celebrity-oriented tabloid, is assumed to appeal to a predominantly male audience, according to its editor (John Vader interview 1987). Although it may be difficult to understand, given the bizarre nature of many stories, it seems many men do read such stories as "informational" and "scientific," employing the accommodative strategy discussed in chapter 4. Men were especially interested in UFOs and wanted to find out more about them: "I also believe in UFOs and I know there is some people who claim that they can teach you where to see UFOs in a regular basis. And how to contact UFO nauts" (letter 7). A Wisconsin man who reads all six tabloids describes his own UFO sighting. He keeps a UFO log and corresponds with a UFO study group in Canada (letter 98).

Although men take the papers personally to the extent that they relate them to their interests, they do not seem actually to relate to the characters in the stories at a personal level. Rather than moving them, the papers inform them. Thus a fifty-nine-year-old Oregon man explains: "OK, if I was narrow-minded and lived in a small community like this here and didn't read that stuff, how would I know that half the girls in the country were upset because they went with a married man for three years and then he went back to his wife—I wouldn't know that, and if I had to carry on a conversation about it, I would be blank . . . so you read it, and it kind of lets you know where everybody's coming from . . . some of these other things, like the one when the boy's face was turned into a balloon or whatever, well, you know those are pathetic but what can I do to help. I can't, so, OK, that should be the end of it" (interview 4). In his earlier letter, this man stressed the need to communicate "information" concisely and without fuss: "Most your stories are usually on one page and I don't have to move around and skip over something to continue reading. . . . Again I say your stories are short enough to keep interest and long enough to get the point across (letter 23).

As this reader suggested, men, like women, do use the information in tabloids as topics of conversation, just as they discuss broadcast or other print news. Lehnert and Perpich (1982) and Salwen and Anderson (1984) also found that both genders do use the tabloids for interpersonal communication, the latter concluding that this fact explodes the stereotype that only women "gossip." However, my interviews suggest that the nature of that interpersonal communication is indeed different, at least from the perspective of the male reader.

The reader quoted above, along with other men, explicitly rejected the idea of tabloids as fuel for "gossip." (I did not use the term unless a reader mentioned it first). According to the Oregon man, others, notably his wife and her friends, may use tabloid stories as sources of "gossip," but he reads them "because it keeps your mind working—reading's the best way to keep an active mind" (interview

4). A fifty-one-year-old man, stressing that "I buy it, so I read it first," passes his papers on to his wife and son, and they might then "discuss" the stories (interview 14). A sixty-nine-year-old from Florida came the closest to describing the kind of sharing of information that many women talked about: "There's so many of us round here in my area that do read 'em, we do hand 'em round each other and then we get to talk about the stories and then we'll say, did you read about that thing in there! Of course it makes a little conversation and then we'll say, oh, you don't believe that, do you" (interview 6). Even he, however, was quick to point out that he could only do this because he was now retired and thus had time on his hands that could be "wasted" in such pursuits. Gossip, as has been frequently pointed out (Brown 1989; Jones 1980), is a pejorative term that is applied to women by dominant culture.

A fifty-year-old Kentucky man succinctly describes the typical male attitude about "information" as opposed to "gossip": "I like to read short true stories about UFO, treasure, ghosts, big feet, adventure, life after death stories, and human interest stories. Also stories of heroism. I do not read gossip, celebrity, crime, or occult articles. I like to read amazing but true stories and true baffeling mysteries." He adds a postscript: "I have been able to use some information from this type of mag. for a grad. bus. class" (letter 19).

## Female Readings and "Gossip"

While men tend to treat tabloids as an informational medium that might be useful when applied to their own lives and interests, women read them more personally. They react to the stories personally, empathizing with the subjects, and they describe using the stories to discuss values and problems. Several used the term "gossip" quite naturally to describe how they read and share the papers.

Thus a Georgia woman says: "All these good stories, and it just makes me happy to know that despite of all the traumas that people go through at the beginning there's always a good ending . . . joy always overcomes sadness. . . . A lot of times I'm near tears when I read the stories, because often I don't dispose of my papers and I read the stories over and over and over" (interview 15). She also credits the *Examiner* with inspiring her own career as a singer, mentioning the many stories about people who made good in spite of problems: "I do owe my career to the paper, because the paper inspired me. Through reading the stories of others, there were other people that had stories like mine. . . . So through reading the stories of others gave me the strength within myself to say, well if they did it, I can do it too." This woman often sends money to unfortunate people featured in the tabloids and feels personally involved in their troubles, as does a woman who "reads all the weeklies from cover to cover." She writes: "I am a sucker for hard luck stories and I do find myself sending get well cards to the children I read about who need help of some kind" (letter 75). A graduate student explained her enjoyment of stories about "ordinary people": "I think part of it is maybe you're not alone in your difficulties or your problems and I think maybe it's just a look at someone else's life—maybe a vaguely more sophisticated form of window-peeking" (interview 16). Another woman describes her reaction to stories like "freak births": "You probably have a little soft spot in your heart somewhere for these things that happen and how these people handle it. You know, was it a shock to the mother, or how does the mother feel about this, how would you feel, you know. . . . I go into San Jose once a week and we talk about these things, we have lunch or whatever and we talk about these things that happen you know, in the same way we talk about what's on TV or that sort of thing or what's going on in the world" (interview 11).

Some readers compared their own lives with those of the people in the stories: "When I read about these other people, I think, I wish they could have some of the luck I've had. I've raised three sons, one daughter and they're all very well off today. They've got good lives, never took drugs, a few of them smoked for a while but they all quit. You know, I look back on my life and I'm happy" (interview 6). Another woman: "Well, I figure somebody else is going through as many problems as I got, I figure that in a pinch, then I can read how they handle their problems." This reader passes on her papers to a sister, a brother-in-law, and a nephew's family—"so they go through five or six—when they get done with 'em, boy, there ain't much left!" (interview 8).

The personal involvement in stories is illustrated in this woman's comments: "What it is, I feel if we can read what's going on in the world, that there are a lot of other people that have more problems than we do and it seems to me, you know, even though it's thousands of miles away from us, we know what's going on, and our problems seem very small when we read about others. . . . I read that about the cobra that killed that man's seven children—me, I would take my two children I had left . . . I'd get those two kids in a hurry and myself too, because I hate snakes" (interview 7).

Many women also mentioned the role of the stories and advice columns in helping them sort through their own problems. "Sometimes I'm in those predicaments too, so you know it kind of helps me, instead of writing in, it kind of helps me to, you know, iron out my situation" (interview 2). Thus the papers serve to dramatize and narrate real-life situations that allow readers to "discuss" their problems, even if that discussion is actually only with themselves. In fact some women talk about tabloid stories and the people in them in much the same terms that they discuss events from their personal experience. For these readers, the tales themselves are "gossip": "I don't always think that listening to gossip is malicious, I think subconsciously we're sort of interested in learning by other people's mistakes hoping that you can prevent them happening to you, that's why I'm interested in gossip, I like to know what's happened to somebody, how it happened, why it happened, what they did about it, and quite often actually when I haven't investigated a subject through gossip and other people's experiences, I've come a cropper" (interview 12). This woman explains that she misses the social network of "real" gossipers she used to have; tabloids now help to fill the role of missing friends: "I was used to my Australian girlfriends where we'd sit down and talk our heads off, and I was missing that, so in reading the papers I found this little gossipy outlet that I wasn't able to have with the people I was mixing with. Definitely in my life [the papers] form a very meaningful part, and when I go to my letterbox and see it there, Oh, it just makes my day just that much brighter, I can see what's going on in the outside world" (interview 12). Another woman explicitly equates reading tabloid gossip with talking about her immediate personal life: "We're people, and so we're naturally interested in what everybody else is doing. If you live in a house, don't you want to know what your neighbors are doing?" (interview 1).

In addition to using the papers to work through their problems and think about issues themselves, many women use them as focal points for discussion and gossip. While men describe passing on the information they have read, women's accounts tell of using the stories as springboards for sharing opinions about their own lives—"what would you do, how would you feel." An eighteen-year-old writes of how she first read the papers when she lived with her grandparents and discussed the stories over dinner. Now she brings them to work, and she and her work mates "end up discussing them most of the day" (letter 29).

Mary Ellen Brown, writing on women talking about soap opera, discusses the pleasurable role of gossip in women's culture: "Women (and on occasion, men) create their own discourse and their own pleasure from the text. Such talk, or gossip . . . is an example of the way the mass media can be mobilized and inserted into oral culture" (1989, 171). She continues: "Gossip then has specific discursive functions in women's culture. It validates their area of expertise (the home), it points out contradictions in institutionally expected behavior as opposed to actual social behavior; it provides entertainment in the form of storytelling, and it provokes a sense of intimacy" (p. 175). Women described their discussions of tabloids (and of other media) very much in these terms. Tabloid stories, like soap operas, "interrogate the boundaries of the family" (Fiske 1987) in the many stories about violation of family norms, problems faced and overcome by families, and the never-ending quest for the perfect marriage and family. Once again, the question of "belief" is relevant here. Both Brown (1989) and Fiske (1987) discuss how soap opera buffs talk about the characters as if they are real, leading critics to scoff at their gullibility, just as tabloid readers are dismissed. Fiske corrects this misunderstanding, describing the role of gossip: "It is a form of 'social cement' which binds together characters and narrative strands in soap opera, binds viewers to each other as they gossip about the show, and establishes an active relationship between viewer and program. It is patriarchally wrong to see women's gossip about soap operas as evidence of their inability to tell fact from fiction: it is, rather, an active engagement with the issues of the program and a desire to read them in a way that makes them relevant to the rest of their lives" (1987, 77).

I have already discussed the playful dimension to tabloid reading, in which readers neither wholly believe nor completely disbelieve but develop and use the stories in their lives. Whether the woman quoted above completely believed the horror story of the murderous cobra, she could think about it, discuss it, play with it, as if it were real. And that way pleasure lies.

## Gendered Readings of Celebrity Stories

For women, tabloid stories, like soap operas, "assert the legitimacy of feminine meanings and identities within and against patriarchy (Fiske 1987, 9). For men, the pleasure comes from obtaining "information" that gives one an edge and from resisting the dominance of mainstream cultural and political attitudes. Nowhere is the different experience of men and women more noticeable than in their readings of stories about celebrities. These of course are a mainstay of tabloid content, yet many male readers claim not to read them at all, saying they couldn't care less about the doings of the rich and famous. In their letters, male readers most often mentioned celebrity stories as the kind they ignored, and this was carried through in interviews. Typical male comments: "Here, one of them today, Robert Wagner and Jill St. John are going to share Thanksgiving Dinner in Aspen, Colorado—who cares!" (interview 4). "I don't care what Liz Taylor and all these are doing because I think their lives are a shambles anyway" (interview 6). "Hollywood is just, I would say it's just a big party, it's a world of make believe to me . . . I like life,

I like the real things in life, things that really happen" (interview 10). One man, a resident of Burbank, California, did express an interest in celebrities, explaining that he had seen many in his home town, and that his interest was in a sense "professional": "I've always had a a secret desire to be an actor myself. I wish I could, you know, break into the movies, that's the reason there really. Yes, I wouldn't mind being an actor myself, if I could go back a little bit, yeah" (interview 14).

My suspicion is that at least some male readers are more interested in celebrity stories than they care to admit. Interviewee 4, who was particularly vehement about celebrity gossip, was remarkably thorough in his dismissal of it, describing in great detail a story about actress Cybill Shepard and her newborn twins before offering it as an example of the "Who cares" type of story. He (and other men) mentioned the *Star* as one of the papers they enjoyed; it would be hard to find much *Star* reading material that is not celebrity related. While some male lack of interest is undoubtedly genuine, I believe that some is related to a cultural perception that interest in celebrity "gossip" is a female vice—men may share the interest, but to discuss it is just not "done." Celebrity stories, unlike the "real people" accounts, are less easy to portray as "information" and more universally characterized as "gossip."

Women, on the other hand, are excited about celebrities and become very involved with them, relating to them at a personal level. A woman in her sixties, for example, felt a special affection for actor Tom Selleck, partly because he was born in the same week and in the same town (Detroit) as her daughter: "I'm just curious about him as a person and I think he's a very likable person, I think he comes from a very personable family. . . . It's almost like a personal relationship" (interview 1). She went on to explain that her knowledge about Selleck made a big difference when watching him perform, increasing the pleasure greatly. Fiske (1987) discusses this pleasurable dimension of television viewing. He argues that many fans interact with TV at three interdependent levels: watching the programs, reading fan magazine gossip, and talking and gossiping about the programs and personalities. Dyer makes a similar point from the perspective of the construction of celebrities: "Star images are always extensive, multi-media, intertextual" (1986, 3). Thus the images of celebrities are constructed not only through their work but also through the many layers of narrative about their professional and personal lives—narratives constructed in the media and in interpersonal gossip. Tabloids, television, movies, and other media reflect and feed into each other, and so to some extent one may only be understood in relation to others. As Turner suggests, "it might be possible to view the ensemble of performative and narrative genres, not as a single mirror held to nature, but as a hall of mirrors" (1985, 245).

Gossip facilitates audience participation and feelings of closeness with both the stars and the characters they portray: "By reading the tabloids, fans may construct parallel narratives about characters and stars as well as metanarratives about the television industry. Indeed, gossip as a mode of audience/text interaction may be seen as a synthesis and serialization of related texts" (Brower 1990, 226). Gossip about celebrities is essentially no different from gossip about other tabloid tales or about people known to the gossipers. It "promotes moral consensus, seeks to generate group esteem for the one imparting guarded information, and places the object of gossip in the dual position of ordinariness (identified with the group because they are discussing him or her) and specialness (possessing unique characteristics worth discussing)" (Brower, 228).

Tabloids help to construct celebrity images at all levels, providing material for gossip and enriching the viewing itself by providing "insider" information. "So the fan with the insider knowledge of the 'real' relationship between, say, George Peppard and Mr. T., can read the ghost image of this relationship as s/he watches Hannibal and B.A. interact on the A-Team" (Fiske 1987, 239). As one interviewee recalled: "This is something I've heard my Mom do more than anything. If I'm at home and the TV happens to be on, she'll say, I read that person's getting married, or I read that person's going to have a child, or I read that person has a drinking problem" (interview 16).

Other women agree: "Well, if you know a bit more about their background, this is something else too, how they got into the movies and how they strived, how they achieved their goal in life, you see this is also important" (interview 11). Another stresses the "insider" pleasure: "These papers—you're the first to know there's trouble, or you're the first to know someone's going to have a baby, so you're ahead of the crowd, that's another thing" (interview 13).

As Richard Dyer puts it, the construction of celebrity personas depends on a encouraging fans to believe they are getting the "truth" about the individuals, and much of tabloid celebrity reporting helps in those constructions. The stories about trouble on the sets of TV shows—of secret romances, illnesses, problems—all help in the construction of a celebrity. "Stars are obviously a case of appearance— all we know of them is what we see and hear before us. Yet the whole media construction of stars encourages us to think in terms of 're- ally'—what is Crawford really like" (1986, 2). Tabloid readers are not oblivious to the hype and the conscious promotion of celebrity images; they do not necessarily believe all the gossip. "And yet those privileged moments, those biographies, those qualities of sincerity and authenticity, those images of the private and the natural can work for us" (p. 15).

Different celebrities strike these cords of "sincerity and authentic- ity" for different readers. Indeed, many women interact with celeb- rity personas even more personally than Fiske's three-level model suggests, reserving their special devotion for stars they feel a per- sonal affinity with and feel they "really" know, as did the Tom Selleck fan. A woman from Eastern Europe, for example, disliked movie star gossip, but read everything about royalty because "I'm from royal blood myself, you know" (interview 4). A young divorced woman talked about her "idol," Sylvester Stallone, showing how her attachment to him affects her personal life: "He's gorgeous! And my boyfriend almost, almost looks like him, almost—he's got like maybe five months to lift weights to look like him" (interview 2).

John Caughey provides some important insight into fan relation- ships with celebrities in his discussion of "imaginary social worlds." He points out that when social scientists study relationships among people, it is "taken for granted that 'social relationships means *ac- tual social relations between real people*' " (1984, 17, italics in origi- nal). Using his ethnographic research from a variety of cultures,

# Gendered Readings

Caughey argues that in all cultures normal individuals have important social relationships with "imaginary" people, whether these be spirits, fantasy figures, media stars, or the characters these stars portray. While some fans strive to achieve an actual face-to-face relationship with celebrities, most do not. Nevertheless, the intensity of relationships with media figures can be very high, as fans create narratives about them in imaginary contexts, construct fantasies about meeting them, and literally fall in love with them. Caughey questions definitions of fans as individuals who simply appreciate the work of a celebrity: "The basis of most fan relationships is not an esthetic appreciation but a social relationship" (p. 40). He describes how "people characterize unmet media figures as if they were intimately involved with them, and in a sense they are . . ." (p. 33). The imaginary relationship takes on many aspects of a real relationship, engrossing much of the fan's time. And, although there are cases of fan involvement so extreme that they could be classed as pathological, Caughey finds that most relationships with media figures are simply an important but perfectly manageable part of everyday life.

Some fans develop an interest in minute details about their idols—often exactly the kind of details that tabloids love to provide. Thus a one-time Beatles fan recalled her devotion to Paul McCartney: "I relished every little detail I could find about Paul. . . . I wanted to know when he woke up, when he went to bed, what color socks he wore, and if he liked french fried or mashed potatoes" (Caughey, 43).

Women tabloid readers often compared themselves with an admired star: "Elizabeth Taylor: She's a gal. When I read her life story. . . . She's a tough old bird, and she's a kid that was beautiful and pampered. Mind you when I was young I was very pretty and pampered, but I never had . . . she's just special. She's one of them I think everyone likes reading about" (interview 13).

Other women referred to stars as role models or ideals: "They're very interesting, and I also somewhat pattern my life after them in a way, . . . I love Joan Collins, I love her, she's very feminate, very ladylike, and I'm often told I'm very ladylike, very feminate, and I'm a Pisces, and they always call me the black Elizabeth Taylor, . . . we like to know how many times they shower a day, how many

– 155 –

brands of lipstick they use, what their love lives are like, whom they date, whom they kiss, what they eat, what do they use on their skin to keep it so flawless and beautiful. . . . everything is so perfect and when they speak it's always, never rushed, it's always very calm, very relaxed, I sort of love to pattern myself on them" (interview 15).

As Caughey points out, these "imaginary relationships" with media figures also facilitate relationships among real people, who use their shared interest in stars and celebrities in the intimate sharing of gossip. Caughey found that both men and women had deep "imaginary relationships" with celebrities; President Reagan's would-be assassin John Hinkley and John Lennon's killer Mark Chapman are examples of those whose obsession became pathological. At the more normal level, it may be that for men the lack of a socially accepted public forum such as gossip may make these relationships less overt. As I have already discussed, many celebrity stories strive to present stars as people who, while rich and famous, have their problems too: "You know, they may be celebrities but they're normal people like us too" (interview 2). Many women liked these stories, again at a very personal level, as they compared their lives with those of the stars, often concluding that their own lives are preferable: "Most people think, you know, that a movie star has got it made, I mean they've got billions, but it's like, you know, the Barbara Hutton story that was on . . . anyway it seems like it happens in real life, that you could have millions upon millions and it really doesn't matter whether you have any at all, you can't buy love, you really can't, there's a lot of things you can't buy, and you know, their problems are a lot worse than ours" (interview 7).

Another woman compares her moral standards to those of celebrities: "For one thing, I don't cheat on my husband—I don't like that. . . . Some of 'em, they're breaking up because, you know, they see 'em on the soap operas and they can't handle it, which I don't think I could either" (interview 3). The Joan Collins fan describes the experience of watching her favorite on TV and "knowing things": "It makes me feel like, they're human just like I am. OK take for example, say I watch Mrs Collins and she went through her divorce, and I say, she have the same problems ordinary people have, you know . . . hey, they suffer, they hurt, they fall in love, they fall out of love, and it makes me feel like if I had the opportunity to relate to one of them, I would feel down to earth with one . . . it's wonderful to know that they, rain fall into their lives just like it comes into ours" (interview 15).

As might be expected from readers who enjoy the tabloids' celebrity coverage, few felt that the papers go too far in their intrusion on celebrities' lives. After all, people who feel a personal attachment to a celebrity naturally wish to know intimate, personal details about that star. The closeness that readers feel to celebrities is underlined by their perception that stars are public property, whose lives can and should be scrutinized by their fans. Some claimed there are limits, such as the woman who mentioned the Carol Burnett case: "It makes the guys maybe stop and think the next time before they manufacture something like that—it isn't right" (interview 8). Others agreed that some tactics went too far but supported the public's "right to know": "Someone dies and they're trying to pay people to take pictures of the deceased. That's going too far, but when you do step from the scene of being an average person, if you're making all the extra money you've got to give up something" (interview 16). Most agree: "I feel once a celebrity, you become the public's and the public has every right to know. If you got a fatal disease, the public has the right to know about you. . . . I feel that they should share with the world" (interview 15).

Behind many of the comments is the view that the public has the right to judge celebrity behavior—gossip always functions to maintain cultural standards and values (Gluckman 1963; Jones 1980; Rosnow and Fine 1976). Thus those in the public eye have an obligation to be good role models. Readers generally agreed that "good news" about stars was preferable to scandal, but if scandal hits, the fans are let down, angry, and judgmental: "I think that once you're in the public eye, in any capacity, whether you're a politician or a movie star or a TV star . . . I think that you're fair game . . . they'd better be clean or they'd better stay out of it" (interview 1). "I think if you're a celebrity you have to expect this. Listen, once you're a celebrity you don't have anything to yourself, you belong to the public. . . . I think a lot of them are a little out of line as far as the way they behave. I think they should live a life that will be respectable" (interview 11). "I think if people know they're going to be spread across the front page of the *National Enquirer*, I really do think it may not give them pause to think at the time, but I think it certainly gives them cause to think later" (interview 12).

While men did not discuss the celebrity stories, except to dismiss them, the one exception was a twenty-eight-year-old man who lives in a small town in Virginia. He cuts out and saves photos from the tabloids and claims to have over 350 signed letters or photos from celebrities. In his words, "It makes them seem more normal, not just a painted feature on the screen or something, they come out, they're more alive to you, more personal to you. I like to see, read something that tells us that the stars have the same problems we do, you know, they're not above getting hurt. . . . I believe the bigger the star, the better I like it, like if they was to have something happen to them, and hear 'em try to overcome it . . . and then if I ever run into a similar situation I might go the same route" (interview 9).

And to me, this man's life-style was significant. A high-school graduate, he has never worked outside the home, but for the last ten years has devoted his life to caring for a mentally ill mother and disabled father—the kind of role and life-style far more frequently expected of women in our society. In addition, his devotion to his parents had allowed him little social life—his social relationships appeared to be entirely with an array of media figures.

This man also explained his love of celebrity stories in terms of escape, just as many women did: "I love to watch public television and when I see that and I see 'em show pictures of Australia and places all over the world, I escape there, I do, because I know that in reality I'll never get to see those places, so I just escape . . . and I can pick up the *National Enquirer* and all of a sudden I'll be with that star that they're talking about, I feel that I'm with that person, I can relate to them" (interview 9).

The Georgia woman similarly explains her enjoyment of stories about royalty: "She seemed like a fairy tale and I tell you, to read about Princess Diana is like therapy, when I look at my life-style and I look at hers. I picture myself sometimes as being Lady Di. I say, 'Oh I would carry myself gracefully in this way. . . .' I read a book once, it was an Italian book about how you dress to attract the right kind of people, I mean like the kings and queens and the upper-class people on this earth. So to read about the princess makes me feel that, hey, I'm living in a real-life fantasy" (interview 15).

Radway, in her study of romance readers, discusses how women, being cast in the role of nurturer, often go unnurtured themselves, needing to escape into a fantasy world where they will be loved and made special. Her observations about romances could just as easily be applied to tabloids: "Like an individual prevented from dreaming, who then begins to hallucinate in waking life to compensate for the reduction in symbolic activity, a woman who has been restricted by her relative isolation within the home turns to romances for the wealth of objects, people, and places they enable her to construct within her own imagination" (1984, 113).

The female reading of celebrity stories has an ambivalent feel—adoration of the sumptuous life-styles of the rich and famous, coupled with a desire to pull them down, to know "just enough dirt to make human beings out of larger-than-life idols" (Levin and Arluke, 1987, 32). It would, perhaps, be too painful if the stars were really perfect, so it becomes necessary to tell oneself that really one's own life is better, has more meaning, and in some sense is what the stars themselves are striving for. The fantasy, then, can be enjoyable and nondisruptive, giving one pleasure but confirming that things are the way they should be. The female reading of celebrity stories is essentially accommodative; readers would say they enjoyed the idea of the liberated, autonomous life-styles of female stars, but their own values were superior and made for a happier life. As Young writes, "The widespread appeal of the mass media rests . . . on its ability to fascinate and titillate its audience and then reassure by finally condemning" (1981a, 328).

The dominant reading of tabloids places them as an example of what Young (1981b) calls "the accommodative culture" of the working class, a culture which, although accommodated within the dominant ideology, may be at odds with it. I believe the tabloids are to some extent an alternative way of looking at the world that may be valuable to people who feel alienated from dominant narrative forms and frames of reference. Like romance novels (Radway 1984), tabloids are situated within the dominant ideology in that they offer no radical alternatives. At the same time, they may still offer a "space" within that ideology, through which there may be some limited appropriation of and dispute over conventional constructions of reality.

And the question of gender is vital in understanding the tabloid reading experience. The male reading of tabloids is less obvious from the perspective of the dominant ideology, which finds it difficult to perceive the papers as informational. The female reading is clearer. Tabloids value emotion, the impact of the personal, the appeal to a private, narrowly bounded world that is the experience of women more than men. Like sensational "tabloid television" shows (Weiss 1989), the papers dramatize threats to the ideal world of family harmony, allowing readers to explore these threats vicariously and compare others' problems with their own good lives. In doing this, they tell their readers that what is most important is family, friendships, and other relationships, and that these need to be worked on. Murphy attributes exactly this to the tabloids of the 1920s, which he saw as "legitimizing the emotional response to human experience" (1984, 66). Celebrity gossip does the same thing, telling readers that stars need love and family too, and that money does not buy happiness. At the same time, the celebrity stories also provide a fairy-tale escape route: deep-down the stars are human, but they also live lives of incredible excitement and glamour. Like romances and soap operas, the tabloids provide idealized stories of beautiful, desired, and often very liberated women. They offer scope for some resistance to everyday realities and material for play—the game becoming "If I were Elizabeth Taylor" just as it could be "If I won the lottery."

A useful concept for understanding the appeal of tabloids is the idea of the "melodramatic imagination," which, as discussed by Ang in her study of the viewers of "Dallas," "should be regarded as a psychological strategy to overcome the material meaninglessness of ev-

eryday existence, in which routine and habit prevail in human relationships as much as elsewhere. The melodramatic imagination is
therefore the expression of refusal, or inability, to accept everyday
life as banal and meaningless, and is born of a vague, inarticulate
dissatisfaction with existence here and now" (1985, 79). As Martin
Weyrauch, assistant managing editor of the old *Evening Graphic*,
said of his readers: "They tread their daily grind in the home, the
office, the workshop; but they are potential adventurers—we all are"
(Murphy 1984, 63).

# 6

# Writers, Text, and Audience

## Tabloids as Folklore

Embalmed in their arresting pictures and bold headlines are the happenings and persons which comprise the folklore of our times, more so than in the conventional newspaper because from the start the tabloid identified itself completely with the common people. It concentrated upon their interests, dramatized their heroes and villains, responded with keen sensitivity to their needs and spoke their language.

—Simon Bessie, 1938

For ease of study, it is convenient to look at content, producers, and consumers of tabloids as separate entities. In doing this, however, it becomes easy to lose sight of the interdependence of all three elements, since writers produce stories with readers in mind, perhaps more so in tabloids than in many other cultural texts. As Richard Johnson (1983) writes, in describing "cultural studies," a full understanding of any text must take into account the complexity of the relationship between the three components. He argues that this relationship should be seen as circular rather than linear, in that producers incorporate readers in their production of texts, and texts in turn may have an impact on readers, whose response then feeds back into the text.

One way to examine tabloids in their full cultural context is to study them as related to folklore. Folklorists have an emphasis on oral communication; their focus is on texts as fluid, changeable products of people who are often creators and audiences at one and the same time. Media scholars, on the other hand, have traditionally tended to view texts as fixed entities made by producers and then consumed by audiences. Tabloids, however, are best understood as lying somewhere in the intersection between fixed, producer-oriented text, and flexible, audience-oriented performance. Tabloid writers make the content, but that content is shaped by an understanding of the narrative schemata of their readers, which it then in turn reshapes, in a continuing circular process.

## Folklore and Media

Folklore, the orally transmitted traditions of any given group of people, has rarely been considered by communications scholars, remaining the province of anthropologists and specialized folklorists. Yet the transmission and maintenance of folk traditions are complex communication processes which are important in constituting the world view of any culture. Through folklore, such as tales, jokes, legends, and rumors, a culture reaffirms its values and offers answers to perplexing questions. Rodgers (1985), one of the few communications scholars to look closely at folklore as communication, offers an explanation for the importance of "urban legends"—the apocryphal tales that circulate orally about phantom hitchhikers, cats in microwaves, or celebrities in unusual situations. Drawing on the work of Brunvand (1981; 1984) and others, Rodgers explains the importance of such legends in constituting and reconstituting a culture's world view, a view that often appears unscientific, distrustful of government and technology, and reliant on stereotypical views of gender and various ethnic groups. Brunvand's study of urban legends points out that, although the tales are told as entertainment, they depend on a degree of plausibility and authentication, confirming and revitalizing existing fears and stereotypes by articulating these in narrative form. The legends will continue to circulate in different, ever-changing variants as long as there is a reason to tell them. Almost all make some overt or implicit point; a lesson is learned in the telling.

Rodgers argues for the importance of analyzing oral tradition as popular communication, pointing out that folklore is a thriving process in contemporary, urban communities. Rodgers's work is unusual in bringing folklore into the realm of communications research, particularly in the study of media, which has until recently often been characterized by a tradition that emphasizes effect rather than process and the discovery of the uniqueness of media messages rather than their cultural context and history (Kepplinger 1979).

Folklorists, on the other hand, traditionally emphasized the study of oral genres, often trying to distinguish between "genuine folk tradition" and the media contribution to it (for example, Degh and Vazsonyi 1973). Researchers such as Brunvand (1981) and Hobbs (1978) showed how newspapers sometimes pass on urban legends, taking the approach that, although newspapers are primarily concerned with "facts," sometimes they get duped.

More recently, however, scholars from both disciplines have begun to converge in their concern for an understanding of the totality of culture. We see a new awareness that contemporary "folk" are surrounded by messages from countless sources, both mediated and face to face, and that contemporary media draw, consciously and unconsciously, on a range of long-established narrative conventions. Thus Chaney points to the "necessity of shared representational conventions, a frame, in staging of fictional performances" (1977, 452). Fiske (1987) argues that popular television programming draws on oral traditions and in turn feeds those traditions, indeed that it must do this in order to be truly popular. Robins and Cohen (1978) argue that the popularity of kung fu movies among British working-class youths is at least in part due to the correspondence of narrative conventions in the movies with existing oral traditions. There is a growing body of literature that analyzes all kinds of media in terms of their relationship to ritual, storytelling, and myth (for example, see essays in Carey 1988).

Folklorists like Smith (1986, 1989) argue that the conventional genres and transmitters of folklore must be reexamined and often collapsed, as narratives mutate and restructure across generic boundaries. Legends, for example, are "persistently disseminated through a wide range of technologically based techniques (films, literature, photocopiers and so on)" (1989, 93). Boyes shows how news and folklore intersect: "The operation of news values and the generic processes of rumour legend intersect and interact to produce a near-identity of values and interest between media and legend performers" (1989, 124). Research on the nature of news and its parallels with traditional storytelling has burgeoned in the last few years (Bird and Dardenne 1988). Oring, for example, calls for the "conceptualization of a single ideological domain to which folklore, news, literature, and court cases belong" (1990, 170).

D. A. Bird was one of the first scholars to point to the relationship between mediated and oral forms of communication: "Folklore and mass communications share common frameworks of defined situations, structure, function, and tradition. Communication—whether folkloric or mass—frequently takes place through media and contains verbal and non-verbal expressive forms and common symbols that are often ritualistic and ceremonial. Mass communication in itself is a social, cultural phenomenon worthy of study by the folklorist" (1976, 285–86). The crucial point here is the assertion that mass communication in itself is worthy of study—not just the way folkloric themes sometimes filter into the media but the process of the media message itself, taking into account the interaction of the consumer in receiving and interpreting the message.

In this chapter, I bring together some of the approaches of folklore and media research to show the intertextuality of oral and mediated forms of communication in tabloids. Tabloids certainly draw on and transmit established oral legends, but they themselves also work like urban legends in restructuring diffuse beliefs, uncertainties, and stereotypes in narrative form. People construct a view of reality from all the culturally embedded messages they encounter, whether these are oral, written, or electronic. Furthermore, the media in general, and tabloids in particular, develop their themes and tell their stories in ways that are not unlike the process of oral transmission. As we have seen, readers receive and use the narratives in oral communication.

Schechter, speaking particularly about the *Weekly World News* and the *Sun*, argues "that tabloid tales aren't simply analogous to folklore; they are a form of folklore: dreamlike, or nightmarish, fantasies spun (like the magical thread in 'Rumpelstiltskin') from the most homely materials" (1988, 116). Schechter's analysis is incomplete, in that he seems not to appreciate any real difference between face-to-face sharing of traditions and mediated, and thus asymmetrical, dissemination. Nevertheless, his insights into the folkloric nature of tabloids are a useful starting point.

The *Weekly World News* and the *Sun*, along with at least parts of the *Examiner*, are the most overtly "folkloric" of the tabloids. These papers are full of mythical figures and phenomena that have fascinated people for generations—ancient Egyptian curses, Atlantis, Bigfoot and other monsters, mermaids, reincarnation, fortune-telling and psychic powers generally, and the more modern folk beliefs about UFOs and alien invaders. Random examples—countless others could be culled from any issue of the three tabloids—include such stories as the discovery of "Secret UFO Base in Grand Canyon: Aliens Stealing Our Minerals and Power" and the revelation that "I've Been Married to Space Alien for 12 Years" (*Examiner*, July 30, 1985; Oct. 25, 1988). The *Weekly World News* covers "Atlantis Rising from the Sea," and declares the "Mystery of the Loch Ness Monster Solved" on one cover (July 28, 1988).

In addition, the three tabloids often develop stories directly from folk ideas—in medicine, for instance. Thus the *Examiner* staff has found that garlic, a universal folk cure for all manner of ailments, is a good cover feature. Garlic is pictured as one of several "Miracle Herbs" that will help prevent strokes and heart attacks (Mar. 7, 1989); a "healing cocktail" of garlic and vinegar will melt flab, flush body poison, and lower blood pressure (May 17, 1988). The garlic and vinegar combination returns as a diet (Apr. 17, 1990). In 1985, garlic was hailed as a "new fertility drug" (*Examiner*, Oct. 29), while it has even been suggested, although not given much credence, as a possible treatment for AIDS (*Sun*, Feb. 27, 1990). Characteristically, folk remedies cluster around ailments that are not easily treated with conventional medicine, such as arthritis, or that go away naturally, such as colds, and these are exactly the kinds of medical problems that all the tabloids cover regularly.

Also, the tabloids' human-interest stories often bear a striking resemblance to legends, with, as Schechter points out, motifs from traditional literature abounding. The March 6, 1990, issue of *Weekly World News* features: "Poodle Squashed Flatter Than a Pancake—in Trash Compactor," about a family pet sent to its unfortunate fate by a toddler in Atlanta. The mother laments, "he was no bigger than a cigarette pack and just as flat" (p. 6). The moral point that characterizes tabloid tales and legends is underlined with another quote from the mother: "That could have been Benjamin [her son] in there." The story is instantly reminiscent of the many modern legends about mishaps to pets, often occasioned by household appliances such as microwave ovens (Brunvand 1984). The *Sun*'s hemorrhoid ointment story discussed in chapter 2 is similar, as are many that depict "the grisly fates of ordinary men, women, and children who fall victim to the blood curdling terrors of diabolical household appliances, malevolent plumbing fixtures, and fiendish convenience foods" (Schechter 1988, 119)

Another story with a familiar ring is: "Shocking Reason Why Stew Tasted So Bad: This Isn't a Rabbit—It's DOG Meat!" (*News*, Mar. 6, 1990, 36). This cautionary tale reports: "A wife and husband were hospitalized in shock after they found out the rabbit they bought from a butcher and stewed for dinner was actually a dog!" The victims, Paul and Melissa Gilbert, from Chicago, were living in Mexico City at the time of this outrage. A similar story appeared in the *Enquirer* in the 1960s (see chapter 1), and the general theme of alien societies and their disgusting preference for dog meat is widespread. Fine (1989) points out that Mexicans, one of our nearest "alien" neighbors, are frequent targets of American warning stories about foreign food habits.

Two popular, related themes are "wild" children raised by animals (Glenn 1989) and human/animal matings resulting in fearful hybrids, both motifs that have ancient roots (Carroll 1984). One such story, about a chimpanzee pregnant with a human baby, led to a campaign against tabloids in Rockland, Massachusetts (*New York Times* 1987).

As Schechter argues, "the contents of these papers are updated, unmistakably American variants of narrative motifs well-known throughout the world" (1988, 106), and he cites the frequent appearance of motifs such as the shrewish wife, old lovers reuniting, and unnatural parents. He emphasizes that the "truth" of a story is not the issue here—many stories in the tabloids, even the *Sun* and *Weekly World News*, are derived from actual occurrences. But, "On those occasions when a true and verifiable story does make it into the *Weekly World News*, for example, it is invariably reported in the language of myth and folklore" (p. 99). In other words, tabloid writers learn how to recognize a theme, to "find the story," and that story frequently turns out to be one that has been told and retold many times before.

The "language of myth and folklore" is most often anonymous, not marked as the original creation of any individual. Unlike high art, or even some genres of popular culture, the author or originator of folk tradition is either unknown or generally forgotten, since folklore has become communal property. With folk traditions, originality is relatively unvalued; familiarity is prized. Attribution, on the other hand, may be important, especially in narratives that, like legends, are "told for true." The narration of modern legends and folk beliefs is almost always accompanied by a reference to the source of the information—a friend, relative, or, quite often, a medium such as a newspaper or television report. Legend scholars have coined the term "Foaf," for "friend of a friend," to refer to these ubiquitous sources (Brunvand 1984, 50–52).

Tabloids often report their retellings of legends in much the same way, peppering their stories with attribution, even if the sources are unnamed "insiders" or "friends." Referring to the *Sun* and *Weekly World News*, Schechter argues that they assume the role of the "foaf": "They disseminate the most brazen fabulations in a tone of devout, even urgent, sincerity, very much in the manner of a neighborhood gossip swearing to the honest-to-God truth of some (clearly apocryphal) incident" (p. 98).

Schechter makes the point that much popular literature, like folklore, has a certain anonymous quality: "Like fairy tales and legends, popular fiction is distinguished by a special kind of immortality: what remains alive is not the language of the original text or even the name of the creator but simply the story itself" (p. 9). Indeed, tabloids are, as Ong puts it, high in "residual orality." As he discusses, "print created a new sense of the private ownership of words" (1982, 131), yet tabloid writers make little attempt to place any kind of individual stamp on their stories. In fact, one might say that the mark of a good tabloid writer is that he or she can turn out story after story that fits the appropriate mold.

Certainly, tabloid stories are bylined—it is important that they conform to the formulaic conventions of a "news story." A byline may actually be the writer's name, but often it is not, since tabloid writers usually write under several aliases, most frequently on the papers with smaller staffs, such as the *News*, *Sun*, and *Examiner*. According to *Examiner* Photo Editor Ken Matthews, the reason is practical: "it looks silly to have a writer's byline on more than one story on a page." Editor Bill Burt agrees: "People feel cheated if they think one guy's writing five stories in the paper, so we give them a house name."

There is, however, a little more to it than simply not having enough writers. The byline is also another way of giving some sense of credibility to a story, another aspect of tabloid as "foaf." Tabloid writers are under no illusion that readers notice specific bylines; as Matthews comments: "Nobody reads bylines anyway—you find that out the first week as a news reporter. . . . Nobody cares who wrote the story except somebody who's angry." The point of the byline is to make the story "look right," as an attributed news story, just as the "I heard this from a friend of a friend" hallmarks a legend. Burt explains that writers on the British tabloids where he used to work used multiple bylines: "If I was writing a story that would have more credibility if it was an Irish name, they would put Murphy or Kelly on the thing. If it would have more credibility if it was written by a woman, they would give me a woman's name." Thus Phil Brennan at the *Examiner* writes under his own name but becomes "Eve Savage" for stories on diets and beauty. Associate Editor Cliff Linedecker also writes as "Linda Decker" and under other names while Matthews becomes "Kenji Matsamoto" for stories originating in the Orient. The *Star* and *Enquirer*, which have larger editorial staffs (sixty at the *Star*, as opposed to twenty-six at the *Examiner* and thirteen at the *Sun*), seem to follow this practice to a lesser extent. Nevertheless, "appropriate" bylines do appear, as in the *Enquirer*'s "Whiz Kid" story written by Paul Einstein.

The more "respectable" tabloids, such as the *Enquirer* and the *Star*, with their emphasis on less bizarre human-interest and celebrity stories, are not as obviously folkloric as the *Sun* or *News*. They do not tend to invent sources and events; nevertheless, the sources and stories they create likewise conform to standard narratives and incorporate standard motifs. Celebrity stories, like other kinds of human-interest tales, are also formulaic and predictable: the names change, but the themes remain the same. As we have seen, editors frequently develop celebrity stories in predetermined directions—the star who desperately wants a baby, the search of all celebrities for a perfect marriage. The lives of individual stars become molded to the established repertoire of celebrity sagas.

Thus, for example, my sample week's issue of the *Star* casts comedian Roseanne Barr in the time-honored role of the "TV queen" whose life is coming apart because of her success. The "good money quote," also paraphrased in a photo caption, is attributed to a "friend": "Roseanne believes she's destroyed her three children. Her rocket to stardom has brought divorce and tragedy and the kids can no longer bear it. Roseanne wants to quit TV and take the children and return to their simple life in a trailer park" (Feb. 27, 1990, 32). Certain celebrities take on a sort of "metapersonality," as they are covered repeatedly, such as the greatest favorite of all, Elizabeth Taylor. "Liz," as she is always called, has developed a persona in the tabloids that is part glamorous princess, part suffering heroine, as she endures constant illnesses and weight problems, and part compassionate and loving humanitarian, as she stands by her friends, even when they are pictured as degenerate and AIDS-infected gays. All the time, she is seeking the love that has eluded her through her many marriages. A *Star* writer calls her the "patron saint of illness," agreeing that she is indeed a "legend" (Murphy 1990, 24).

The folkloric nature of much celebrity coverage is suggested further by a look at the gossip columns. In the chillier post-Burnett climate, tabloids now rarely publish the unfavorable and unsubstantiated rumors about celebrities that Potterton (1969) described. However, a tabloid staple is still celebrity gossip consisting of short anecdotes, most of which are unattributed to any particular source other than the columnist. The difference between these and the often vicious gossip of the past is that the anecdotes generally cast the stars concerned in a favorable light, or at least are not unfavorable, thus heading off lawsuits. While many of the anecdotes may have been witnessed by a columnist, or have some other "reliable source" as their origin, it becomes clear after regular reading that the stories are often essentially folkloric—some incident may have occurred, but in the course of the telling, details are changed or merged. The gossip columnist may be originating the item or simply offering another version of a tale he or she has heard from someone else. Such celebrity tales have been labeled "migratory anecdotes" by Barrick (1976), although they are essentially one variety of urban legend.

A good example of the migratory anecdote, either in the making or doing the rounds, is a tale involving comedian and talk-show host Joan Rivers and rock star Bruce Springsteen, which features in three of the six sample week tabloids. A comparison of parts of the texts shows the folkloric nature of the story. The "World's Hottest Gossip" column in the *Weekly World News* has Rivers taking her "pooch" Spike for a late-night walk outside "a Big Apple hotel" when she "ran smack into Bruce Springsteen. The Boss said he didn't think it was safe for Joan to be walking around alone at that hour—then, like the gentleman he is, he volunteered to accompany the comedienne while Spike did his duty" (p. 13). No explanation is offered as to why Rivers or Springsteen are outside the unnamed hotel. The columnists attribute the story to the New York *Daily News*.

According to the "Star People" column in the *Star*, Rivers was staying at the unnamed hotel because her Manhattan apartment was being renovated. "One snowy day she asked the doorman to walk her dog Spike, but he was busy. She saw a guy outside waiting for a cab and told the doorman to ask him if he'd take $20 to walk the pooch. The guy accepted the money and when he returned the dog, Joan was shocked to discover he was superstar rocker Bruce Springsteen!" (p. 13).

The third variant appears in the *Examiner*'s "Hollywood Hotline" column: "Ladies' man Bruce Springsteen played personal bodyguard for Joan Rivers when the bigmouthed comedienne took her terrier, Spike, for a late-night walk in New York City. When she ran into The Boss on her way out the door of her Manhattan apartment building, Bruce scolded her for venturing out alone at night. Then he grabbed the leash and tagged along" (p. 12).

While the story appears mildly interesting and not especially unbelievable at first reading, the three versions show all the hallmarks of an urban legend or migratory anecdote. The source of the story is vague. Is either Springsteen or Rivers supposed to have shared this information, or is someone supposed to have seen the incident? The location, while always New York City, is either a hotel or Rivers's Manhattan apartment. No explanation is given for the unlikely scenario of Bruce Springsteen loitering around the very apartment or hotel from which Rivers and Spike are about to emerge. My attempts to elicit comment or verification of the incident from the three tabloids, and from Joan Rivers, failed; even if some actual event was the source of the story, the details have mutated in the telling, as they invariably do.

## A Case Study: John F. Kennedy and the Tabloids

We have seen so far how tabloids both pick up and retell existing legends and folkloric tales, and in a more general sense how they restate folk themes by constantly representing them through specific stories. The operation of this process over time is illustrated in tabloid coverage of many personalities; one of these is the tale of President John F. Kennedy. Tabloid interest in Kennedy is consistent with several established themes, and tabloid personnel say he is still a guaranteed attraction on their covers. Many readers described their feelings for Kennedy: "He was just special—he did things, and he did it right. I still cry whenever I see that film of his funeral" (interview 3). One reader was interested in all the Kennedys: "I think I know everything about the Kennedys. I might know how many cavities they have. . . . There's a lot of money there, there's a lot of power there, there's a lot of class there. . . . They have a sort of magnetism and I think they have a strong spiritual awareness about them." She reserved her special devotion for JFK: "I loved him, I was only a young girl, but even to this day I still love the man. . . . He was like a great king and sometimes when someone is that powerful it's almost like they're angelic. . . . He had this power. . . . He's about like Elvis Presley, I can't even begin to tell you. . . . When you see a man like John F. Kennedy you automatically want to bow to your knees. . . . And he was very handsome also, yes, ma'am, a very striking man" (interview 15).

Folk traditions quite rarely grow around politics and politicians; the Kennedys seem to have a special status. Short-lived "joke cycles" frequently arise around political events (Preston 1975), and some politicians, such as Abraham Lincoln and Winston Churchill, live on in anecdotes, usually about their endearing personal foibles (Barrick 1976). A few politicians, such as Gary Hart, have briefly become the subject of both joke cycles and tabloid attention (*National Enquirer*, June 2, 1987). Kennedy, however, is unique in modern times in being the center of folk and popular traditions that still circulate more than twenty-five years after his death.

Kennedy's role as a tabloid hero began to emerge only after his death. Just as there is relatively little lasting political folklore, tabloids generally ignore conventional politics (although they are not apolitical, as we have seen). It was Kennedy's developing status as a popular hero rather than as a president as such that turned him into a tabloid staple. During Kennedy's life, he was just another politician, and thus generally of little interest. Just before the 1960 New Hampshire primary, the *National Enquirer*, in a brief, soon-to-be dropped "political" column, reported that Kennedy's biggest drawback as a presidential candidate was "the vagueness of his popularity with the voters" (Jan. 15, 1960, 15); later that year it commented: "He fears that his youthful appearance will cost him a good deal of support" (Apr. 3, 1960, 10). Even the assassination itself was ignored by the *Enquirer* in 1963, presumably because the paper did not anticipate the growth of a legend.

Not long after Kennedy's death, however, and especially following doubts raised by the Warren commission's findings, the legend was underway: "Suddenly, the dead Kennedy became what he had been for relatively few in life—the hope for the future, the promise of advancement for the underdog, the notion of grace and magic, the hero, the Prince of youth. . . . it was also the age-old horror of the slaying of the priest-king, which Kennedy had not been until he fell" (Edwards 1984, 413).

The legend seemed to spring up in printed and oral contexts simultaneously. Popular printed stories defining the "image" began to appear almost immediately after the assassination. In 1964, for instance, Warden and Childs of New York issued a twenty-five-cent comic book, *The Illustrated Story of John F. Kennedy, Champion of Freedom*. The picture book promised the "story of a great American family, whose history began in poverty and whose story was climaxed by reaching the highest office in the land." The booklet chronicles Kennedy's war heroism, his great work for peace, and finally the assassination, closing with the funeral and a rendering of the famous John Kennedy, Jr., salute. "His mother now stepped forward and to forever bless the memory of her beloved husband, lit the Eternal Flame which shall burn forever by his grave." Kennedy also quickly became the hero of dozens of *corridos*, the orally composed ballads of Mexican Americans (Dickey 1978).

While the corridos celebrated Kennedy primarily as a peacemaker and one who respected ethnic rights, the oral legends and tabloids focused on three themes that have little to do directly with his politics. These themes have changed and developed in the years since the assassination, but an examination of available tabloid stories from the 1960s to 1990 shows that they have remained quite consistent. (Pre-1983 stories are part of a large collection of Kennedy memorabilia owned by Mrs. Mary Ferrell of Dallas; I do not claim to have seen all published tabloid stories on Kennedy).

Perhaps the most striking theme is the "Kennedy-Is-Alive" story. This legend still circulates orally and was first documented in the folklore literature in the late 1960s. De Caro and Oring (1969) document tales collected from oral tradition that describe Kennedy as alive in a "vegetable-like state" in Athens, and the marriage of Jacqueline Kennedy to Aristotle Onassis as a carefully arranged fake, with sources often offering psychic Jeane Dixon as authority for the story. Rosenberg (1976) gives oral variants in which Kennedy is in Parkland Hospital in Dallas or at Camp David.

Rosenberg also discusses the circulation of the story, attributed to Truman Capote, in the Milwaukee *Metro-News* and the *National Informer*, a now-defunct Chicago-based tabloid, again including an explanation for Jacqueline Kennedy's marriage. Baker (1976) offers a variant reported in the *National Tattler* in 1971—Kennedy on a Greek island owned by Onassis. His widow is supposed to have married Onassis only so that she can visit the island without suspicion. The story also appeared in 1971 in the Montreal-based tabloid *Midnight* (which later became the *Globe*). In this story (Oct. 18, 1971, pp. 14–15), the island is identified as Skorpios. The elaborate story includes photographs supposedly taken by a British tourist, and quotes "six unshakable eyewitnesses." The "witnesses" reported that Kennedy was "helpless like a baby. His body was wasted away." In addition, "The entire back of his head was a scarred mass. It had been operated on several times. There was a metal plate under the skin to protect the brain where the bone was broken away." According to a former staff member of that publication, the story and photographs were fabricated and staged and were prompted by the widely known legends circulating orally at the time (interview with Mary Perpich, Aug. 6, 1985). In another issue (Aug. 30, 1971, 10–12), *Midnight* claimed that the story had recently appeared in the British *Sunday Express*, the Italian *Oggi*, and the Belgian *Zondag Nieuws*.

A 1980s version provided a best-selling cover story for the *Na-*

*tional Examiner* (July 26, 1983). In this variant, Kennedy is being kept closely guarded at a retreat in the Swiss Alps. He has regained some of his mental functions, and on good days he has the abilities of an eleven-year-old. The story is reminiscent both of urban legends and of mainstream news accounts in its attention to detail and insistence on attribution to reliable sources. In this case the authority is a Swedish psychic, Sven Petersen, "who contributes to para-psychology newsletters around the world and is especially respected for his experiments in communication with the dead." Throughout the story his expertise is stressed in such language as: "a reputation as one of the world's most skilled mediums," "a considerable reputation for accuracy and veracity." The story also quotes a Dr. Chandra Singh, "a political scientist at the University of Calcutta," who maintains that these circumstances would explain the many discrepancies in accounts of what happened to Kennedy after the shooting. In this version, it is pointed out that Jacqueline Kennedy was not party to the secret, a point that indicates the way she has been gradually cut out of the picture over the years as the image of JFK himself has assumed prominence.

Most recently, the *Weekly World News* resurrected the story yet again (Aug. 21, 1990). The paper's source is a letter purported to have been written by a Polish neurosurgeon who has been attending Kennedy in a secret convalescence center in Poland. After the shooting, Kennedy was apparently spirited away to Poland to prevent a second attempt on his life, and a wax likeness was buried at Arlington National Cemetery. "At least 16 politicians and businessmen as well as the CIA were in on the deception" (p. 46). In keeping with the gradual improvement in Kennedy's health seen in the tales over the years, JFK, although paralyzed, is lucid, and has been advising American presidents in times of crisis. The paper's cover shows an artist's impression of Kennedy as he appears today, and the story offers final "proof" of its veracity with a quote from Dr. Andy Reiss, a "Los Angeles–based psychic and metaphysician," who states: "It may be more than a coincidence that he recently appeared to me in a vision, giving me the feeling that he is still here with us—and very

JFK Is Alive! The *Weekly World News*, Aug. 21, 1990.
Reprinted courtesy of Weekly World News, Inc.

much alive" (p. 46). Once again, the role of Jacqueline Kennedy in all this does not merit a mention.

Apparently encouraged by the success of this story, the *News* returns to the theme a few months later with a cover proclaiming: "JFK photographed in secret hideout!" (Nov. 6, 1990). The paper then launches into a retelling of the "Kennedy on Skorpios" variant, explaining that the photographs "originally appeared in a major news magazine" (p. 2). The news magazine in question is the 1971 issue of *Midnight* referred to above; photographs, sources, and quotes are identical. The *News* ties the tale to its August version, explaining that, after his sojourn on Skorpios, JFK was taken to Poland, and later to parts unknown. In a final flourish, the *News* prints a photograph of a check for $1 million, which it is offering to any reader who can verify the present whereabouts of the president.

Many of the variants of this legend rest on the assumption that readers have a great deal of faith in psychics, an assumption that pervades all tabloid narratives and which also underlies other stories that have developed the "Kennedy-Is-Alive" theme. In these cases, Kennedy has been reincarnated, first in the form of a seven-year-old German boy (*Sun*, July 3, 1984). "Psychics have confirmed that they can communicate with the spirit of J.F.K. through Klaus Zimmerman," the account claims, adding that a U.S. government official "shook his head in amazement" when he interviewed the boy. Again, the details: "He even recalls a 1962 conversation between little Caroline Kennedy and the ambassador of Niger." Psychics quoted in the account predict that Klaus will grow up to be a great leader who will reunite East and West Berlin—echoes of "Ich bin ein Berliner," perhaps.

A month later, a ten-year-old Indian girl is "hailed by scientists and religious leaders as incredible proof of reincarnation (*Examiner*, Aug. 4, 1984). Dr. Chandra Murakajee, "a world-respected parapsychologist and professor of antiquities," is quoted as saying, "there is little doubt that Sharda lived before as President Kennedy." Like Klaus, she suffers headaches that are her recollections of the assassination. Incidentally, the Mexican American corridos also develop the notion of Kennedy living on, although in a more symbolic way.

Dickey (1978, 55) suggests that the corridos "seem to be similar to the many rumors for years after Kennedy's death that he was still alive." He also mentions the case of at least one female *curandera*, or healer, "who invokes Kennedy's spiritual power as well as the power of other 'folk saints' as beneficial forces to help with her cures" (p. 55).

As Rosenberg (1976) points out, the notions of a dead mythic hero (or villain) being alive and ready to return, or returning in the form of another person, are widespread heroic motifs. Tabloids have used the motif repeatedly—among the notables who have refused to die are Hitler (giving the *Examiner* its best-selling cover), James Dean, and of course Elvis Presley.

Tied closely to the idea of Kennedy's return is the theme of a conspiracy that killed him: perhaps he is dead, but it took almost superhuman powers to kill him, a motif also discussed by Rosenberg. This old motif was probably fueled further by the genuine controversy over the Warren commission's conclusions and the uncertainties surrounding the responsibility for the murder. Ambiguity and unsatisfactorily explained circumstances traditionally provide fertile ground for the growth of legend and rumor (Mullen 1972). The circumstances surrounding the assassination thus provide the second main focus for tabloid coverage of Kennedy.

Speculation about responsibility for the murder has raged through the tabloids for years, with the consensus being that a conspiracy was involved, as several tabloid readers I interviewed still believe. A typical comment: "I think they know more about Kennedy's death than the public ever found out. . . . I think some of the people who were in office had something to do with his death. Like Castro, he was mixed up in it. Johnson, he was gonna become president at the time, you know, just a whole lot of things didn't look good" (interview 6). Earlier, the *National Enquirer* (Sept. 2, 1975) had gone so far as to offer $100,000 for proof of a conspiracy, the reward to expire one year later. Although it seems never to have been claimed, the *Enquirer* and other tabloids continued to uncover answers. Thus the *National Tattler* (no longer published) reported in 1975 its discovery of a "conspiracy plot" that would show "that the CIA, in league with other government intelligence agencies, was involved in the assassination" (Sept. 9, p. 2). Another reported affidavit would show a plot "among Communists, the CIA and the John Birch society" (p. 4). The story adds the Mafia to the conspiracy, finally claiming that Richard M. Nixon and Watergate figures Frank Sturgis and E. Howard Hunt may also have been involved. The web is tangled further by the suggestion that Lee Harvey Oswald's killer, Jack Ruby, may have been "infected with cancer cells" in order to kill him. In fact, Ruby may have all the answers himself, since, according to the *Globe*, he also is still alive. He was part of the plot to kill Kennedy, along with the CIA, who later provided him with a new face and a faked death (*Globe*, Nov. 15, 1988, 8–9).

The now-defunct tabloid *Modern People* (Aug. 3, 1975) reported that Oswald was "programmed" to kill Kennedy in the Soviet Union on the auspicious date of April 1, 1961. The Soviets used "a hypnotic technique known as RHIC-Edom" (Radio-Hypnotic Intracerebral Control-Electronic Dissolution of Memory). This used a miniaturized radio receiver surgically implanted in the cerebral region, making Oswald a "robot killer" who would immediately forget his crime. The CIA then used Oswald for its own purposes. According to another story in *Modern People* (July 2, 1975) Jack Ruby and Sirhan Sirhan, the killer of Robert Kennedy, were programmed in the same way. The effect of the conspiracy was dramatic: "You'll learn that on Nov. 22, 1963, our government was overthrown—by a handful of men who hold enormous power, not only in this nation, but throughout the world" (*Modern People*, June 29, 1975, 10).

Several years later, the *Globe* (Nov. 29, 1983, p. 7) reported that "he died because a Buddhist curse guided three independent assassination teams to Dallas on that fateful day, claim two top psychics and a veteran investigator." The curse was invoked in November 1963 by a group of Buddhist monks who blamed JFK for the assassination of the president of Vietnam and his brother. The curse set in motion three forces opposing Kennedy—the Guardians, a clandestine group of international arch-conservatives; CIA elements who said he was a threat to national security; and the Mafia, whose feud with the Kennedys dated back to the 1920s. The *National Enquirer*, in a special issue commemorating the assassination (Nov. 22, 1983), throws a new group into the conspiracy. "Working with top experts on the assassination" (p. 30), it identifies the assassins as French terrorists who hated JFK because of his speeches supporting Algerian independence. Most recently, the *Globe* implicates Charles Harrelson, a convicted murderer with ties to Dallas organized crime, and the father of "Cheers" star Woody Harrelson (Feb. 27, 1990).

A mystical aspect is sometimes added to the conspiracy with the theme that Kennedy apparently knew he was doomed, but like Jesus and other heroes, "he calmly accepted that, and played the role fate had assigned him" (*Globe*, Nov. 29, 1984, 7). The mystical, predetermined aspect of Kennedy's death was an important element in folklore that spread rapidly at the time: "The widespread shock and dismay that followed the assassination of President Kennedy was marked by many attempts to find some sort of mystical connection between the martyred president and Abraham Lincoln. Thus it was shown that the names of both Kennedy and Lincoln have seven letters, while those of their assassins, Lee Harvey Oswald and John Wilkes Booth, have 15. Lincoln was shot in a theater and the assassin ran to a warehouse. Kennedy was shot from a warehouse and the assassin ran to a theater. Both Lincoln and Kennedy were succeeded by men named Johnson, and so on" (O'Connor 1984, 351).

Similarly, the *National Tattler* (Feb. 9, 1975, 17) had drawn parallels between the Kennedy assassination and that of Lincoln, claiming both presidents had premonitions of doom. "He did it [went to Dallas] purposely to test God's power" (p. 17). In 1973 the *Tattler* reported that Kennedy "was aware of the whims of fate. It was almost as if he knew what lay ahead" (p. 15). In the same story, the *Tattler* gave extended treatment to an account by psychic Jeane Dixon of a vision of the future president she had experienced in 1952: "God had given down a prophecy. . . . He had ordained a tragedy that would bring the Eternal Flame to the hearts and minds of men (p. 27). The narrative effect sought here, as throughout the tabloid treatment of Kennedy, is "resonance" (Herrnstein Smith 1981, 225). The stories are intended to evoke in the reader a complex of responses and emotions associated with the cultural heritage of "doomed hero" conventions. The *Enquirer*'s cover photograph for its 1983 special issue is chosen for its resonant qualities, showing Kennedy kneeling, hands folded in prayer, eyes gazing heavenward. In the same issue, the *Enquirer*, following an established tabloid tradition, develops the mystique surrounding the assassination with "a long list of people associated with the J.F.K. slaying who have died mysteriously and often violently since then" (p. 35).

As a kind of subplot, the idea of a "Kennedy curse" developed soon after the death of Robert Kennedy in 1968. The *National Tattler* (Nov. 25, 1973, 14) proclaims, "surely it could be nothing less than a curse—a classic, ancient, and demonic curse—that casts its shadow so darkly over the Kennedy family." In the same issue, it suggests that Edward Kennedy may be the one "who will hurl back the curse for ever" (p. 15). *Midnight* (Dec. 3, 1973, 16) reports a prediction by astrologer Tassia Lutha that Jacqueline Kennedy will be the next victim, and the curse is still cited as a major factor in such tragedies as the death of David Kennedy (*National Enquirer*, May 15, 1984, 30–35; *National Examiner*, May 15, 1984, 11; *Star*, May 15, 1984, 16–17). A strange echo of the living Kennedy theme appears in a *National Examiner* story that asks, "Was David Kennedy buried alive?" (Nov. 20, 1984, 27).

A final prominent theme of the Kennedy story is JFK's prowess with women, an aspect that has grown to "heroic" proportions since his death. As Owen Jones writes, "A hero is a man whose deeds epitomize the masculine attributes most highly valued within a society" (1971, 341), and prowess with women is certainly one of these. News of Kennedy's womanizing was suppressed by the media during his life (Gans 1979, 484), and for many years afterward, mainstream media continued to play it down, preferring to present Kennedy as a more sanitized hero. It appears that, at least for several years after his death, even the tabloids preferred to present Kennedy as a virtuous husband and father, but more recently Kennedy's sexuality has become a major part of the legend. Even in more mainstream media this aspect of Kennedy's image has come more to the fore, in spite of the scruples of "responsible" writers: "We've heard all this before in the *National Enquirer* and elsewhere, but it says

The Kennedy Legend. The *National Enquirer* twentieth
anniversary special issue, Nov. 22, 1983. Reprinted
courtesy of National Enquirer, Inc.

something about our culture that it can appear as well in a biography whose title declares it celebratory. This, then, is yet another of the roles Kennedy played: Don Juan. Accompanied by winks, it too has become part of the myth-verification that the hero of World War II and the Cuban missile crisis was, in the same macho terms, heroic in bed as well" (Hochschild 1984, 56).

The development of tabloid treatment of Kennedy's reported liaison with Marilyn Monroe demonstrates the change in the treatment of his sexuality. *Midnight*, in a March 11, 1974, cover story, claims to reveal Kennedy's personal diary, in which he declares his love for Monroe. He is portrayed as a man torn between duty and the powers of a seductress: "He was a man who loved and adored his wife and loved his children, and yet he could not ignore Marilyn's beauty, that mysterious sensual look in her eyes. . . . It tortured him too with the thought that he should never have been unfaithful to Jackie in the first place, that he should never have succumbed to Marilyn's charms" (p. 17). Reporting that Kennedy "worked hard and loved passionately," the article appears to suggest that the affair, while wrong, was simply a symptom of his strong, noble character. After all, what red-blooded man could resist "the siren song of Marilyn Monroe?" (p. 17).

A little later, the *Star* (June 15, 1976), reports on the "sizzling affair" between Kennedy and Judith Campbell Exner, describing him as "the world's most perfect lover—active, warm, considerate, and above all, tender" (p. 4). By this point, there is little mention of any guilt, and the pattern of Kennedy's apparently insatiable appetites is being established. By the 1980s, the tabloids had become tireless in their listing of the women Kennedy supposedly seduced, including Judy Garland, Veronica Lake, Angie Dickinson, and Gene Tierney. The various affairs described provide not only a vivid picture of the "heroic" male role ascribed to Kennedy but also of conventional images of female sexuality—from helpless innocent, through insatiable slut, to untouchable princess. Most of the affairs share a feature that raises Kennedy's prowess to a mystical level. By now, Kennedy is invariably the active partner; the women involved could not help themselves, but fell completely under his spell, while he remained always in control. They were conquests to him, but he was the love of their lives.

Thus, Veronica Lake "would have given up Hollywood in a flash for the chance to be his bride," while Gene Tierney "succumbed to JFK's charm and fell very much in love" (*Globe*, Nov. 29, 1983, 4). Marielle Novotny was said to be an eighteen-year-old Soviet spy who was ordered to seduce Kennedy and obtain state secrets. "But the Russian scheme backfired when Novotny succumbed to J.F.K.'s charms and fell madly in love with him." According to her husband, "J.F.K. was her first and probably her only true love" (*Globe*, Nov. 29, 1983, 4). Florinda Bolkan, a Brazilian actress, was said to be Kennedy's last lover. "He was handsome, young, rich, intelligent, and at the height of his power. He could have had any woman he wanted" (*Globe*, Dec. 13, 1983). Bolkan is quoted: "We were so close in that short time before his death that I believe he has watched over me ever since. There was something strange, almost supernatural, in our meeting. . . . He was my first love, and my last."

By the 1980s, even Marilyn Monroe is no longer the "siren" but merely a victim of her own lust. According to the *National Examiner*, Monroe had sexual relations with both John and Robert Kennedy and was pregnant by Robert when she died (July 3, 1984, 1; Oct. 23, 1984, 35). She was also used by the Soviet Union, who extracted "pillow talk" secrets from her through a spy who became her lover and eventually murdered her. She is portrayed as a woman who had numerous lovers, most of whom, like Kennedy, used her. She has become almost the mirror image of the "heroic" portrayal of Kennedy—showing a clearly double standard at work. This image of Monroe is not unique to the tabloids; Dyer (1986) describes the public image of Monroe as a helpless, suffering, nymphomaniac victim whose name "became virtually a household word for sex" (p. 23).

One woman, however, was apparently special—she who in the tabloids became a mythic princess comparable to Kennedy's prince, and who seems to represent the other side of Monroe's sad nymphomaniac. Both the *National Examiner* and the *Globe* report on the "secret romance" between JFK and Princess Grace of Monaco. Like others, "Grace fell almost immediately under the sway of the president" (*Globe*, Nov. 29, 1983, 7). In recurring verbal formulae, Kennedy is compared to Prince Rainier: "Kennedy at the height of his power and glamor, was almost embarrassingly superior in every way to the paunchy Prince of a tiny country devoted to gambling and vacations." According to the *Examiner*, "he was at the height of his power—the most powerful man in the world and one who had brought a message of hope and peace for all" (Sept. 13, 1983).

According to the *Globe*, Kennedy traveled secretly to Nice to meet Grace seven times, although there was some question as to whether the relationship was sexual. The *Examiner* is more specific: "Grace, of course, was too principled ever to launch into an affair with Kennedy, but who's to say if her heart was ever her own, or Rainier's, after this momentous meeting" (Sept. 13, 1983). On Kennedy's part, "who could blame him if for an instant, it crossed his mind that she would have been the perfect wife to reign with him in Camelot" (Sept. 13, 1983).

Kennedy's actual wife, Jacqueline, seems to have almost disappeared from recent tabloids, apart from occasional appearances in gossip round-ups and as peripheral to stories about the other Kennedys. One rather odd exception is a story describing how JFK installed listening devices ("bugs") in his wife's brassieres so that he could hear her conversations with aides (*National Examiner*, Sept. 4, 1984, 1). Kennedy's total control over women, including his own wife, seems to reach an absurd level in this account.

However, the image of Jacqueline Kennedy has not remained static, but went through several permutations before the tabloids decided to ignore her as anything other than a minor celebrity. These changes were directly related to, and effectively made necessary by, the development of Kennedy's sexual image. Initially, she was the devoted, grieving widow, who would keep the Eternal Flame alive. Her marriage to Aristotle Onassis destroyed that image. While early stories (mentioned above) sought to explain the marriage as a cover for visits to her injured husband, several tabloids later engaged in vicious character assassination. In 1969, the *National Tattler* accused Jacqueline of using "pep pills, energy shots and so-called speed treatments" while she was First Lady (July 13, p. 13). Later that year, the *Tattler* claimed, "The true picture of Jacqueline Kennedy Onassis is beginning to emerge from the Camelot legend—like a slap in the face" (Nov. 16, p. 24). Describing her as a "selfish, demanding, materialistic and relatively unfeeling woman" (p. 24), the paper attributes this to her being "flat as a board," and "that, in itself, can have horrendous psychological effects on a woman" (p. 24). The *Tattler*'s coverage seemed to reflect readers' opinions, such as that of a letter-writer from Indianapolis: "She never did like our country. She travelled outside it during her time as First Lady. She left our country for a rich Greek" (*Tattler*, July 26, 1970, 14).

Taking up the theme, *Midnight* (Feb. 14, 1972, 16) reports that, in his personal diary, JFK wrote "Jackie can be a real bitch," and that he had considered divorce. Later, *Midnight* called Jacqueline "the world's merriest widow," claiming that "the world is shocked at her behavior" (May 26, 1975, 2). The same year, the now-defunct *National Insider*, in an article on JFK's love life, dismissed Jacqueline as a wronged wife, reporting that she held "nude parties with handsome bucks" while her husband was away (July 27, p. 3). The derisive tone of the accounts of Jacqueline's supposed excesses contrasts markedly with those of her husband's, in which JFK is described as "a hard-driving sex machine" (p. 11). White House secretaries "would tell me what they would give for only one night with that man" (p. 11). A late appearance of the hostile genre was a 1989 story in which the *Examiner* reveals a "secret FBI report" on a cruise she reportedly took with Aristotle Onassis a month before Kennedy was killed (Dec. 5, pp. 8–9). FBI chief J. Edgar Hoover, "a man of stern moral principles," was supposedly "appalled at the First Lady openly cavorting with such a man," described as "a fabulously wealthy pro-Nazi."

It seems that, once the picture of Kennedy as heroic lover began to become clearer, it became necessary to discredit his wife in order to justify Kennedy's reported affairs, a task made easier by her unpopular marriage. Later, it became possible largely to ignore her.

## Implications

From this summary of tabloid stories, we have a picture of Kennedy as a mythic hero, potent both politically and sexually. He can only die as a result of treachery and in the face of exceptional odds, and his charisma transcends death itself. The question arises, then, whether the tabloid media create narratives, of Kennedy or other tabloid themes, and then foist them upon their readership—as traditional media effects research would tend to suggest—or, conversely, whether tabloids merely passively reflect the image of the world already held by their readers. The answer is, I believe, more complex than such simplistic models would suggest.

The image of Kennedy that emerges from the tabloids is not unique to them but includes elements that appear both in oral tradition and in other media (see, for example, Epstein 1975). Kennedy, like James Bond (Bennett and Woolacott 1987), Robin Hood (Smith 1989), or Elvis Presley (Fenster 1988), has become a figure encrusted with narratives that intersect with each other differently according to the reading of different individuals. Underlying the three general themes described here, for instance, are other narratives—the Kennedy family's Irish Catholic rags-to-riches background, the tragic histories of many of JFK's siblings, the virtually legendary tales of his World War II heroism. In addition, specific stories about Kennedy are often resonant with association that goes beyond him as an individual—conventional narratives of hero, lover, national leader, and so forth.

The tabloids appear to pick up on existing ideas and beliefs, restating them in narrative form, performing much the same function as the teller of an urban legend. It is likely that some readers will then pass them on orally through conversation and gossip. This is not to say that reading a tabloid is identical with hearing an oral legend, but if with Herrnstein Smith we agree that narrative of all kinds is a "social transaction" (1981, 228) involving frames of reference shared by teller and audience, we may see them as comparable processes. According to Ellis, the telling of a legend invites a response, and "demands that the teller and the listener take a stand on the legend: 'Yes, this sort of thing could happen'; 'No, it couldn't'; Well, maybe it could'; . . . a legend is a narrative that challenges accepted definitions of the real world and leaves itself suspended, relying for closure on each individual's response" (1989, 34).

This is exactly the kind of reaction tabloid writers are looking for—the "Hey, Martha" story is supposed to provoke readers into drawing someone else's attention to the tale and thus encourage the carrying on of the story. Legend scholars, who used to debate fiercely the question of "belief" as a necessary element in legend telling, have now started to see "belief" as a less black-and-white concept. They suggest that what is involved in legend telling and hearing is more accurately a suspension of disbelief, during which a participant plays with notions of reality, involving other people in the game (Ellis 1989; Bird 1989). And it should never be assumed that all participants, whether tellers or listeners, are identically involved in the legend—presence and degree of belief are extremely variable (Bennett 1988). As discussed in earlier chapters, readers' comments about reading tabloids suggest the same kind of approach.

A really effective "Hey, Martha" may become an open-ended dialog between tabloids and readers, as readers generate more developments in the story. Perhaps the most successful example of this has been the long-running "Elvis Is Alive" story. This legend was not confined to the tabloids, having been the subject of books, television news shows, and other media. Gary Trudeau satirized the tale in his "Doonesbury" strip, showing a middle-aged, balding Presley explaining his absence as a UFO abduction—"Them tabloid papers actually got it right!" (Aug. 31, 1988).

The first major tabloid cover story on this theme ran in the *Weekly World News* on May 24, 1988, claiming Presley had faked his own death to escape the pressures of stardom. Readers then claimed to have seen Presley at various locations all around the country, thus generating more stories. Other tabloids got in on the act, the *Examiner* running a series of out-of-focus photographs of "Presley" visiting Las Vegas (Oct. 4, 1988). This story was followed by another claiming that Presley attended his daughter Lisa Marie's wedding (Oct. 25, 1988). It was based on eyewitness testimony from two *Ex-*

*aminer* readers who recognized Presley from the pictures in the tabloid they had with them as they watched Elvis enter and leave the church where the wedding took place.

The *News* countered with "actual proof" that Presley still lives—a letter he sent to an old friend and fan in West Germany (Nov. 15, 1988). The story takes on added dimensions with a fan's velvet Elvis picture that weeps real tears (*Weekly World News*, Nov. 1, 1988). The tabloid tale/legend, in other words, became a self-perpetuating, evolving narrative that needed both readers and tabloid writers to speed its growth. Boyes (1989) describes a similar phenomenon in Britain, where newspapers, predominantly tabloids, covered a series of unconnected events associated with a popular print that had apparently survived several fires. Over many months, the papers molded the events into a coherent "jinxed picture" narrative that developed a life of its own, with the help of readers. (The *Star*, incidentally, emphasizing its role as the most skeptical and newsy of the tabloids, ran a story on Nov. 22, 1988, with the teasing headline "Elvis Presley's Amazing Life after Death" that turned out to be a thorough analysis of Presley's posthumous popularity, including the Elvis-is-alive legend, quoting psychologists and experts on popular culture.)

Far more than newspapers, tabloids rely on reader response and involvement. Reader letters and weekly circulations are tracked, and because of the over-the-counter nature of most sales, reader preferences can be seen and acted upon quickly. Pleasing the customer (and thus selling more papers) is the only major consideration for tabloids, unencumbered as they are with a sense of needing to inform. As the *Examiner*'s Ken Matthews says, "it does no good for me to analyze the appeal of Kennedy or anything else. All we need to know is it works—when we put Kennedy on the cover people buy more of them than when we put somebody else on there." The tabloids themselves have no need to create a belief in reincarnation, conspiracies, or the inevitability of personal sorrow for the famous—only to rearticulate it. The readers then pass on these stories, not so much in the form of detailed urban legends, but in gossip and rumor. As Rosnow and Fine (1976) have pointed out, the media often act as brokers of such rumor, the audience and media existing in a symbiotic relationship. Tabloid writers actively work to produce the sense of interdependence between text and audience with frequent opportunities for readers to respond and participate—whether writing for advice, sending money to handicapped children and disaster victims, advising stars on their weight problems, or voting for an actor to play GI Joe. The *Globe* has even advertised a "Globe Spotters" program, in which readers are invited to send in story ideas, with varying financial rewards as an incentive.

Like traditional storytellers, journalists often work by taking general themes and structuring them into a coherent narrative, using established formulae. Like the purely oral storytellers described by Albert Lord in his classic analysis of formulaic oral composition, journalists have to work quickly and efficiently, slotting new information into frameworks that are understood by both teller and audience. These constructed narratives then fragment back into oral tradition, only to be restructured by another storyteller, in a continuing, cyclical process. Lord notes the effect of themes that recur over and over in slightly different forms: "This common stock of formulas gives the traditional songs a homogeneity which strikes the listener or reader as soon as he has heard or read more than one song, and creates the impression that all singers know all the same formulas" (1971, 49).

News is often similar. Graber observes that "most stories are simply minor updates of previous news or new examples of old themes" (1984, 61), while Rock comments: "The content may change, but the forms will be enduring. Much news is, in fact, ritual. It conveys an impression of endlessly repeated drama whose themes are familiar and well-understood" (1981, 68). As Chibnall writes, "you can put six reporters in a court and they can sit through six hours of court verbiage and they'll come out with the same story" (1981, 86). While reporters might like to think this kind of congruence is somehow inherent in the events covered, the more plausible explanation is that it is a consequence of journalists' grasp of established narrative conventions. For example, Sibbison (1988a) concluded that mainstream publications like *Newsweek*, the *Los Angeles Times*, and the *Boston*

*Globe* consistently cover medical stories according to the conventions of the "medical breakthrough story" even when such an approach cannot be justified by the facts—much as tabloids often do.

Hughes (1968) suggested that there are a number of particular human-interest stories, such as "the lost child story," that appear repeatedly, each one feeding into those that follow and determining how "the story" or "the angle" is perceived and developed, much as tabloid writers describe it. The importance of the selection of "the story," and the learning of the narrative conventions that guide that selection, are stressed in journalism textbooks, although not always described as such. Instead, budding journalists are encouraged to develop their journalistic intuition, their "nose for news." Thus Fedler comments that journalists "rely on their intuition: Their instinct, experience and professional judgment" to recognize what is newsworthy in events (1984, 140). Mencher approvingly quotes a reporter whose definition of journalism sounds remarkably similar to that of the tabloid writers: "You know—what you want to write and how you want to write it while you are doing the reporting" (1983, 110). While Mencher goes on to explain that sometimes such plans have to be modified in light of the evidence, the message is clear: find the story, and then accumulate facts to bolster it. Stocking and Lamarca (1990) suggest that, at least when covering nonbreaking news, journalists routinely develop stories designed to confirm preexisting hypotheses.

Ong (1982) contrasts oral and literate culture, demonstrating that orality inevitably produces and values the familiar and the standardized. By its very nature, journalistic storytelling must retain a high level of residual orality. Most journalists simply do not have the time to compose each article as an original work of art; they function by using the talents of the traditional storyteller. Tabloid journalists, like their readers, consciously value the particular features that characterize oral narratives, such as cliché, hyperbole, and standardized language, so their stories are even more markedly oral in nature.

As we have already seen, Cohen observed the relationship between oral and print communication when analyzing nineteenth-century ballad and newspaper stories of a murder, both of which "distorted facts to accommodate a shared pattern of storytelling." Her assumption was that "these formulae are shared also by large numbers of the reading and listening public who accept and preserve these narratives" (1973, 4–5). Darnton argues that this relationship is also a contemporary one. Recalling his experience as a *New York Times* reporter, he describes the way journalists could obtain quotes for particular, standard stories: "When I needed such quotes I used to make them up, as did some of the others . . . for we knew what the bereaved mother and the mourning father should have said, and possibly even heard them speak what was in our minds rather than in theirs" (1975, 190).

This kind of practice, while perhaps not standard in daily journalism, is rampant at the tabloids, where "quotes" are often the yes/no answers to questions phrased by the reporter. The reporter, of course, phrases her or his questions using standardized frameworks. Thus individual slices of experience, such as Henry Dempsey's survival while clinging on to his plane, become moulded into the standard "heroic survival" story, complete with religious overtones. It seems likely, furthermore, that sources themselves may actually phrase their quotations in "appropriate" form, even without direct feeding from the reporter. We know, for example, that Dempsey did not give any direct quotes to the *Star* or *Enquirer*, but both papers claimed to have interviewed acquaintances about what he told them. It is certainly possible that these sources, knowing the kind of utterance that was expected of them, gave the tabloids the quotes they needed. Journalese, after all, is a language we all have internalized; one can sometimes see sources when interviewed on television slipping into standard phraseology to interpret an event to a reporter. Standardized storytelling, in other words, is indeed transactional; stereotyped "stories" are recognized by journalists, sources, and readers. Like the romance novel, the tabloid is an endless retelling of a few basic stories and, therefore, "can be valued as much for the sameness of the responses it evokes as for the variety of the adventures it promises" (Radway 1984, 63).

## An Unequal Transaction

The relationship between writers and readers of tabloids is not the same as that between traditional storytellers and their audiences, although it is comparable. We should remember that even in completely oral cultures not everyone is an active, creative storyteller. Specialists often tell the stories, and most people listen and comment. Nevertheless, in oral cultures everyone potentially is a storyteller; in the tabloid writer/reader relationship, no matter how much input readers have, the stories are inscribed on the pages of the paper. The role of the reader can be active and creative, but, as Siikala writes: "Mass-produced narrative has ousted the majority of the narrative genres. Even though tales are produced commercially, people are still left with scope for interpretation. Nowadays, instead of the narrator, we increasingly come across the commentator expressing opinions on the narratives transmitted by the media" (1984, 152).

Perhaps most important, tabloid writers do not belong in the community of their readers, even though they are greatly skilled in writing for that community. As Williams writes, "professionals who shared nothing of the lives that they were reproducing learned to produce an extraordinary idiomatic facsimile of those lives" (Heath and Skerrow 1986, 8). Tabloid writers do not tend to share the values of their readers, as would oral storytellers—they are more likely to belong to the liberal, affluent elite. *Examiner* staff, for example, assert that they do not talk down to their readers, that they respect their values and beliefs. I believe this is true, but at another level they show cynicism and a certain degree of mockery of their readers, suggested, for example, in Smilgis's accounts of tabloid writers' swapping "best headlines" in a Florida bar (1988). This is illustrated at its height in the persona of "Ed Anger," a *Weekly World News* columnist whose musings are a one-note tirade of right-wing, ethnocentric, antifeminist, antigay, "good old boy" attitudes. The writer is reputed to be a classic liberal who simply writes "180 degrees away from his real views," according to Ken Matthews of the *Examiner*. Matthews finds him "a scream," and he is a star favorite of the "self-conscious readers" set—a cruel parody of what they see as the attitudes of "real" readers. And indeed, while many readers find Anger extreme or laughable, some do like him very much. One interviewee remarked, "most of the time he has a pretty good head on his shoulders" (interview 8).

News of any kind is obviously mediated not only through the journalist but through the institutional structures of the newspaper and society at large. Thus Hall acknowledges the social transaction between newspapers and readers, commenting, "successful communication in this field depends to some degree on a process of mutual confirmation between those who produce and those who consume." He cautions, however, that "at the same time, the producers hold a powerful position vis à vis their audiences" (1975, 22) and thus will tend to set the agenda. As Nord (1980) points out, formulaic popular genres are a product not only (or primarily in his view) of mutually understood frameworks. They are also a product of economic forces that make formulaic potboilers easy and profitable to turn out.

Nevertheless, a purely economic view begs the question of where the formulae came from in the first place, and the answer, reinforced by the evidence of folklore and popular culture, is that they are not imposed from above. Popular culture is popular because of its resonance, its appeal to an audience's existing world view. As Schechter writes, successful popular art needs "people with a talent for dreaming up the very fantasies that the mass audience (with or without being aware of it) craves, at a given moment, to hear or read or see. But these fantasies . . . turn out to be precisely those stories which have always amazed, amused, titillated, or terrified listeners . . . stories, in short, with both the function and essential form of traditional folk tales" (1988, 86). Tabloid writers, when they talk about reworking a story nugget and writing it "properly," that is, in tabloid style, are describing a skill similar to that of oral storytellers. The end product may be more clichéd than poetic, given that tabloid writers have to grind out story after story aimed at a mass readership, while traditional storytellers had the time to retell, polish, and develop their repertoire, tailoring it in each performance to a specific audience.

The successful tabloid writer learns that he or she should abandon any personal style along with great attachment to a "real" byline: "if (with the calculation of the hack) he is adept at exploiting the news he is also (with the instinct of the born storyteller) highly skilled at hitting upon those themes and motifs which never seem to grow old" (Schechter, 95). Slater, in one of the few studies that specifically compares media and folkloric communication, also argues that media framings are in large part determined by an awareness on the part of journalists of existing folk schemata. She quotes a writer of the popular *literatura de cordel* in Brazil, in which she finds some clear similarities to tabloids: "It does no good to write about a child who was born with two heads if there is not already a rumor to the effect, if people are not already talking about it in the streets" (1982, 53).

Similarly, tabloid writers tended to write stories that picked up on tales and images of JFK that already existed, in turn helping to keep these alive and circulating. We may notice gradual changes in the tabloid image of Kennedy over the years—changes that, while refining details, do not radically alter the basic thread of the legend. In folklore as well, Brunvand (1986) notes a defining characteristic of both continuity in overall story and variation of individual details as circumstances change. We see this continuity of themes throughout the tabloids, even as particular stories vary and emphases change over the years in response to competition in the tabloid market.

Young (1981b), while agreeing that both economic considerations and maintenance of a dominant ideology are fundamental to the functioning of modern mass media, argues that those media that must sell to working-class audiences must represent the culture of their audiences. As Carey (1975) writes, news may be seen not so much as information-giving but as ritual or play, as social values are defined and celebrated through the telling of stories that lay out cultural codes. The power of media's "ideological effect," as discussed by Hall (1977) and others, derives not from coercion and forcing audiences to consume a product they dislike but from using familiar narrative structures to frame stories in ways that reinforce hegemony. Tabloids, although they embrace the nonmainstream, continually reinforce the status quo, always stressing that readers are better off where they are.

# Writers, Text, and Audience

According to Cawelti's discussion of "artistic matrices," face-to-face oral transmission might belong to the "communal matrix," where "there is a lack of distance between its elements and the absence of mediating figures within the system" (1978, 296). Closely related to this is the "mythological matrix" which "resembles the communal model in that there is a high degree of identification between creator-performer and audience, and the genres are a communal possession rather than individual creations" (p. 298). Through this matrix, a culture's values and beliefs are dramatized in such media as news and other popular culture, but with the "mythmaker" retaining control over the product. A dialectical relationship exists between symbolic systems and society so that, as Geertz (1973) notes, these symbolic systems are both a model of and a model for society, both reflecting and re-presenting value systems. It is here that media such as tabloids are situated, as they pick up existing folk ideas, re-presenting them as story, and helping to reinforce and reshape the folk world view.

The folk world view of tabloid readers is not always shared by the culture as a whole. The "accommodative culture" of which tabloids are an example belongs firmly within the dominant ideology, but it may be at odds with that ideology. Tabloids emphasize the personal over the political, as well as the unexplained, the mystical, and conspiracy theories of government, which are all reflected in the Kennedy myth. By doing so, they represent aspects of the folk world view of their targeted audiences, just as mainstream newspapers, with their emphasis on official sources and scientific explanation, represent the folk world view of theirs (with a considerable overlap between the two, of course). Although much of the mystical view did permeate the "quality" press and other media, it dominated the tabloids, which dealt exclusively in Kennedy's personality and charisma, responding to their primarily working-class readers. We see the "paradox of charisma," as Geertz has termed it. Although "charisma is rooted in the sense of being near to the heart of things . . . a sentiment that is felt most characteristically and continuously by those who in fact dominate social affairs . . . its most flamboyant expressions tend to appear among people at some distance from the center, indeed often enough at a rather enormous distance, who want to be closer" (1983, 143–44).

Through tabloids, readers may feel that they are indeed getting closer to "the heart of things." The tabloids are permeated with a feeling of distrust of government, an assumption that those who run the country are guilty of waste, mismanagement, and constant coverups—whether these are of UFO sightings, cars that will run without gas, or the Kennedy assassination. The appeal of Kennedy seems at least in part due to a perception of him as having been outside and above the establishment, even though, as a liberal Democrat, his domestic views were not shared by most tabloid readers. For example, a conservative fundamentalist reader admired Kennedy deeply, at least in retrospect: "He was firm, firm on his foundations and he stood for the United States, he was for our country 100 percent" (interview 7).

Kennedy's outsider status is reinforced by the proliferation of conspiracy theories that consistently link government agencies both to the assassination and the "cover-up." Tabloids offer their readers some answers, and perhaps some feeling of control and power. A *National Tattler* reader once declared: "I have read several stories in *Tattler* about the no-fuel engine, the oil company rip-offs and the cover-up of the JFK assassination. . . . I am glad that someone is trying to inform the people about what is going on in this country. . . . Even the dumbest of us know that we are being duped by most of the big companies. And these companies are being assisted by the government . . ." (*Tattler*, June 1, 1975, 2).

We cannot assume from this analysis of tabloids that their millions of readers receive the bulk of their political information from the papers. As already mentioned, Kennedy is one of the few politicians even to appear in tabloids. However, this analysis of the Kennedy "legend" may be useful in showing some features of a view of the world that is rarely acknowledged—a view where personality, aura, and mysticism are more relevant than policies and other details. This world view is not confined to tabloids, but merely more visible in them. Graber, in her study of political news processing, reported that the news most people remembered best consisted of "human interest" stories that "served no work-life or civic-life purposes" (1984, 86). Even in "straight" newspapers, Graber found that political coverage seemed to acknowledge reader's interests, stressing candidates' personal qualities over professional capabilities.

Of course, there is no neat cause-and-effect relationship such that only people who read "quality" papers hold "nonmystical" images of Kennedy, or that only tabloid readers have heard that Kennedy is alive. Most people are exposed to information from a myriad of sources. The point is simply that, in a world where mass media and oral transmission go hand in hand, people's perceptions derive from communication processes of all kinds. As Blaustein points out: "The folklorist is essentially a student of human communication. In contemporary American society, the folklorist must take account of the bewilderingly complex mesh of communication channels through which our culture is generated, transmitted and perpetuated" (1969, 2).

Distinctions between communication channels and genres may not be as relevant to the "folk" in constructing a particular view of the world as they have been to folklorists and communication scholars. As Johnson writes, "texts are encountered promiscuously; they pour in on us from all directions in diverse, coexisting media, and differently-paced flows. In everyday life, textual materials are complex, multiple, overlapping, co-existent, juxta-posed, in a word, 'inter-textual' " (1983, 41).

Journalism and folklore are not only related on the occasions when newspapers report an "urban legend" as fact. Media, particularly such media as tabloids, are not merely good sources of folklore. Rather, media and oral tradition are comparable, though not identical, communication processes, during which narratives are constructed from familiar themes that repeat themselves over time. People do not necessarily transmit folklore and attend to media in different ways and for different purposes. Both are part of the complex way in which cultural "reality" is constructed—the "bricolage" that Lévi-Strauss described (1966). The "truth" about John F. Kennedy, as about any topic that appears in tabloids, differs among

# For Enquiring Minds

people, but whatever that perceived truth or image might be, it is a dynamic one that is fed by many kinds of interdependent communication processes. Tabloid texts are produced by writers, but those writers depend on the cultural codes around them, specifically those of their readers, to produce the cultural phenomenon that is a tabloid.

# Conclusions

## A Word on Cultural Studies and Optimism

Supermarket tabloids virtually define the word "trash"—sensational, excessive, gossipy, stereotyped. They are so unvalued that they are completely ephemeral; loyal readers may keep favorite issues and stories, but libraries shun them. While critics often call them sleazy, sexy, or immoral, the papers in fact cast themselves as guardians of a particular kind of moral code that sits well with their regular readers.

Fifty years ago, Bessie (1938) suggested that the 1930s tabloids were despised at least in part because the United States, more than any other country, denies class differences and antagonisms. Since tabloids largely address working-class concerns, their existence, now as then, may be troubling to those who cannot understand their appeal. In the 1980s, Fiske points out the class-based nature of much criticism of popular culture: "Casting the popular as the degraded, the illegal, or the immoral justifies the policing action of the bourgeoisie in their constant attempts to devalue or curb it" (1987, 228). It is easier to condemn tabloids than to understand why so many millions of Americans find a valued place for the papers in their lives. The tabloids are popular precisely for the reasons they are also despised—they are exciting yet predictable, formulaic yet titillating; they celebrate excess and ordinariness at the same time. They value gossip and speculation; they are nosy and fascinated with people and the way they cope, or might cope, with what life throws at them.

Just as the papers themselves are "trashed," so by extension are their readers. A central aim of my study has been to provide an informed reassessment of tabloid reading, in accord with the reassessment of popular culture developed by the cultural studies tradition. Responding to the Frankfurt School's indictment of the "culture industry" and its negative effects on working-class consciousness, cultural studies scholars have worked to reinterpret the popular culture audience, showing that people are more active, even critical, readers than has been assumed. Fiske restates the guiding axiom that "There is no pleasure in being a 'cultural dope'" (1987, 9)—people do not simply accept what is fed to them. Such writers as Fiske (1986; 1987) and Grossberg (1983–84; 1984), drawing on influential interpretations like that of Hebdige (1979), suggest that people make an almost infinite range of meanings from texts, and that these meanings are potentially and actually subversive.

Taking up de Certeau's concept of the popular culture reader as "poacher," Fiske (1987) points out that of the vast array of popular cultural artifacts offered every day, only some become truly popular, apparently striking a responsive chord that others miss. I have suggested that tabloids have succeeded because they do indeed strike that chord. Their writers have successfully carried on a formulaic tradition in which stories that dramatize and explore the values and beliefs of their readers can be retold again and again, producing a predictable pleasure that readers can count on week after week. Budd, Entman, and Steinman (1990) point out that cultural studies work has failed to distinguish sufficiently between popular, usually subcultural, media that genuinely represent their audience's schemata and mass cultural forms. The former tend to be more responsive to their audiences because they are paid for largely from sales while mass media like television gain their revenue from advertising, responding to their customers' requirements to "serve up" a demographically valuable audience. Tabloids are unusual in that, while hardly subcultural, given their enormous audiences, they are relatively independent of large advertisers, who see their readers as undesirable targets. There is, therefore, an unusually close fit between the world view portrayed in the papers and that of their readers.

Even allowing for this close fit, I suggest that readers are more

# Conclusions

active and playful than many might think. Readers take what they want from the papers, and this practice varies greatly among them. To some, tabloids are information; to others they are gossip. Belief in their claims depends upon existing ideas and preconceptions. The papers provide hope, escape, inspiration, and validation—both in the reading and in the insertion of the narratives into continuing oral communication. The picture of an active, creative reader making her or his own meanings from a text is an attractive one. Cultural studies is indeed a "humane and optimistic discourse" (Morris 1988, 20). The comparison of tabloids with folklore also suggests an optimistic approach—folklore being active, ever-changing narratives that allow creativity from their bearers. There is no doubt that tabloids draw on and feed the array of narrative conventions already known by their readers; that it one reason for their popularity.

However, even before much of the recent surge in cultural studies interpretations, Grealy saw a danger in the optimism of this type of discourse. He pointed to a problem in the approach taken by a founding father of the tradition, Raymond Williams: "because of Williams' social democracy, his idealism of popular culture, the crucial element is missed: popular culture is the culture of a subordinate class; it is the site of a symbolic order within which the subordinate class lives its subordination" (1977, 7).

Morris, in a telling critique of cultural studies as it has developed in the last few years, argues that the discovery of an active reader producing multiple meanings from the text has become the only theoretically "correct" conclusion: "I get the feeling that somewhere in some English publisher's vault there is a master-disk from which thousands of versions of the same article about pleasure, resistance, and the politics of consumption are being run off with minor variations" (1988, 15). And as cultural studies becomes institutionalized, she discerns a move "to commodify an appropriate theoretical style for analyzing daily life" (p. 6). Morris particularly regrets what she sees as the loss of the "polemological edge" in cultural studies, which began as an analysis of class-based experience and offered a capacity to articulate feelings of "loss, despair, disillusion, anger" (p. 25). The real disempowerment felt by audiences in their daily lives is muted in the constant assertions that they are able to "resist" or "subvert" the dominant ideology through creative readings of popular texts.

She also suggests that the multiple readings discovered in the "voxpop style of cultural studies" (p. 21) may often exist only in the mind of the critic, who uses "the people" as a kind of talisman; the "people" actually "represent the most creative energies and functions of critical reading. In the end they are not simply the cultural student's object of study, and his native informants. The people are also the textually delegated, allegorical emblem of the critic's own activity. Their *ethnos* may be constructed as other, but it is used as the ethnographer's mask" (p. 17). Others have remarked the same tendency for cultural studies of audiences to represent a kind of intellectual exercise, where critics examine all the "readings" that may be possible. In stressing the ways popular culture may empower its fans, empirical evidence for such assertions is often lacking. "The audience . . . has been (like the weather) something that everybody talks about and nobody does anything about" (Schudson, 1987, 60). Lull also points out the dearth of of real audience research in cultural studies: "What is presented in much cultural studies writing about audiences is actually the writer's position, his or her relation to media content, to the family, to the social environment" (1988, 240). Modleski critiques the approach of cultural studies writers such as Grossberg, whose interpretations essentially explore their own enjoyment of popular culture: "immersed in their culture, half in love with their subject, they sometimes seem unable to achieve the proper critical distance" (Modleski 1986, xi).

Not surprisingly, the end result can be a completely optimistic view that sees all forms of popular culture as empowering their audiences, offering "the sanitized world of a deodorant commercial where there's always a way to redemption" (Morris 1988, 21). My research on tabloid readers suggests that an important element in their readings is indeed a form of resistance to dominant values—an awareness, for example, that they "should" be reading about news and current affairs but find these boring and irrelevant. The perception that tabloids offer "untold stories" about anything from govern-

# Conclusions

ment waste to a movie star's romance is important to them because it suggests some sense of knowing and control over things that are really out of control.

But a sense of pleasure in a feeling of control is not the same as actually having control. And resistance is not subversion. Readers may feel empowered, but that does not change their subordinate position in the class structure. There may be a range of possible readings of tabloids, but a radical reading is not one of them. As Budd, Entman and Steinman write, there is a danger that exceptional, oppositional readings may be taken as the rule. Thus one individual's apparently anomalous tabloid reading described in chapter 4 could be extended to produce a celebratory interpretation of tabloid reading as an exploration of gender role diversity. In actuality, "Most people don't rewrite texts freely, but understand them through a limited number of coherence-producing schemata" (1990, 171). It is highly improbable that the most creative reader could, for instance, construct a feminist, secular, or liberal reading of tabloids. In effect, what tabloids seem to do very effectively is show that being subordinate really is not so bad. Maybe this is helpful for liberal intellectuals who want to find only good things to say about popular culture, but "There's something sad about that, because cultural studies emerged from a real attempt to give voice to much grittier experiences of class, race, and gender" (Morris 1988, 21).

In fact, tabloid readers are, for the most part, people with little real power who would dearly love to have more. But they are not radicals; they are not out to change the system. Willis discusses aspects of working-class experience: "A quite marked degree of disenchantment with the prevailing system and a degree of knowledge of exploitation . . . can coexist with a calm acceptance of the system and belief that there is no systematic suppression of personal chances in life. Suppression is recognized, but as no more than a random part of the human condition" (1977, 165). And if suppression is random, change may also be random, and subject to the many faces of fate that are presented in tabloids. While Willis was writing about Britain, his point is easily transferable to the United States. In fact, it may be even more relevant here, where a sense of "working-class" consciousness is less developed. Ideals of individualism—the dream that any ordinary person might become a star or a president—tend to ensure even less a of a sense of "systematic suppression" in this country.

As Gitlin points out, the optimistic interpretations of cultural studies appear to claim resistance to dominant ideology as a political act, when it clearly is not: "it is pure sloppiness to conclude that culture or pleasure is politics" Gitlin (1990, 192). In fact, the pleasure that tabloid readers derive from the political message of tabloids may actually replace real political action, giving as it does an illusion of "insider knowledge." The feeling of getting closer to the power center, based on the erection of widespread conspiracy theories, may seem empowering; actually it just confirms that, in reality, they are infinitely far from the center. The tabloids offer fables and moral tales that help readers cope with their disenchantment, giving them undeniable pleasure. But because there is pleasure in learning to live with and enjoy aspects of subordination, including the possibility that fate may intervene, does not mean that there is no pain, no frustration, no anger that the Wheel of Fortune has passed by yet again.

Another troubling point that emerges from a consideration of the "banality of cultural studies" (Morris 1988) is the question of relativism. The optimistic voice of cultural studies suggests that there are innumerable readings of a text and that readers will choose the one that works best for them. We have seen, for example, that some people may read tabloids as scientific, and that may indeed be a strategy of resistance against what is seen as a dominant scientific establishment. From an optimistic, relativistic standpoint, there is no problem with this; if it gives a reader pleasure, it is positive. Shweder writes of "divergent rationalities": "theories, doctrines and concepts often classified by outside observers as symbolic, delusional, ideological, supernatural, or religious, not only are viewed as reasonable, natural, and objective to the insider, but are also sufficiently explained by reference to processes legitimately classified as rational" (1986, 191).

But there is a problem. Schudson applauds the more recent view of consumers of mass culture as active and creative. "But this is not

# Conclusions

or should not be to admit all cultural forms equal, all interpretations valid, all interpretive communities self-contained and beyond criticism" (1987, 66). Tabloids themselves are supremely relativistic. Tabloid writers repeatedly absolve themselves from responsibility with their assertions of objectivity; they do not have to believe anything, merely to find someone authoritative who does. We have seen that few if any readers believe everything in the tabloids. But the message of tabloids is that anything is potentially believable, and all things are possible. Do we accept and even celebrate the "divergent rationality" of readers who think fossilized dinosaur eggs can hatch or that the earth is regularly visited by aliens? Is it such a wonderful, constructive thing that some tabloid readers firmly believe they will win the lottery, or that celebrities' lives are really much worse than their own? Petrified eggs do not hatch, and anyone who believes they do is likely to be dismissed by the educated as stupid, uneducated, or both. Espousing many aspects of the "divergent rationality" of the tabloids simply ensures that proponents advertise their subordinate class to the world. As Willis writes, resistance against dominant ideology, although pleasurable, may actually block people from upward mobility. "Resistance is thus an intimate part of the process of reproducing capitalist-class relations" (1977, 82).

In an enthusiasm for the power of the audience, it is easy to invest too much in an empowerment that may be illusory. There is not one, single, "reading" of tabloids; there are not even only two or three. But there are not infinite numbers of readings, either; tabloids cannot be anything to anybody. Like much popular culture, tabloids consistently preach the lesson that there is little anyone can do to change the world except hope for a miracle. In that respect, they are again much like a great deal of folklore. While in certain situations folklore can be genuinely subversive in a way tabloids are not, most folk narratives help people cope with daily existence and their position in the pecking order by telling tales that dramatize values that are essentially conservative. They provide rich material for fantasy and hold out hope of sudden, magical change, but people who are overly ambitious or greedy meet bad ends. For while it has rarely been analyzed as such (Green, 1983), folklore too is ideological in that it reinforces and repairs hegemony, "defining a reality that citizens freely accept, a reality whereby the natural or inevitable right of the ruling class to rule is popularly taken for granted" (Schudson 1987, 53).

Schudson writes of his discomfort with much recent research that has offered "a salutary new valuation of popular culture combined with an undiscriminately sentimental view of it" (1987, 51). Like Morris, he points out the other side of the optimistic view of cultural studies: "with the recognition of the active role of audiences in constructing the works they engage, there is a danger of romanticizing and sentimentalizing audiences as they exist in certain inhumane social conditions" (p. 64).

For example, my interpretation of female readings of tabloids suggests that women read actively and creatively, inserting tabloid narratives into their oral culture and their lives. They value tabloids highly because the papers validate their concerns for family and interpersonal relations. Yet many had lived or were living very difficult lives, victims of spouse abuse, lack of money, and the generalized oppression of being an "old-fashioned housewife." Tabloids, like romances, help them cope with their lives and feel good about themselves, but they do not give them power to change their lives. As Allor writes, commenting on Modleski's (1982) work on romance reading, "Reading women's narratives is simultaneously pleasure and capture within patriarchal representations" (1988, 223). I have tried to show how female tabloid readers take a creative and active pleasure in tabloids, which positively value such aspects of life as nurturing and personal relationships that are often devalued elsewhere for no other reason than their labeling as "female." Nevertheless, as a feminist I believe there is a danger in sentimentalizing oppression, whether based on class or gender.

In sounding a cautionary note about the optimism of cultural studies, I do not wish to risk returning to the theoretical minefield of the "cultural dope." I have stressed throughout this study that stereotypes of tabloids and their readers are offensive and elitist, based largely on a perception of what people "should" be interested in and the correct style in which such media should be presented. I have tried to help tabloid readers break the stereotype in their own words; in fact,

# Conclusions

I have tried to show them as more than "tabloid readers." Rather, they are people who find a place for tabloids that complements their use of other media, other recreation, and other aspects of their identity. To some, tabloids are an important and central medium; to others they are relatively peripheral.

Schudson (1987) wonders whether the "playful" readers suggested in many theoretical cultural studies really do exist. My research suggests that they do, and in that sense, I add a voice to the "optimistic discourse" of cultural studies. However, we must temper optimism with a reassertion that media like tabloids are indeed the "site of a symbolic order within which the subordinate class lives its subordination" (Grealy 1977, 7). To be successful, tabloids must answer the demands of their readers—the "audience function," as Young describes it. But they are also guided by the "control function," through which producers "try to keep the commodity within the political and moral limits that they find acceptable" (1981b, 411). Tabloid readers may find excitement and hope in the papers, but that hope is often illusory—the tabloid may indeed be a "fetish of hope for the helpless" (Schroeder 1982, 180). As Young writes, "In order to sell their commodity the controllers open up a Pandora's Box: calamity and mischief fly out and it is their task to keep the lid only partially open and to charm the creatures that they have revealed. But the lid has to be kept open if they are to compete for and retain audiences" (1981b, 411).

In this study, I have tried to narrate a previously "untold story" of the supermarket tabloids. Working within the theoretical tradition of cultural studies, my aim has been to understand the relationship between tabloid writer, text, and audience, an interplay that succeeds in producing a supremely popular cultural commodity. The tabloid charms its readers and beckons them into a world where life is dangerous and exciting. But when the journey is done, it soothes them with assurances that, be it ever so humble, there really is no place like home.

# Appendix

## Letter Writers Cited

Although all readers' letters were read and their views incorporated in the text, not all were cited directly. Letter writers cited are listed anonymously below. If the writers were also interviewed, the interview number is given. Where available, information is given on gender, age, marital status, occupation, and hometown.

1. Female, 62, married, homemaker employed part-time, Bellaire, Mich. (Interview 3: Nov. 14, 1987.)
2. Female, 38, county schools tutor, Troy, Tenn. (Interview 7: Nov. 19, 1987.)
5. Male, 21, graduate premedical student, Columbus, Ohio.
6. Female, 62, married, telephone company worker, Dunedin, Fla. (Interview 5: Nov. 14, 1987.)
7. Male, Tucson, Ariz.
9. Male, 69, single, retired baker, Defuniak Springs, Fla. (Interview 6: Nov. 17, 1987.)
10. Female, 67, widow, retired—volunteer work, Lake Worth, Fla.
12. Male, 39, unemployed, two years college, Detroit, Mich.
14. Female, 63, married, retired, college graduate, Pleasanton, Tex. (Interview 13: Dec. 2, 1987.)
15. Female, 56, unemployed because of disability, Columbus, Ohio.
18. Male, 40, serving 60-year sentence for murder, Attica, N.Y.
19. Male, married, retired farmer, Richmond, Ky.
20. Female, divorced, Webster, Mass.
23. Male, 59, married, construction company owner, Coos Bay, Oreg. (Interview 4: Nov. 14, 1987.)

26. Female, 60, semi-retired from ministry, San Jose, Calif. (Interview 11: Nov. 22, 1987.)
27. Female, 28, divorced, housewife/mother, Hilo, Hawaii.
29. Female, 18, single, mailroom clerk, Philadelphia, Pa.
31. Female, 68, married, housewife, Springfield, Mass.
32. Male, 44, married, machinist, Pearl, Miss. (Interview 10: Nov. 22, 1987.)
34. Female, married, housewife, Fostaria, Ohio.
36. Female, 54, married, housewife, Ohio.
37. Female, 25, divorced, beauty consultant/fast-food cashier, Burton, Ohio. (Interview 2: Nov. 12, 1987.)
39. Male, 46, nuclear security guard, Brewerton, N.Y.
40. Female, 33, married, Little Rock, Ark.
41. Female, 56, married, nursing aide, Mass.
42. Male, 80, retired, Spring Grove, Minn.
43. Male, 46, single, scientist, Canada.
46. Female, 57, divorced, retired, Waupaca, Wis. (Interview 8: Nov. 21, 1987.)
50. Male, 27, at-home care giver, Henry, Va. (Interview 9: Nov. 21, 1987.)
51. Female, 68, widow, retired circus performer, Lindstrom, Minn. (Interview 1: Nov. 10, 1987.)
54. Female, 59, nursing aide, Halifax, Nova Scotia, Canada.
55. Male, geologist, Penn.
56. Female, 38, unemployed, New Orleans, La.
58. Female, 52, divorced, insurance office clerk, Columbus, Ohio.
62. Female, 74, married, housewife, Brazil, Ind.
64. Female, 36, Atlanta, Ga.
67. Female, 39, singer, Decatur, Ga. (Interview 15: Dec. 7, 1987.)
70. Female, 48, Axton, Va.
72. Female, homemaker and small business operator, Nashville, Ga.
74. Male, 36, holiday business owner, King's Lynn, England.
75. Female, 65, single, retired factory worker, Jacksonville, Ark.
78. Female, 75, widow, retired, Grand Rapids, Mich.
79. Male, 45, motor company inspector, Louisville, Ky.
81. Female, 58, married, substitute teacher, Baltimore, Md.
82. Female, 89, widow, retired, Miami Beach, Fla.
86. Female, 57, divorced, unemployed, McKinleyville, Calif.
87. Female, 58, housewife, Long Beach, Calif.
88. Male, 31, parapsychologist/entrepreneur, Columbus, Ohio.

# Appendix

90. Female, 54, married, Kissimmee, Fla.
91. Female, 57, married, retired entrepreneur, Floral City, Fla.
93. Female, 63, married, retired professional secretary, Columbia, Md. (Interview 12: Nov. 23, 1987.)
95. Male, 51, married, punch press operator. Burbank, Calif. (Interview 14: Dec. 6, 1987.
97. Male, 37, single, jewelry store clerk, Lima, Ohio.
98. Male, 58, single, retired car worker, Kewaunee, Wis.
99. Female, 44, psychic, Perryville, Ark.
100. Female, 53, married, housewife, Spartanburg, S.C.
101. Female, 47, receptionist, Dallas, Tex.
103. Female, 84, married, retired bookkeeper, Chico, Calif.
104. Male, 32, magazine editor/publisher, Henderson, Ky.
106. Male, 51, Rosebud, Mont.
107. Male, Burlington, Ky.
108. Male, Burlington, Ky.
109. Male, Burlington, Ky.
110. Male, Burlington, Ky.
111. Male, Burlington, Ky.
114. Female, 51, housewife/part-time work, Roanoke, Va.

Female, 23, graduate student, Iowa City, Iowa. (Interview 16: April 14, 1987. Interviewed following advertisement in local newspaper seeking tabloid readers.)

# Bibliography

Specific tabloid stories are cited only in the text.

Agar, Michael. 1980. *The Professional Stranger: An Informal Introduction to Ethnography.* New York: Academic Press.

Allor, Martin. 1988. "Relocating the Site of the Audience." *Critical Studies in Mass Communication* 5: 217–33.

Ang, Ien. 1985. *Watching "Dallas": Soap Opera and the Melodramatic Imagination.* London: Methuen.

Anonymous. 1964. *The Illustrated Story of John F. Kennedy, Champion of Freedom.* New York: Warden and Childs Inc.

Bailey, Dennis. 1989. "Ghost Writers in the Sky." *Columbia Journalism Review* 28 (1): 10–11.

Baker, Ronald L. 1976. "The Influence of Mass Culture on Modern Legends." *Southern Folklore Quarterly* 40: 367–76.

Barber, Simon. 1982. "The Boss Don't Like Swindle Make It Robbery." *Washington Journalism Review*, July–Aug., 46–50.

Barkin, Steve M. 1984. "The Journalist as Storyteller: An Interdisciplinary Perspective." *American Journalism* 1 (2): 27–33.

Barrick, Mac E. 1976. "The Migratory Anecdote and the Folk Concept of Fame." *Mid-South Folklore* 4: 39–47.

Bennett, Gillian. 1988. "Legend: Performance and Truth." In Gillian Bennett and Paul Smith, eds., *Monsters with Iron Teeth: Perspectives on Contemporary Legend* 3. Sheffield, U.K.: Sheffield Academic Press, 13–36.

Bennett, Tony, and Janet Woollacott. 1987. *Bond and Beyond: The Political Career of a Popular Hero.* New York: Methuen.

Bent, Silas. 1927. *Ballyhoo: The Voice of the Press.* New York: Boni & Liveright.

Ben-Yehuda, Nachman. 1985. *Deviance and Moral Boundaries: Witchcraft, the Occult, Science Fiction, Deviant Sciences and Scientists.* Chicago: Univ. of Chicago Press.

Bernstein, Basil. 1973. *Class, Codes and Control.* London: Paladin.

Bessie, Simon Michael. 1938. *Jazz Journalism: The Story of the Tabloid Newspapers.* New York: E. P. Dutton.

Bird, Donald A. 1976. "A Theory for Folklore in Mass Media: Traditional Patterns in the Mass Media." *Southern Folklore Quarterly* 40: 285–305.

———. 1986. "'E.T. Star's Daddy Is a Skid-Row Bum'; 'Goetz Gets a Break'; 'Doc Errs, Drug Perils Mom-to-Be': Rhetoric and Style of Selected Tabloids." Paper presented at Sensationalism and the Media Conference, Ann Arbor, Mich.

———. Undated. "The National Weekly Tabloid Phenomenon: An Analysis of Themes, Values and World View." Unpublished manuscript in author's possession.

Bird, S. Elizabeth. 1989. "Playing with Fear: Interpreting the Adolescent Legend Trip." Paper presented at annual convention of International Communication Association, New Orleans.

———. 1990. "The Kennedy Story in Folklore and Tabloids: Intertextuality in Political Communication." In R. L. Savage and D. Nimmo, eds., *Politics in Familiar Contexts: Projecting Politics through Popular Media.* Norwood, N.J.: Ablex, 247–68.

———. 1990. "Travels in Nowhere Land; or, Ethnography and the "Nonexistent" Audience." Paper presented at annual convention of Association for Education in Journalism and Mass Communication, Minneapolis.

Bird, S. Elizabeth, and Robert W. Dardenne. 1988. "Myth, Chronicle, and Story: Exploring the Narrative Qualities of News." In Carey, ed., *Media, Myths, and Narratives,* 67–87.

Blaustein, Richard. 1969. "Horatio Alger Is Alive and Well: The Rags to Riches Syndrome and the Reaffirmation of Belief in the *National Enquirer.*" Unpublished manuscript, Indiana Folklore Archive.

Boyden, Donald P., and John Krol, eds. 1990. *Gale Directory of Publications and Broadcast Media.* Gale Research Inc.

Boyes, Georgina. 1989. "Women's Icon, Occupational Folklore and the Media." In Smith and Bennett, eds., *The Questing Beast,* 117–32.

Brogan, Patrick. 1979. "The Best and Worst of the U.S. Press." *Journalism Studies Review,* July, 39–41.

# Bibliography

Brower, Sue. 1990. "Inside Stories: Gossip and Television Audiences." In
Sari Thomas and William A. Evans, eds., *Culture and Communication*
4. Norwood, N.J.: Ablex, 225–35.

Brown, Mary Ellen. 1989. "Soap Opera and Women's Culture: Politics
and the Popular." In Kathryn Carter and Carole Spitzack, eds., *Doing
Research on Women's Communication: Perspectives on Theory and
Method*. Norwood, N.J.: Ablex, 161–90.

Bruner, Edward M. 1984. "The Opening up of Anthropology." In E. M.
Bruner, ed., *Text, Play, and Story: The Construction and Reconstruc-
tion of Self and Society*. Washington, D.C.: American Ethnological
Society, 1–16.

Brunvand, Jan Harold. 1981. *The Vanishing Hitchhiker*. New York: W. W.
Norton.

———. 1984. *The Choking Doberman and Other "New" Urban Legends*.
New York: W. W. Norton.

———. 1986. *The Study of American Folklore*. New York: W. W. Norton.

Buckley, William F. 1981. "Bravo Burnett." *National Review*, Apr., pp.
508–9.

Budd, Mike, Robert M. Entman, and Clay Steinman. 1990. "The Affirma-
tive Character of U.S. Cultural Studies." *Critical Studies in Mass
Communication* 7 (2): 169–84.

Burt, Olive Woolley. 1958. *American Murder Ballads and Their Stories*.
New York: Oxford Univ. Press.

*BusinessWeek*. 1983. "Now the Story Can Be Told! How Tabloids Survived the Recession." Nov. 7., pp. 145–46.

Byrne, John A. 1983. "Slugging It Out in the Supermarkets." *Forbes*, Mar.
14, pp. 78–79.

Carey, James W. 1975. "A Cultural Approach to Communication."
*Communication* 2: 1–22.

Carey, James W., ed. 1988. *Media, Myths, and Narratives: Television and
the Press*. Beverly Hills, Calif.: Sage.

Carroll, Michael P. 1984. "The Folkloric Origins of Modern "Animal-
Parented" Stories." *Journal of the Folklore Institute* 21 (1): 63–85.

Caughey, John. L. 1984. *Imaginary Social Worlds*. Lincoln: Univ. of
Nebraska Press.

Cawelti, John G. 1978. "The Concept of Artistic Matrices." *Communication* 5: 283–305.

Chaney, David. 1977. "Fictions in Mass Entertainment." In Curran et al.,
eds., *Mass Communication and Society*, 440–51.

Chibnall, Steve. 1981. "The Production of Knowledge by Crime Reporters." In Cohen and Young, eds., *The Manufacture of News*, 75–97.

Chodorow, Nancy. 1974. "Family Structure and Feminine Personality." In M. Z. Rosaldo and L. Lamphere, eds., *Women, Culture and Society*. Stanford: Stanford Univ. Press.

_____. 1978. *The Reproduction of Mothering*. Berkeley: Univ. of California Press.

Cohen, Anne B. 1973. *Poor Pearl, Poor Girl: The Murdered Girl Stereotype in Ballad and Newspaper*. Austin, Tex.: Publications of American Folklore Society Memoir Series, no. 58.

Cohen, Stan. 1981. "Mods and Rockers: The Inventory of Manufactured News." In Cohen and Young, eds., *The Manufacture of News*, 263–79.

Cohen, Stan, and Jock Young. 1981. "Effects and Consequences." In Cohen and Young, eds., *The Manufacture of News*, 423–40.

Cohen, Stan, and Jock Young, eds. 1981. *The Manufacture of News: Social Problems, Deviance and the Mass Media*. London: Constable.

Collison, Robert. 1973. *The Story of Street Literature: Forerunner of the Popular Press*. London: J. M. Dent.

Corkery, P. J. 1981. "Enquirer: An Eyewitness Account." *Rolling Stone*, June 11, pp. 19–21, 62.

Curran, J., M. Gurevitch, and J. Woolacott, eds. *Mass Communication and Society*. London: Edward Arnold.

Darnton, Robert. 1975. "Writing News and Telling Stories." *Daedalus* 104: 175–94.

De Caro, F. A., and E. Oring. 1969. "J.F.K. Is Alive: A Modern Legend." *Folklore Forum* 2 (2): 54–55.

Degh, L., and A. Vazsonyi. 1973. *The Dialectics of Legend*. Indiana Univ. Folklore Preprint Series 1 (6).

Dickey, D. W. 1978. *The Kennedy Corridos: A Study of the Ballads of a Mexican American Hero*. Austin: Univ. of Texas Center for Mexican American Studies.

Dyer, Richard. 1986. *Heavenly Bodies: Film Stars and Society*. New York: St. Martin's Press.

Eason, David L. 1981. "Telling Stories and Making Sense." *Journal of Popular Culture* 15 (2): 125–29.

_____. 1988. "On Journalistic Authority: The Janet Cooke Scandal." In Carey, ed., *Media, Myths, and Narratives*, 205–27.

Edwards, O. D. 1984. "Remembering the Kennedys." *Journal of American Studies* 18 (3): 405–23.

# Bibliography

Ellis, Bill. 1989. "When Is a Legend? An Essay in Legend Morphology." In Smith and Bennett, eds., *The Questing Beast*, 31–54.

Emery, Edwin. 1972. *The Press and America: An Interpretive History of the Mass Media*. Englewood Cliffs, N.J.: Prentice Hall.

English, Philip W. 1990. "Bash, Bash, Bash: Cultural Warfare on Television." Paper presented at first Reading X Conference on American Culture, Apr., Duluth, Minn.

Engstrom, John. 1984. "Tabloid Fever!!" *Chicago Tribune Magazine*, June 3, pp. 20–23, 26–30.

Epstein, E. J. 1975. "History as Fiction." In his *Between Fact and Fiction: The Problem of Journalism*. New York: Vintage Books.

Evans, William A., Michael Krippendorf, Jae H. Yoon, Paulette Posluszny, and Sari Thomas. 1990. "Science in the Prestige and National Tabloid Presses." *Social Science Quarterly* 71 (1): 105–17.

Fedler, Fred. 1984. *Reporting for the Print Media*. New York: Harcourt Brace Jovanovich.

Fenster, Mark. 1988. "Elvis: The Consumption and Use of the Popular Figure." Paper presented at annual convention of International Communication Association, New Orleans.

Fine, Gary Alan. 1989. "Mercantile Legends and the World Economy: Dangerous Imports from the Third World." *Western Folklore* 48 (Apr.): 153–61.

Fiske, John. 1986. "Television: Polysemy and Popularity." *Critical Studies in Mass Communication* 3: 391–408.

_____. 1987. *Television Culture*. New York: Methuen.

_____. 1988. "Meaningful Moments." *Critical Studies in Mass Communication* 5: 246–51.

Fox, Roy F. 1988. "Sensationspeak in America." *The English Journal* 77 (Mar.): 52–56.

Francke, Warren T. 1986. "Sensationalism and the Development of Reporting in the Nineteenth Century: The Broom Sweeps Sensory Details." Paper presented at Conference on Sensationalism and the Media. Ann Arbor, Mich.

Frazier, Kendrick. 1984. "Touting Psychic Wonders in the Mainstream Media." *Skeptical Inquirer* 9 (2): 106–9.

Friedrich, Otto. 1987. "New Age Harmonies." *Time*, Dec. 7, pp. 62–72.

Gans, Herbert. 1979. *Deciding What's News*. New York: Pantheon.

Geertz, Clifford. 1973. *The Interpretation of Cultures*. New York: Basic Books.

# For Enquiring Minds

_____. 1983. *Local Knowledge: Further Essays in Interpretive Anthropology.* New York: Basic Books.

_____. 1988. *Works and Lives: The Anthropologist as Author.* Stanford: Stanford Univ. Press.

Gilligan, Carol. 1982. *In a Different Voice: Psychological Theory and Women's Development.* Cambridge, Mass.: Harvard Univ. Press.

Gitlin, Todd. 1990. "Who Communicates What to Whom, in What Voice and Why, about the Study of Mass Communication?" *Critical Studies in Mass Communication* 7 (2): 185–96.

Glenn, William M. 1989. "Debate Rages over Shocking Half-Human/Half Animal Babies." *Alternatives* 16 (21): 32, 35, 37.

Gluckman, Max. 1963. "Gossip and Scandal." *Current Anthropology* 4: 307–16.

Goldstein, T. 1985. *The News at Any Cost: How Journalists Compromise Their Ethics to Shape the News.* New York: Simon and Schuster.

Graber, Doris A. 1984. *Processing the News: How People Tame the Information Tide.* New York: Longman.

Grealy, Jim. 1977. "Notes on Popular Culture." *Screen Education* 22: 5–11.

Green, Archie. 1983. "Interpreting Folklore Ideologically." In Richard M. Dorson, ed., *Handbook of American Folklore.* Bloomington: Indiana Univ. Press, 351–58.

Greenwell, J. Richard. 1987. "The Tabloids That Time Forgot." *Newsletter of the International Society of Cryptozoology* 6 (2): 9–10.

Grossberg, Lawrence. 1983–84. "The Politics of Youth Culture: Some Observations on Rock and Roll in American Culture." *Social Text* 8: 104–26.

_____. 1984. "'I'd Rather Feel Bad Than Not Feel Anything at All': Rock and Roll, Pleasure and Power." *Enclitic* 8 (1–2): 94–111.

Gourley, Jay. 1981. "'I Killed Gig Young' and Other Confessions from inside the *National Enquirer.*" *The Washington Monthly*, Sept., pp. 32–38.

Hall, Stuart. 1975. Introduction to A. C. H. Smith, *Paper Voices: The Popular Press and Social Change, 1935–1965.* London: Chatto and Windus.

_____. 1977. "Culture, the Media and the Ideological Effect." In Curran et al., eds., *Mass Communication and Society*, 315–48.

_____. 1982. "The Rediscovery of 'Ideology': Return of the Repressed in

# Bibliography

Media Studies." In M. Gurevitch et al., eds., *Culture, Society and the Media*. London: Methuen.

Heath, Stephen, and Gillian Skerrow. 1986. "An Interview with Raymond Williams." In Modleski, ed., *Studies in Entertainment*, 3–17.

Hebdige, Dick. 1979. *Subculture: The Meaning of Style*. London: Methuen.

Herrnstein Smith, B. 1981. "Narrative Versions, Narrative Theories." In W. J. T Mitchell, ed., *On Narrative*. Chicago: Univ. of Chicago Press, 209–32.

Hinkle, Gerald, and William R. Elliott. 1989. "Science Coverage in Three Newspapers and Three Supermarket Tabloids." *Journalism Quarterly* 66 (2): 353–58

Hobbs, Sandy. 1978. "The Folktale as News." *Oral History* 6 (2): 74–86.

Hobson, Dorothy. 1982. *Crossroads: The Drama of a Soap Opera*. London: Methuen.

Hochschild, A. 1984. "Would J.F.K. Be a Hero Now?" *Mother Jones*, Feb.–Mar., 56–57.

Hofstadter, Douglas R. 1982. "Metamagical Themas." *Scientific American* 246 (Feb.): 18–26.

Holden, Larry. 1977. "The Incredibly Rich Tabloid Market." *Writers Digest*, July, pp. 19–22.

Hughes, Helen M. 1968. *News and the Human Interest Story*. Chicago: Univ. of Chicago Press.

Jahoda, Gustav. 1971. *The Psychology of Superstition*. Harmondsworth, England: Penguin.

James, Barry. 1990. "France Possessed by the Occult and Irrational." *Skeptical Inquirer* 14 (3): 232–33.

Jameson, Frederic. 1984. "Postmodernism, or the Cultural Logic of Late Capitalism." *New Left Review* 146: 53–92.

Jensen, Klaus Bruhn. 1986. *Making Sense of the News: Toward a Theory and Empirical Model for the Study of Mass Communication*. Århus, Denmark: Århus Univ. Press.

———. 1987. "Qualitative Audience Research: Toward an Integrative Approach to Reception." *Critical Studies in Mass Communication* 4: 21–36.

Johnson, Richard. 1983. *What Is Cultural Studies Anyway?* Birmingham Univ. Centre for Contemporary Cultural Studies General Series SP 74.

Johnson, Otto, ed. 1990. *Information Please Almanac*. Boston: Houghton Mifflin.

# For Enquiring Minds

Johnston, Winifred. 1935. "Newspaper Balladry." *American Speech* 10: 119–21.

Jones, Deborah. 1980. "Gossip: Notes on Women's Oral Culture." *Women's Studies International Quarterly* 3: 193–98.

Kelley, Lane. 1989. "Mad Slasher Comes Calling at the *National Enquirer.*" *Duluth* (Minn.) *News-Tribune* (Knight-Ridder), Nov. 26, p. 7C.

Kepplinger, Hans M. 1979. "Paradigm Change in Communication Research." *Communication* 4 (2): 160–71.

Klaidman, Stephen. 1975. "Upbeat *Enquirer* Thrives on Supermarket Sales." *Washington Post*, Aug. 17, pp. G1–G2.

Klare, Roger. 1990. "Ghosts Make News: How Four Newspapers Report Psychic Phenomena." *Skeptical Inquirer* 14 (4): 363–71.

Landro, Laura. 1987. "Murdoch Quietly Becoming Formidable in Magazines." *Wall Street Journal*, Feb. 5, p. 6.

Lehnert, Eileen, and Mary J. Perpich. 1982. "An Attitude Segmentation Study of Supermarket Tabloid Readers." *Journalism Quarterly* 59: 104–11.

Lévi-Strauss, Claude. 1966. *The Savage Mind.* Chicago: Univ. of Chicago Press.

Levin, Jack, and Arnold Arluke. 1987. *Gossip: The Inside Scoop.* New York: Plenum Press.

Levin, Jack, Amita Mody-Desbarau, and Arnold Arluke. 1988. "The Gossip Tabloid as an Agent of Social Control." *Journalism Quarterly* 65 (2): 514–17.

Lord, Albert B. 1971. *The Singer of Tales.* Cambridge, Mass.: Harvard Univ. Press.

Lull, James. 1982. "The Social Uses of Television." In E. Wartella and D. Whitney, eds., *Mass Communication Review Yearbook* 3. Beverly Hills, Calif.: Sage, 397–409.

———. 1988. "The Audience as Nuisance." *Critical Studies in Mass Communication* 5: 239–42.

MacDougall, A. Kent. 1989. "Memoirs of a Radical in the Mainstream Press." *Columbia Journalism Review* 27 (6): 36–41.

Malinowski, Bronislaw. 1954. *Magic, Science and Religion.* New York: Doubleday.

Mano, D. Keith. 1977. "Enquiring." *National Review*, Feb. 18, pp. 209–10.

McDonald, Daniel. 1987. *"Enquirer* Stories Worth Thinking About." *ETC* 44 (4): 392–94.

# Bibliography

McDonald, Deborah M. 1984. "The Derived Image of the Supermarket Tabloid." Ph.D. diss., Ohio State Univ.

Mencher, Melvin. 1983. *Basic News Writing*. Dubuque, Iowa: Brown.

Mendez-Acosta, Maria, Piet Hein Hoebens, Michael Hutchinson, Dick Smith, Henry Gordon, and Michel Rouze. 1984. "Special Report: The State of Belief in the Paranormal Worldwide." *Skeptical Inquirer* 8 (3): 224–38.

Modleski, Tania. 1982. *Loving with a Vengeance: Mass Produced Fantasies for Women*. Hamden, Conn.: Archon Books.

———. 1986. Introduction to Modleski, ed., *Studies in Entertainment*.

Modleski, Tania, ed. *Studies in Entertainment: Critical Approaches to Mass Culture*. Bloomington: Indiana Univ. Press

Morley, David. 1980. *The Nationwide Audience: Structure and Decoding*. London: BFI.

———. 1986. *Family Television: Cultural Power and Domestic Leisure*. London: Comedia Publishing Group.

Morris, Meaghan. 1988. "Banality in Cultural Studies." *Discourse* 10 (2): 3–29.

Mott, Frank Luther. 1963. *American Journalism: A History, 1690–1960*. New York: Macmillan.

Mullen, Patrick B. 1972. "Modern Legend and Rumor Theory." *Journal of the Folklore Institute* 9: 95–109.

Murphy, James E. 1984. "Tabloids as an Urban Response." In Catherine L. Covert and John D. Stevens, eds., *Mass Media between the Wars: Perceptions of Cultural Tension, 1918–1941*. Syracuse Univ. Press, 55–69.

Murphy, Ryan. 1990. "America's Fascination with Liz." *Duluth* (Minn.) *News-Tribune Magazine* (Knight-Ridder), June 24, p. 24.

Nerone, John C. 1987. "The Mythology of the Penny Press." *Critical Studies in Mass Communication* 4 (4): 376–404.

*Newsweek*. 1969. "From Worse to Bad." Sept. 8, p. 79.

*New York Times*. 1987. "Moral Trailblazing in Rockland, Mass." Dec. 20, p. 50.

Nord, David P. 1980. "An Economic Perspective on Formula in Popular Culture. *Journal of American Culture* 3: 17–31.

———. 1988. "Teleology and News: The Religious Roots of American Journalism, 1630–1730." Paper presented at annual conference of Association for Education in Journalism and Mass Communication, Portland, Oreg.

Nordheimer, Jon. 1988. "In Bland New World, Tabloids to Imitate *Reader's Digest* (Well, Not Quite)." *Minneapolis Star-Tribune*, Feb. 14, pp. 1EX, 4EX.

Nordin, Kenneth D. 1979. "The Entertaining Press: Sensationalism in 18th Century Boston Newspapers." *Communication Research* 6 (3): 295–320.

O'Connor, John W. 1984. "Misperception, Folk Belief, and the Occult: A Cognitive Guide to Understanding." *Skeptical Inquirer* 8 (4): 344–54.

O'Leary, Noreen. 1989. "The Untold Story of the *Enquirer* Acquirer." *Adweek* 39 (May 29): 30, 32.

Ong, Walter. 1982. *Orality and Literacy: The Technologizing of the World.* London: Methuen.

Oring, Elliott. 1990. "Legend, Truth, and News." *Southern Folklore* 47, 163–77.

Owen Jones, M. 1971. "(PC + CB) x SD (R + I + E) = Hero." *New York Folklore Quarterly* 27: 243–60.

Pauly, John J. 1988. "Rupert Murdoch and the Demonology of Professional Journalism." In Carey, ed., *Media, Myths, and Narratives*, 246–61.

Peer, Elizabeth, and William Schmidt. 1975. "The *Enquirer*: Up from Smut." *Newsweek*, Apr. 21, p. 62.

Pfaff, Fred. 1987. "Headway for the Headliners: Those Screaming Checkout Tabloids Are Being Heard on Madison Avenue." *Marketing and Media Decisions* 22 (May): 66–68, 72–73.

Porter, B. 1989. "The Scanlon Spin." *Columbia Journalism Review* 28 (3): 49–54.

Potterton, Reginald. 1969. "I Cut Out Her Heart and Stomped on It!" *Playboy,* Apr., pp. 117–18, 120, 204, 206, 208, 212.

Press, Andrea L. 1990. "Class, Gender, and the Female Viewer: Women's Responses to *Dynasty.*" In Mary Ellen Brown, ed., *Television and Women's Culture: The Politics of the Popular.* Newbury Park: Sage, 158–82.

Preston, Michael J. 1975. "A Year of Political Jokes (June 1973–June 1974); or, the Silent Majority Speaks Out." *Western Folklore* 34: 233–44.

Radway, Janice. 1984. *Reading the Romance: Women, Patriarchy and Popular Literature.* Chapel Hill: Univ. of North Carolina Press.

Reilly, Patrick. 1989a. "Deflated *Enquirer*: $400 Million Sale Price Is More Like $200 Million." *Advertising Age*, Apr. 3, pp. 2, 61.

# Bibliography

_____. 1989b. "Where New Owner Can Pare *Enquirer.*" *Advertising Age*, Apr. 17, pp. 2, 84.

Ressner, Jeffrey. 1988. "Enquiring Minds: A Walk on the Sleazy Side with the New Breed of Tabloid Reporters." *Rolling Stone*, June 30, pp. 53–56, 64.

Robins, David, and Philip Cohen. 1978. *Knuckle Sandwich: Growing Up in the Working Class City.* Harmondsworth, England: Penguin.

Rock, P. 1981. "News as Eternal Recurrence." In Cohen and Young, eds., *The Manufacture of News*, 64–70.

Rodgers, R. S. 1985. "Popular Legend and Urban Folklore as Popular Communication." Paper presented in Popular Communication Interest Group, annual convention of International Communication Association, Honolulu, Hawaii.

Rollins, Hyder Edward. 1969. *The Pack of Autolycus; or, Strange and Terrible News of Ghosts, Apparitions, Monstrous Births, Showers of Wheat, Judgements of God, and Other Prodigious and Fearful Happenings as told in Broadside Ballads of the Years 1624–1693.* Cambridge, Mass.: Harvard Univ. Press.

Rosenberg, B. A. 1976. "Kennedy in Camelot: The Arthurian Legend in America." *Western Folklore* 25 (1): 52–59.

Rosenbloom, Mike. 1979. "Selling a Magazine with Television." *Broadcasting*,. Jan. 8, p. 11.

Roshco, Bernard. 1975. *Newsmaking.* Univ. of Chicago Press.

Rosnow, R. L., and G. A. Fine. 1976. *Rumor and Gossip: The Social Psychology of Hearsay.* New York: Elsevier.

Rothman, Andrea, and Gail DeGeorge. 1989. "Peter Callahan: An Acquiring Mind." *BusinessWeek*, May 15, pp. 139–40.

Rudnitsky, Howard. 1978. "How Gene Pope Made Millions in the Newspaper Business." *Forbes*, Oct. 16, pp. 77–78.

Sagan, Carl. 1990. "Why We Need to Understand Science." *Skeptical Inquirer* 14 (3): 263–69.

Salwen, Michael, and R. Anderson. 1984. "The Uses and Gratifications of Supermarket Tabloid Reading by Different Demographic Groups." Paper presented to Association for Education in Journalism and Mass Communication, Gainesville, Fla.

Sandhage, Doug, and William Brohaugh. 1977. "More Tabs to Check at the Checkout Counter. *Writer's Digest*, July, pp. 27–28.

Schardt, Arlie. 1980. "Hollywood's Stars vs. the *Enquirer.*" *Newsweek*, Dec. 8, p. 86.

Schechter, Harold. 1988. *The Bosom Serpent: Folklore and Popular Art.* Iowa City: Univ. of Iowa Press.

Schiller, Dan. 1979. "An Historical Approach to Objectivity and Professionalism in American News Reporting." *Journal of Communication* 29 (4): 46–57.

_____. 1981. *Objectivity: The Public and the Rise of Commercial Journalism.* Philadelphia: Univ. of Pennsylvania Press.

Schroeder, Fred E. H. 1982. "*National Enquirer* Is National Fetish! The Untold Story!" In Ray B. Browne, ed., *Objects of Special Devotion: Fetishes and Fetishism in Popular Culture.* Bowling Green, Ohio: Bowling Green Univ. Popular Press, pp. 168–81.

Schudson, Michael. 1978. *Discovering the News: A Social History of American Newspapers.* New York: Basic Books.

_____. 1982. "The Politics of Narrative Form: The Emergence of News Conventions in Print and Television." *Daedalus* 111 (4): 97–112.

_____. 1987. "The New Validation of Popular Culture: Sense and Sentimentality in Academia." *Critical Studies in Mass Communication* 4: 51–68.

Shepard, Leslie. 1978. *The Broadside Ballad: The Development of the Street Ballad from Traditional Song to Popular Newspaper.* Hatboro, Pa.: Legacy Books.

Shweder, Richard A. 1986. "Divergent Rationalities." In Donald W. Fiske and Richard A. Shweder, eds., *Metatheory in Social Science: Pluralities and Subjectivities.* Chicago: Univ. of Chicago Press, 163–96.

Sibbison, Jim. 1988a. "Covering Medical 'Breakthroughs.'" *Columbia Journalism Review* 27 (2): 36–39.

_____. 1988b. "Dead Fish and Red Herrings: How the EPA Pollutes the News." *Columbia Journalism Review* 27 (4): 25–28.

Siikala, Anna-Maria. 1984. "The Praxis of Folk Narratives." In Bengt R. Jonsson, ed., *ARV: Scandinavian Yearbook of Folklore* 40. Stockholm.

Singer, B., and V. A. Benassi. 1981. "Occult Beliefs." *American Scientist* 69: 49–55.

Slater, C. 1982. "The Hairy Leg Strikes: The Individual Artist and the Brazilian *Literatura de Cordel.*" *Journal of American Folklore* 95: 51–89.

Smilgis, Martha. 1988. "In Florida: The Rogues of Tabloid Valley." *Time,* Aug. 15, pp. 13–14.

Smith, Paul. 1986. "On the Receiving End: When Legend Becomes

# Bibliography

Rumor." In Paul Smith, ed., *Perspectives on Contemporary Legend.* Sheffield, U.K.: Sheffield Academic Press, 197–215.

———. 1989. "Contemporary Legend: A Legendary Genre?" In Smith and Bennett, eds., *The Questing Beast*, 91–102.

Smith, Paul, and Gillian Bennett, eds. 1989. *The Questing Beast: Perspectives on Contemporary Legend* 4. Sheffield, U.K.: Sheffield Academic Press.

Spradley, James P., and David W. McCurdy. 1988. *The Cultural Experience: Ethnography in Complex Society.* Prospect Heights, Ill.: Waveland.

Spivak, John L. 1942. "The Rise and Fall of a Tabloid." In George L. Bird and Frederic E. Merwin, eds., *The Newspaper and Society.* New York: Prentice-Hall, 378–80.

Steele, Janet E. 1990. "The 19th Century *World* versus the *Sun*: Promoting Consumption (Rather Than the Working Man)." *Journalism Quarterly* 67 (3): 592–600.

Stein, George. 1988. "Generoso Pope: Millionaire Owner of National Enquirer." Obituary. *Los Angeles Times.* Oct. 3, p. 16.

Stephens, Mitchell. 1988. *A History of News: From the Drum to the Satellite.* New York: Viking.

Stocking, S. Holly, and Nancy LaMarca. 1990. "How Journalists Describe Their Stories: Hypotheses and Assumptions in Newsmaking." *Journalism Quarterly* 67 (2): 295–301.

Thorn, Patti. 1989. "Tabloid Tales! Believe It or Not! The Truth behind Claims is Truly Sensational." Albuquerque *Tribune* (Scripps-Howard), June 23, pp. D1, D5.

*Time.* 1972. "Goodbye to Gore." Feb. 21, pp. 64–65.

Tuchman, Gaye. 1974. "Making News by Doing Work: Routinizing the Unexpected." *American Journal of Sociology* 79: 110–31.

———. 1978. *Making News: A Study in the Construction of Reality.* New York: Free Press.

Tuchman, Gaye, Arlene Daniels, and James Benet, eds. 1978. *Hearth and Home: Images of Women in the Mass Media.* New York: Oxford Univ. Press.

Turner, Victor. 1985. *On the Edge of the Bush: Anthropology as Experience.* Tucson: Univ. of Arizona Press.

Underwood, D. 1988. "The Boeing Story in the Hometown Press." *Columbia Journalism Review* 27 (4): 50–56.

# For Enquiring Minds

Wagner, M. W,. and M. Monnet. 1979. "Attitudes of College Professors toward Extra-sensory Perception." *Zetetic Scholar* 5: 7–17.

Waters, John. 1985. "Why I Love the *National Enquirer.*" *Rolling Stone*, Oct. 10, pp. 43–44, 71–72.

Weiss, Philip. 1989. "Bad Rap for TV Tabs." *Columbia Journalism Review* 28 (1): 38–42.

Welles, Chris. 1979. "The Americanization of Rupert Murdoch." *Esquire*, May 26, pp. 51–59.

Wells, Jeff. 1981. "Profitable Nightmare of a Very Unreal Kind." *Skeptical Inquirer* 5 (4): 47–52.

Whitby, Gary. 1982. "The Penny Press and the Origins of American Journalistic Style." *Studies in Journalism and Mass Communication: A Review from the Texas Journalism Education Council Annual Conference*, pp. 23–34.

_____. 1985. "Sinners in the Hands of an Angry Preacher: Jimmy Swaggart's Televangelism as Popular Communication." Paper presented at annual convention of International Communication Association.

Willis, Paul. 1977. *Learning to Labour: How Working Class Kids Get Working Class Jobs*. London: Saxon House.

Wolkomir, Richard. 1987. "With Tabloids, Zip! You're in Another World!" *Smithsonian* 18 (Oct.): 240.

Woodress, Frederick A. "Here at the *National Enquirer.*" *Writer's Digest*, July, pp. 24–26.

Young, Jock. 1981a. "The Myth of Drugtakers in the Mass Media." In Cohen and Young, eds., *The Manufacture of News*, 326–34.

_____. 1981b. "Beyond the Consensual Paradigm: A Critique of Left Functionalism in Media Theory." In Cohen and Young, eds., *The Manufacture of News*, 393–421.

# Index

# Index

*Il Progresso*, 24
*Independent*, the, 21
intertextuality, 2, 4, 153; of folklore and media, 163-66

Jackson, Janet, 72
Jackson, Michael, 69, 84
Jagger, Bianca, 69
"jazz journalism," 20
*Jet* magazine
Jewett, Helen (murder case), 14-15
*Justice Weekly*, 32

Kaplan, Richard, 36, 95, 108
Kennedy, David, 182
Kennedy, Edward, 182
Kennedy, John F.: tabloid coverage of assassination of, 63, 179-82, 188, 190, 196, 197-98; growth of tabloid legend of, 172-74; is reincarnated, 178-79; sex life of, 104, 182-87; is still alive, 175-78
Kennedy, Robert F., 180, 182, 185
"Knots Landing," 40, 70, 72

Lake, Veronica, 184, 185
Laughton, Charles, 27
Lavin, Audrey, 83
Leggett, Anthony, 60, 80, 81, 99, 119-20
Lennon, John, 156
Letterman, David, 69
Lewis, Harold, 81
Liberace, 83
Light, Judith, 48

Lincoln, Abraham, 173, 181
Lindbergh, Charles, 21
Linedecker, Cliff, 32, 39, 47, 63, 64, 74, 76, 79, 80, 81, 82, 86, 88, 89, 94, 99, 170
*London Illustrated Police News*, 15
*Los Angeles Times*, 191

McCartney, Paul, 155
McCaskie, Sonja (murder case), 26
McCormick, R. R., 19
McEnroe, John, 83
McEwen, Arthur, 18
MacFadden, Bernarr, 7, 21, 35
MacFadden Holdings Inc., 7; buys *National Enquirer* and *Star*, 30, 35, 36
Mather, Cotton, 11
Matthews, Ken, 33, 49, 80, 81, 82, 88, 89, 91, 92, 96, 102, 103, 116, 169, 170, 190, 194
Maxwell, Robert, 35
Mengele, Josef, 90
*Miami Herald*, the, 91
*Midnight*, 31, 32, 175, 178, 182, 184, 187
*Midnight Globe*, 31
Milano, Alyssa, 48
*Milwaukee Metro-News*, the, 175
*Modern People*, 33, 59, 180
Monroe, Marilyn, 184-85
Mr. T., 153
Munsey, Frank A., 18
Murdoch, Rupert, 29-30, 68, 95, 106
Murphy, Eddie, 71

# Index